For Cindy,

History is most easily
learned through fiction.
Enjoy the trip,

Louise M. Coffman

Abner's Journey to America

Telling of the joys and sorrows, adventures and hardships of a group of Pennsylvania Dutch on their way to America in the 1730s

By

Louise M. Coffman

authorHOUSE™

1663 LIBERTY DRIVE, SUITE 200
BLOOMINGTON, INDIANA 47403
(800) 839-8640
WWW.AUTHORHOUSE.COM

First published by AuthorHouse 02/21/05

ISBN: 1-4208-0862-1 (sc)

Printed in the United States of America
Bloomington, Indiana

This book is printed on acid-free paper.

Scripture: King James Version
Cover: Unknown artist

DEDICATION

To my children, Dane, Nancy and Janet

ACKNOWLEDGEMENTS

I especially thank Mary Stephenson. When she was Women's Editor of the York Sunday News she encouraged me and gave me the opportunity to write a column. I thank Phyllis and Leroy Bechtel for help with the Pennsylvania Dutch language, directions for preparing food, and willingness to give a thought whenever I asked. I thank Paul and Hilda Shaffer for the information about butchering. I thank Sammi Lehman for being a great source of general knowledge of the period and the use of her research on indentured servants. I thank Beth Breen for the use of her books, her knowledge of the early days and her encouragement. I thank the Reverend Nancy Jones for answering my questions about the Brethren Church and for reading my manuscript for errors in their general beliefs. I thank Kathleen Lehman and Janet Dempsey for editing the manuscript and for suggestions and critical comments. I thank Sara Coffman, Steve Dempsey and anyone else who gave me aid and comfort, helped me with the computer or listened to me go on and on. I thank my friends in our little writers' group, Laura Hess and Karen Julian for a great deal of encouragement. Finally, I wish to thank my husband Dean for bringing me here where some of the people still think that everyone else in the world talks funny.

PREFACE

Although the time of this story is 1735, eighty years after the end of the Thirty Years' War, the effects of that war remained in central Europe. It had been an ugly war between Catholics and Protestants. The German states had been devastated by it and the population of central Europe was less than half what it had been before the war began. In the 1630s, twelve years into the war, the Protestants ran out of money. France was a Catholic country but King Louis XIV and Cardinal Richelieu saw the chance to gain territory without going to war. The French began giving large sums each year to the Swedish king to continue fighting for the Protestants. In the 1640s, Karl Ludwig[1] was elected king of the German States. He saw that there would be nothing left of his country if the war continued. After years of negotiations, he managed to get all parties to agree on certain points and the Treaty of Westphalia was signed in 1648. One of the points of the treaty provided that considerable land that had been part of the German States was to be given to France. Later France made further claims on German territory.

---

[1] In the German States, kings were chosen by electors. Sons did not necessarily succeed their fathers. Electors' positions were hereditary. If a bishop, the office was hereditary.

The claims were uncalled for but when they were refused a French army invaded the Rhine Valley, burning villages, killing cattle, blowing up castles, tearing out orchards and ruining vineyards so that no one else could benefit from the land.

There were sixteen German states. These states were divided into nearly three hundred principalities, each governed by a prince. Another point of the treaty was that the prince of each principality dictated which church his people would attend. He could be Roman Catholic, Lutheran, or Reformed, that is, Calvinist. No other denomination or sect was allowed. Confusion came about when a prince who belonged to one church was succeeded by one who belonged to another. Then by law, everyone in that principality was supposed to change to the church the new prince dictated.

Anabaptist[2] sects such as the Mennonites, Brethren, Moravians or Schwenkfelters[3] were pacifists and they had not fought in the war. No provision was made for them in the treaty and it became unlawful for anyone to be an Anabaptist. They were fined, imprisoned, tortured, drowned, burned and dragged to death. They had their property confiscated, were forced to be galley slaves and sometimes their children were sold into slavery.

In this fictional story, Abner's family, the Hartzells, belong to a Brethren group. The villagers ignore the law because the Brethren, especially Abner's grandfather, Frederick Hartzell, are good people. No one objects to their presence until a new magistrate and a new Protestant minister insist that the law be upheld. These two men stir up the villagers,

---

[2] Anabaptists believe that a person should choose the time of his/her baptism when old enough to understand the significance. Most Anabaptists were also pacifists.

[3] The Amish sect broke away from the Mennonites at a later date.

whereupon the Brethren elder and one of the boys are killed. The rest of the Brethren are forced to flee for their lives. This is the reason that Abner and his family are refugees on a boat going down the Rhine River. They know that Pennsylvania is the only place where they will be safe, but the cost of getting there is high.

CHAPTER ONE

"Look, Schotzy! Look!" Abner shouted excitedly to his best friend. "It's a boatful of ugly men and I do believe they're trying to catch up with us." He pointed to a skiff that had begun following the boat that the refugees hoped would take them down the Rhine River to safety. They still had a long way to go to escape the danger that had driven them from their homes in the German state of Bavaria.

"You're right!" Schotzy shouted back. "They are a greistlich[4] bunch for sure. Take notice how hard they're rowing. It wonders me why for they're trying to catch up with us."

"They might be river pirates," answered Abner. "I heard the captain telling Cousin Jake something about river pirates. He said that if they catch up with us, they'll take alls we got."

"I better would take my brother and my dog to the front of the boat," gasped Schotzy as he grabbed Reuben's hand and Werner's leash. "Nothing better wouldn't happen to my brother or my puppy!"

"Pick up the oars, men!" shouted the captain as soon as he spotted the pursuers. "It's river pirates! You've got to fight them off. Pass the word."

---

4   greistlich: ugly

Herr Hartzell, Abner's grandpa, calmly replied to the captain, "Sir, my people do not fight. Instead of fighting, we pray. That's what we believe will help and that's what we'll do." He turned to Abner and added, "See that all of the women and children go to the front. Tell them I said there's nothing to get fussed up about. They should just stay calm and pray. This battle is the Lord's." Abner grasped Pearl's leash and followed Schotzy as Herr Hartzell fell to his knees.

The captain's mouth dropped open in disbelief. He gulped, "Old man, you gotta understand, they're tough, these pirates, and they have no mercy. They'll make off with alls you got and that includes the boys, young women and girls. They don't mind killing the men. I must bribe them to keep in business so I daresn't fight them myself, but I don't stop my passengers from protecting themselves and their property."

Herr Hartzell lifted his head and repeated, "The battle is the Lord's. He said that if we keep our vows,[5] thank Him and give Him the glory, He will protect us in time of trouble. I'm believing that He means what he says in the Book."

Abner, a good looking, well built ten year old, with dark eyes, fair skin and very black hair, returned to his grandfather and reported, "Everyone in our group is praying. All of ours are calm, but the strangers are screaming and carrying on."

Abner, followed by his dog, walked to the rail and stood there. He closed his eyes and prayed for protection, but he had a difficult time keeping his mind on his prayers. After a short while he could not resist looking to see what was happening. He had seen several miracles since the trouble had started in his village two months before. Nevertheless, he was pretty sure his faith was not as strong as his grandfather's.

He sat on the deck, held his dog close and worried. *What if they do board our boat? What if they do steal all our money? It wonders me what would happen to us then. We can't go*

---

[5]   Psalm 50:14, 15

back. Our old neighbors have moved into our houses and they'd probly kill us before they'd let us have them back. Dear God, save us. We have to keep going until we get to Pennsylvania. Cousin Jake says that it's the only place in the world where we'd be welcome and able to worship God without having a king or anybody else telling us whatfer way we have to do it. He says that only in Pennsylvania will we be safe.

As the pirates drew nearer, some of the passengers, including Herr Schmitt, the blacksmith, and Willy Gruver, one of the boys from the village, picked up oars and prepared to fight them off. Herr Schmitt was not a member of the religious group; and Willy had said before, "My folks don't believe in fighting. It's all right if it works, but it seems to me that a man needs to fight for what belongs to him and his family."

Captain Garber steered the boat into the swiftest part of the current and kept his eyes on the river for anything that would hinder it. "Dunner vetter! Watch out!" he shouted. "See those riffles up ahead? In the water there's something. Hold on!" He swerved hard to the left, and the boat narrowly missed the roots of a submerged tree that had fallen into the river during the heavy rains. "Mein Gott!" he said reverently. "Close, that was. They must be working, your prayers. Look at the pirates." Abner jumped up and saw that the skiff had snagged against a root of the submerged tree. The little boat had overturned and dumped the pirates into the water.

"Praise God," said Herr Hartzell. Turning to the captain, he added, "I told you that God keeps his promises and looks after his own."

"Maybe so," said the captain. "So half I do believe, and then again, not."

Abner watched the pirates swim towards the river's edge and climb out. "Do pirates stop you often?" he asked the captain.

"Not that often. What we're really stopped for the most is tolls. Wherever it's narrow, the river, like here, the natives make a living by stringing chains or ropes from one side to the other. The boats can't go on until every passenger pays something. See those castles and big houses? They were no doubt paid for with tolls."

"How often is this likely to happen?" asked Jacob Altland who had just joined them. Jake was an agent for the William Penn Land Company, the secular leader of the group, and Abner's mother's cousin.

"Pretty many times," the captain replied.

"How many times? You must tell me so I can prepare my people. They've been through a lot already, and they'll go through more before we get where we're going, but it's harder if it comes as a surprise."

"Like I said, pretty many times."

Cousin Jake is a good leader who watches out for us, thought Abner. *He doesn't like the way the captain is avoiding the question.*

"How many times?" Jake's voice took on a sharp edge that told the captain that Jake Altland was not a person to be trifled with.

"You don't have to get smart with me," the captain shot back. "You want to know, I'll tell you: probably fifteen times between here and Frankfurt, and ten more times between there and Der Lorelei where you change boats. That's where I turn around."

"That *is* pretty many times. And how much will they want from each of us?"

"A pfennig or a piece of jewelry. Most of them like jewelry."

"Do these people look like they would have jewelry?" Jake asked impatiently. "These people are poor."

"Don't try to pull that one over on me," objected the captain. "I've observed them before. Most of them will have some money or something of value hidden on themselves or in something that they've brought along, even the poorest looking ones."

"I'll give you that these people are frugal and watch after what they've got, but they've been through a lot over the years," said Jake. "I know for certain that two families among us have lost children because they starved to death. Does that sound like they have money? They and their surviving children are going to have to become indentured servants to pay for their passage. In fact, more than half of the ones in this group are going to have to work two, four, or more years to pay for the cost of this trip."

"So, why are they leaving this country?"

"We've been persecuted because we refuse to worship the way the government says we must," put in Herr Hartzell. "William Penn invited us to come to Pennsylvania. His land company has given us a chance for a better life in his colony in America."

The captain scratched his head, thought a bit and said, "I'll see what I can do to help you. When we're stopped, group the families together and tell the toll taker the number of families. Then some of them will charge per family instead of by the head."

"Thank you. That's good to hear. You're very kind, and we appreciate it," said Jake as he reached out to shake hands with the captain.

Abner began to worry again, thinking of how much it might cost to go down the river. He knew it would not be free, but to be charged every few miles was scary. *Papa was robbed of alls he had. I know Mama has some money on her and some jewelry, too, but I'm afraid the tolls with cost us dear. Who knows how much it will be to cross the ocean? No doubt a lot. It wonders me if maybe I could be bound out. Living with strangers, working for them, learning what they want and eating their food isn't my choice, but I might have to get used to it. Mama was bound out to hateful people, and Grandpa was bound out as a whipping boy for the prince. It was hard on her, and it was hard on him, but for him it was a blessing. He learned to read and the queen gave him a Bible. I'll have to pray that if the time comes for me to be sold into bondage, I will have a good master who will treat me right and teach me a trade. Then maybe everything will be all right.*

The thought of becoming an indentured servant made Abner shiver, even though it was a warm summer day. He made his way to where his mother and the rest of the group were huddled together praying. He stood quietly for a moment and then shouted, "Our prayers are answered! You should a saw it! No one even had to begin to fight. The captain by near hit a tree that had fallen into the water, and then the pirates got snagged on its roots. Over they went into the drink, and their little boat, it got away from them." He laughed and added, "They'll hafta earn a honest living now, ain't?"

All of the children jumped up and shouted, "Hallelujah!" Since it was a beautiful day, and such a relief to know they were safe from the pirates, some of the little ones began to run wildly around the deck. It was not long before the captain blasted on a horn and said, "Now mind! We can't have this! One of youse nix nookses[6] is going to end up overboard, and the rest of you will no doubt fall and hurt yourselves." He turned around and asked, "Who is in charge of these kinder?[7] Make them settle!"

---

[6] Nix nookses: mischievous or naughty children, particularly boys

[7] kinder: children

Abner's grandpa, his father Matthias Hartzell, his Cousin Jake Altland, and all of the mothers pointed to the deck and commanded, "Settle!" The children knew what that meant. They sat down quickly and looked at each other. Next to Abner was Ephraim Schotzenberger, better known as Schotzy. He had been Abner's only friend since they both were toddlers. Schotzy's mother had died when he was little; then his father, a woodcutter, died the previous summer when a tree had fallen on him. Soon after his father's death, his grandmother who had been sickly, passed away. The family was down to just Schotzy and his grandfather, also a woodcutter. The winter just passed had been very hard on Schotzy. His grandfather refused to go to the forest after his son's death, and spent all of his money at a biergarten. Schotzy and his pappaw, as he called him, went hungry many times. Then Herr Schotzenberger died. At his funeral the church bells would not ring because some boys from Abner's church had tied rags around the clappers. This angered the authorities who clamped down on the Brethren forcing them to flee for their lives.

Abner looked at Schotzy and noticed how thin he was. His thick, curly, nearly white hair always needed to be combed, and he wore clothes that were made of secondhand, nearly worn out material. Schotzy was easy to get along with and generally accepted everything that came his way, even though he had recently inherited fifty large pieces of gold from his mother's father. No one except Schotzy, Abner and his grandfather were supposed to know this, but Abner, who could not keep a secret, had mentioned it to Trudy by mistake. Trudy was Widow Schneider's thirty year old daughter, promised to marry Cousin Jake as soon as they arrived in Holland. Schotzy was not a member of the religious group. He came along because he had been bound out to Herr Hartzell before the magistrate told them about the inheritance.

Sitting next to Schotzy was Reuben, a boy who seemed to be about six. When Abner and Schotzy first saw him in a village along the way, he had been a filthy beggar dressed in rags. Schotzy immediately wanted to help him because he could see that the little boy was worse off than he had ever been. A woman in the village said that Reuben's parents had been refugees just passing through. Both died, leaving the little boy to the mercy of strangers. Unfortunately, there was little mercy to be found in that village, and he had lived with animals. When Abner and Schotzy found him, he was just as likely to bark as to speak. He rarely spoke, but when he did, no one in the group understood what he said. Even though Schotzy was not yet ten years old, he was determined to take care of the little fellow, to teach him to talk, and to provide him with whatever he needed. Frau Grim, a widow who joined their party shortly after Reuben did, gave him clothing that had belonged to her son who had just died. After being bathed, combed, and dressed decently, Reuben was a slender, handsome boy with wavy brown hair and light brown eyes.

Sitting next to Reuben was Abner's feisty cousin, Minnie Ness, who was a little younger than Abner. A redhead with a disposition to match, she had joined the group the day that the refugees had been forced to leave their village. That day had been the worst of Abner's entire life, and she had added to his misery. He had been staying at his grandparents' home for over a week because someone had thrown rocks at him, knocking him out and giving him a concussion. For several days, Abner could not remember what had had happened or what day it was. The doctor prescribed bed rest until his memory returned. In trying to rescue him, Rachel, his mother, fell and broke her wrist. Since she could not take care of him and his father was away, Herr Hartzell, his grandpa, insisted that Abner and Rachel stay at his house until they were better, even though Abner's grandmother was not well.

Abner's father, a master mason, had been pressed into service by the king nearly a year before to work on building a new palace. Grandpa figured that until things settled down, he could handle the situation with Trudy's help. However, things did not settle down. There had been a riot and some of the village people had broken into Abner's house. Several of the village rowdies vandalized it and stole everything of value. Even though his home was only a block away, Abner was never to see it again.

Abner loved his grandmother very much, and early on that awful day she died. Later the same day his grandfather had been accused of heresy, theft and murder. He was arrested and was being led away to be burned at the stake when he was miraculously saved while Abner and his mother were praying. The accusers had fallen into a trance allowing Abner's family and their religious group to escape.

Just as they were preparing to leave, Abner's father and Cousin Jake arrived, bringing Minnie with them. She was very different from Abner, or anyone else he had ever known. He had been raised in a strict but loving family, protected from the world and taught that he must not fight because it was the wrong to do. Besides, if he fought, he knew he would be severely punished. Minnie, on the other hand, had been raised rough. Her mother had had her single, and Minnie had learned early that she had to use her wits and fight for survival.

Minnie had arrived at Abner's village dirty and uncombed, and he had called her Minnie Mess instead of Minnie Ness. She had retaliated by hitting him in the belly as hard as she could. He did not let on how much it hurt, but from then on he showed her respect. That worst day ended at midnight after almost all of the congregation of Brethren became refugees. The next day was his birthday and he turned ten years old.

Since Abner and Minnie looked at the world from two totally different points of view, it was natural that they did not get along. Minnie picked at Abner day after day until he lost his temper and started a fight with her. Because she had fought all of her life and he had never been allowed to, she won easily. He not only had to suffer the humiliation of losing to a girl, he had been whipped by his father. Then thirteen year old Martina, the blacksmith's daughter and oldest girl in the group, persuaded the other girls to shun Minnie until she apologized to Abner. Minnie refused, maintaining that it was not her fault that he got into trouble.

When Abner asked Minnie why she couldn't be nice, she had replied, "I ain't never gonna be nice because the nice ones in my family get bound out to low down miserable people. But the nasty ones don't get bound out because nobody wants 'em. Then the nice ones come home with a baby they don't want and give it to the grandma to raise. But nobody wants that baby, and it goes around being made fun of until it's old enough to be bound out. It goes on like that."

Abner shook his head in disbelief and said, "It can't be that bad."

Minnie had replied, "You wanta bet? Where do you think I came from?" After that, Abner kept as far from Minnie as possible until Father Werner, a compassionate priest who had given them shelter, asked him to take notes while he taught Minnie about plants and their healing properties. During the lesson, he had realized that Minnie was really very smart. The next day, which was the last day before they reached the river, Abner decided to teach her how to read. He figured that if she could read, she would not bother him when she wanted to know something that was in the notes.

CHAPTER TWO

Now all of the children were sitting together on the deck observing the little riverside villages, the huge castles, the neat vineyards, the differently dressed people who were hoeing grape vines, plowing fields, visiting neighbors, walking dogs, fishing, eating at riverside cafes, and doing all of the other interesting things that can be seen while floating down a river in the heart of Europe during the summer.

Schotzy looked around at the group, rumpled Reuben's hair and said, "None of us wanted to leave home, but if we hadn't, I would never have met Reuben, and he wouldn't be my brother. This poor little mansly[8] would still be a beggar in Kittzheim. That is, if he hadn't died yet."

"You're right," said Abner. "If we hadn't left home, we would never have met Father Werner and learned that Catholics can be nice." He petted the half-grown German shepherd that Father Werner had helped him get and added, "And I wouldn't have my Pearl, a little girl dog just like I always wanted."

"And I wouldn't have my boy dog, Werner," added Schotzy. "I've got a nice brother and a good dog. Before I didn't have nothing. That's glichlich[9] if you ask me."

---

8   mansly: little man
9   glichlich: luck, prounounced glicklick

Martina began to speak. Her dark blond hair was braided and wound into a bun. Her light blue eyes looked around the little group as she confessed, "It was good that Herr Hartzell pointed out to me that shunning Minnie was not right. I believed that by shunning people who didn't act the way I thought they should, I was giving them punishment that they had coming. I didn't realize that it wasn't my job to punish people, and I was as bad as the person I was shunning." She looked at Minnie and added, "I'm sorry I shunned you and persuaded the other girls to shun you, too."

Minnie looked surprised and teary-eyed as she hugged her little sister Mary. She started to say something, but Reuben spoke first. "Glad Schotty for budder." He smiled broadly showing where he had recently lost a tooth. He looked around shyly and added, "Good budder."

"You're right," said Minnie, nodding her head. "Schotzy is a good brother and a good friend. He was willing to risk his life to go back with me to get my little sister Mary. I never knew that there could be a person like Schotzy." She smiled at him, and he looked down in confusion. He was not used to receiving compliments, and Minnie was not used to giving them. She ran her hands through her hair and rubbed her ear nervously as her face turned red. Then she added, "I'm glad we are on this trip because we met Father Werner, and he gave me the portfolio about plants that heal, how to use them, and how to make salves and teas. He asked Abner to write it all down, and then yesterday, Abner began to teach me how to read what he had written. Otherwise, I wouldn't know much about plants and healing." Suddenly she began to cry.

"What's a matter?" asked Martina's middle sister Alice. "Why for are you brutzich?"[10] Alice was a sweet little blond

---

[10]   brutzich: whining or crying, rhymes with foot sick

somewhat younger than Minnie and Abner. She had bright blue eyes and a winning smile. It would have been hard not to like her, and Abner did, though he did not let on about it much.

Minnie shook her head and wiped her nose on her sleeve. "What I said wasn't altogether true. I know I must stop lying and start telling only the truth." When she had regained her composure, she wiped her eyes and continued, "I guess I'd better tell you something, and then you'll know what a bad person I really am."

The rest of the children turned and stared, not believing that Minnie was talking that way. It was totally unlike her. She did not seem to notice and continued, "When I was just little, my mama's husband, not my papa - I never knew who my papa was – anyways my mama's husband took me to Herr Flickinger, the powwow doctor. We called him Old Flick. One of his eyes went this way, and the other eye went that way, and he walked crooked." She motioned with her hands and continued. "He was old, and he had greasy gray hairs and a long dirty beard. He combed my hair, cut off some of it and kept it. Do you know that when someone has a lock of your hair or your fingernail clippings, they have power over you?"

"That's just superstition," said Abner.

"That's what you think," Minnie shot back. "He had power over me. I had to do what he said, and I was afraid of him. I'm not afraid of many people, but I was like his slave. If I didn't obey, and I mean quick, he beat me. He took me to different towns and villages to help him on market days. He did magic tricks and sold his magic tonic. After that anybody who wanted powwowed for[11] got in line. He didn't charge for powwowing but people had to give him something. If

---

[11]   powwowed for: to have a faith healer pray for or cast a spell for healing, wart removal, etc

they didn't, he might put a hex [12] on them. That's how he made his living. When he put hexes on people, I listened and learned how. People gave him money and other good stuff to put hexes on their enemies. Sometimes when Old Flick got tired, I put on the hexes. It wasn't long before the word got around that my hexes were more powerful than his. He didn't like that. He didn't stop me, but he took everything that people gave me. After market closed he always told me to get lost while he went to a biergarten. I had to steal if I wanted anything to eat." All of the children sat very still, listening to the story, finding it hard to believe.

"When I was in those different towns, I began going into churches just for a place to rest while I waited for him. Everything was awful right then. I was hungry. I hated stealing and that day someone caught me and beat me. My mother was sick and near to dying, and I knew that my stepfather planned on binding me out to Old Flick. Nothing worse than that could ever happen!" Minnie stopped, wiped her nose again and continued.

"You're going to have a hard time believing this, but I'm going to tell you anyways. I was sitting in the church, and Jesus came down out of one of the windows and talked to me. I wasn't even surprised. I talked to Him, and told Him that if I could get away from Old Flick and find someone who cared for me so I wouldn't have to steal, and if someone would teach me to read, I would follow Him. I even told Him I would be nice. When I got home that day, Cousin Jake was there. He was nice to me and he said he would take me to live with Abner's mother and father for awhile. Then when he was ready to go to Pennsylvania, he would come back for me and take me along."

---

[12] hex; curse

"Is that right?" said Abner. "I thought we'd be stuck with you forever."

"Stop it, Abner," said Minnie. "You're my cousin. If you didn't like me, you wouldn't be teaching me to read." Hugging her sister again, she went on, "One part of my promise was answered, but then I wished that I had included Mary in my bargain." Turning to Schotzy she said, "Thank you, for going along with me to get my sister. It got you in trouble, and you knew it would. Thank you, too, for being my friend. I never had a friend like you before."

No one said anything for awhile, and then Minnie spoke again. "I still have something else I have to say, even though I don't want to say it." Looking ashamed she turned to Martina, "You're lucky that Herr Hartzell told you to stop shunning me and be nice because I was about to put a powerful hex on you. I thought that if I got rid of you, the rest of the girls would like me."

Martina gasped and turned pale as Minnie continued, "When I came downstairs that morning at Father Werner's after I went to get Mary, everyone smiled. I couldn't get over it. Then Herr Hartzell told me to get used to having people care for me. The second part of my bargain with Jesus was answered. Then yesterday, Abner started teaching me to read. The third part was answered, and last night I said my prayers for the first time in my whole life. I even asked Jesus to show me how to be nice." She smiled and added, "Youse'll just have to get used to me being nice."

"We'll believe it when we see it, ain't?" Abner said, looking around at the rest.

Minnie ignored him. "This morning I remembered that my mother often told me I should be sorry for every time I was nasty to people, and then ask Jesus and them to forgive me. Now I know she was right." She took a deep breath, let it out, and then added, "Abs, I've been mean to you. That's the way everybody always acted in my family. I picked until you lost your temper and your papa whipped you. I'm sorry."

"That's all right," Abner answered. "I got over it."

Minnie went on, "I'm sorry, too, that I took the money from the thief's bedroll. Abner, you saw me do it, but you didn't let on. I was afraid of what would happen when I joined the group again. I thought maybe you'd blabbed it all over, and I'd be in big trouble. I just heard that the money belongs to Trudy's mother. I'll give it to her. And thank you for teaching me to read. I've always wanted to read."

"It was fun," replied Abner. "I didn't know if I could do it or not, but I tried. You're catching on quick." He looked down as if he were ashamed, and then continued, "You don't have to apologize. I started it by picking the first day I saw you. I called you Minnie Mess, so will you forgive me?" Minnie nodded, and he added with a grin, "From now on, I won't pick if you don't pick, except for maybe a little."

"Deal," she answered.

Alice smiled and cut in. "Minnie, I'll be your friend," she said. "I really should be your friend because when Abner and I get married, you'll be my cousin. It's a good idea for me to be your friend."

Alice did not notice Abner's frown and continued to chatter. "Me and Abner are gonna have a nice house when we get married and live in Pennsylvania. Herr Altland could tell us what it's like. We're gonna live there, and we need to know. I saw a stork this morning. I hope there are storks in Pennsylvania, 'cause we're gonna have lots of babies." She turned to Abner and said, "Storks bring babies. Did you know that?" Abner turned red and looked down at his dog. Alice did not notice his embarrassment and kept on chattering. "It wonders me if the birds are the same there as they are here. What do you think, Abner? Do you think they're the same?"

Couisn Jake who was sitting nearby heard her and saved Abner from answering. "Alice, I'll be glad to tell you about the birds in Pennsylvania and about the trees and animals, too," he said. "The storks are pretty much the same and so are the robins, except the American robins are fatter and bigger than these here. I'd say most of the birds there are different from the birds here in the old country. There are some little green birds that our people call distelfinks and the Englishers call parakeets. They are related to parrots. Our people like to paint pictures of them and decorate fracturs[13] with them. They're pretty and I like to see them, but farmers kill them as fast as they can because they eat the seeds as fast as the farmers plant them. Passenger pigeons are birds the farmers slaughter for food because they eat their crops. There are millions of passenger pigeons and when they fly over, a flock can be several miles long and darken the sky. Men and boys go to their nests at night and take the young ones called squabs. They're very good eating."

"Is there any food over there that we don't have here?" asked Martina.

"Ya," nodded Cousin Jake. "As a matter of fact there is. There are potatoes and yams. They grow under the ground sort of like beets. The potatoes are good fried, baked or in stew. The yams are sweet and are very good baked. There's corn. It grows on a tall stalk, and the part you eat is called the ear."

Reuben laughed and then reached up playfully and touched Schotzy's ear. "Eat ear," he said, and his eyes lit up with glee. The children couldn't help laughing with him as Schotzy reached over and gave him a love tap.

"There are lots of kinds of nuts in Pennsylvania. Chestnuts are plentiful, more plentiful than here. You know how good

---

[13]   fractur: A decorated birth or marriage certificate.

they are. There are also little nuts related to chestnuts that the Indians call chinquepins. They grow on bushes. Hickory nuts are plentiful and so are black walnuts and hazelnuts. In the fall there are nice grapes and something called pumpkins and squash that you have to get used to."

"When we get to Pennsylvania, will we have to travel far to get where we are going?" asked Schotzy.

"It's pretty far, more than one hundred miles," answered Cousin Jake. "It's not nearly as far as from your village to where we got on the boat, so it won't take as long. They started a new road from Philadelphia to Lancaster that might be done by now."

"How about William Penn?" said Martina. "Can you tell us about him?"

"Ya, well," said Cousin Jake, stopping to think. He scratched his head and began his history lesson, "William Penn's family is very rich, and his father was a friend of the king of England. In his country, everyone is supposed to worship in the Anglican Church, but William refused to do so because he had become a Quaker. Quaker beliefs are not very different from the Brethren's. He was thrown in prison and his father bailed him out. He said that all people are created equal in the sight of God. We believe that, too. It is the custom everywhere to bow to a king and for men to take off their hats in the king's presence. Well, William Penn nearly got in trouble because he refused to do that. He said that the king was no better than he was. If the king hadn't taken it as a joke, William Penn could have been thrown in jail for a long time. The king owed his father, Admiral Penn, a great deal of money and could not repay him. When the admiral died, the king owed the money to William. The king asked him if he had any suggestions. This is what he had been praying for. He said that he would gladly accept the wooded land between the colony of New York and the colony of Maryland as full payment. The king agreed and suggested that it be named for William Penn's father. At first it was called Penn's Woods, and then the name was changed to Pennsylvania which means the same thing." Jake looked around and saw that the boat was about to be stopped. "I'll tell you more later," he said. "We are being stopped by some toll takers, and I must go talk to them."

There were two toll takers and four soldiers: a corporal and three privates. They saluted the captain smartly, and the corporal said, "We're looking for men who have deserted the king's service. We have reason to believe that there are several on board this boat. Deserters think that the river makes for an easy getaway." Rubbing his hands together in anticipation, he grinned showing yellow teeth. "They have another think coming. We get'em by the hundreds."

When Abner looked at the corporal and heard him speak, his whole being filled with fear. *That soldier's voice is so evil, and my father is a deserter. Will they figure out that he is putting on an act and not a dumkopf like he will pretend to be? He left the king's service, and that's against the law. The king said he must work on his new palace but the king already has a castle and a palace. Why did he have the power to make my papa leave his family to work on a place he doesn't need? I wish I understood these things.* Abner sat down on the deck, put his arm around his dog and continued to worry. He knew he wasn't supposed to worry, but he could not help it. *What will these soldiers do to my papa? I hate to think about it.*

Abner's father was hoping to get out of the country and into Holland where he would be safe. Another deserter in their party was Klaus Schneider, a soldier, who was making his way overland. That was risky, too, but he figured it would be safer for him to go alone and meet the others when they got to Holland. Klaus was a neighbor who had joined the army years before. He had deserted to help the people of his village escape when he saw that Herr Hartzell was likely to be burned at the stake.

There were many deserters in that country because men and boys had been forced to join the army. Their king was paid by the king of another country to send men to fight the other king's wars. The second king paid well for the services of these soldiers, called mercenaries, but the soldiers themselves did not receive much of the money. Their king and government kept most of it.

The soldiers who had come aboard the boat looked at each man and teenage boy carefully. Even if the person they were looking at had not been in the army, they might take him anyway. *It wonders me what my papa will do. I hope they don't hurt him. He was beat up yesterday.* Abner watched closely as the soldiers approached Matthias. "What is your name and where are you going?" barked the corporal.

Matthias was hunched over on the deck. *He does not look right,* thought Abner. *He looks vacant minded. His mouth is crooked and hanging open so drool is running down his face. He looks like an idiot. He's a good actor, no doubt about it.*

"Stand up, Dumkopf. Look at me and tell me your name," the corporal ordered. As Matthias acted as if he could not get up, one soldier turned to another and said, "He's umglich."[14]

Matthias began to groan as he tried to get up. He was putting on, but even so, Abner knew that getting up was hard because Matthias was sore from the beating he had got the day before. "Ya, umglich," he muttered as he slowly arose. "Das es recht,[15] umglich. After us dey come, der debils, ya, after us dey come. Dey make awful." Matthias waved his hands about excitedly and kept on muttering, "Den der engles[16] dey come outen der sky and vas carrying on somesing vonderful. Dey

---

[14] umglich: not right
[15] das es recht: that's right, recht rhymes with wrecked
[16] engles: angels

vanted us, der debils, but der engles dey make mit flapping der wings unt vouldn't let 'em. Dat vas somesing youse von't see much."

The corporal laughed, rolled his eyes and with a swift punch, knocked Matthias down. "I told you to stand up and look me in the eye! Now stand up." Every time Matthias tried to stand, the corporal knocked him down. "You're ferdudst,"[17] he taunted, and then began to kick him before he could get up.

Abner could see that the other soldiers did not like what he was doing but were afraid to interfere. Abner stood watching, wondering, torn up inside. He glanced at Minnie and saw her clenching her fists.

"How can you just stand there like that?" she hissed. After one more second, she tore into the corporal just as she had gone after Uncle Simon when he called her a Hunky. She scratched his face, pulled his hair, kicked his shins and tried to pull him away from Matthias. At that, Abner could stand by no longer. He jumped in and so did Willy, Seth, and Otto. The corporal let go of Matthias, slammed Minnie to the deck and began pounding on Abner. The privates punched the three boys, knocked them down and kicked them.

When the soldiers decided to look for more victims, a number of people grabbed Willy, Seth and Otto. Then Abner heard his Aunt Edda yell, "Run and hide you stupid fools. Do you want to be hanged?" The boys ran.

The corporal decided to take his anger out on Abner. He picked him up and shook him like a dachshund shakes a rat. Then he turned him upside down, held him by the heels and shook him some more. At that, one of Schotzy's gold coins that had been sewn into Abner's waistband came loose and rolled out onto the deck.

---

[17]   ferdudst: not right in the head, dud rhymes with stood

Everyone scrambled for the coin. The corporal dropped Abner, pulled his sword and demanded the coin. When he had it in his hand, the other soldiers stripped Abner, searched his clothes, and found the second gold coin. Then the corporal slapped Abner several times on his bare bottom, laughed loudly and said, "That was the most fun I've had in a long time. Thanks for the two big pfennig." Abner hung his head and covered himself with his hands while his mother put his clothes over him.

"They're all ferdudst," the corporal said, as he dusted himself off. Then he winked at Minnie and asked, "You want to join the army? I do believe you'd win any war you were in." He laughed again and saluted her. All of the soldiers left the boat in high spirits, having forgotten about Otto, Willy and Seth.

After the soldiers were gone, the toll takers demanded money. After they were paid, the boat was allowed to proceed. As Abner felt his lip begin to swell and his head ache, he wondered what his punishment would be for fighting. *I expect Grandpa will tell me how disappointed he is that I did not stand by and let the soldier beat up my papa. But how could I, especially when Minnie was brave enough to take them on? They could have killed my papa and me, and there would have been nothing that anybody could have done about it. Besides that, I've lost Schotzy's gold coins. I don't know what to say to him.* Strangely enough, no one ever said anything about the incident.

CHAPTER THREE

Next time Cousin Jake talked about Pennsylvania, he told about a man named Jakob Hochstetler who settled in Lancaster County.

"The Hochstetler family belonged to the Mennonite Church. Just like us Brethren, they did not believe in warfare. Herr Hochstetler told his wife and children that if Indians came they were to give them whatever they asked for. One day when he and his son, John, were away at a mill, a raiding party came to their home. Frau Hochstetler didn't listen to what her husband had said and refused to give them anything. The Indians killed her and the children who were home, burned their cabin and barn and took their horses. When Herr Hochstetler and his son returned, the Indians captured them and made them walk a long way over the mountains to their village. As prisoners, the father and son worked hard for the Indians, teaching them their ways, such as how to build a cabin with a chimney. They showed the Indians that gentleness, kindness and helpfulness were better than war. After twelve years, the Hochstetlers were released and allowed to return to Lancaster County. They both married and had many more children." Jake looked around at the children and added, "I'm telling you this because I want you to remember that when we get to Pennsylvania, we must be kind to the Indians. We must give them what they ask."[18]

As the Brethren continued on their journey, each day was different and yet the same. They often saw boats coming towards them being pulled by horses on the towpath that ran along the edge of the river. When there was a bend or a rocky place, the towpath would change to the other side. Then men with long poles would guide the boat to horses that were waiting for the ropes on the other side. Abner could see that it was very hard work. Once they saw a boat being pulled by men instead of horses. "Those men are prisoners," explained the captain. "They are being punished for breaking the law." *Just as we could be*, thought Abner as he whispered a prayer for the men being punished in such a cruel way.

Now that the toll takers were there so often with their chains across the river, Cousin Jake and the women were more careful with their money; and the food was not as plentiful as before. Still, the group did not go hungry. The cow gave a bucketful of milk twice a day, and there was a barrel of sauerkraut on board. They ate a lot of that, as well anything that could be bought at a bargain whenever the captain stopped at a town or cities along the way. One day there were eels in the market, and some of the people proclaimed that they were a great treat. Abner tasted them, made a face and spit them out. "Ach, them are horrible. They are bony, greasy and strong." He shivered, then looked up and saw Widow Schneider watching him. She was from his home village and had caused him considerable trouble.

The widow frowned and said, "You're sneaky,[19] just plain sneaky." She looked him up and down and added, "I know you from a long way back. Spoiled, you are. Spoiled rotten.

---

[18]   This is a true story.
[19]   sneaky: finicky, difficult to please

You had it so good all of your life, you can't take a little something out of the ordinary." Abner was about to say it was not true when his dog showed her teeth and growled. Abner reached down and patted her thinking, *Good for you, Pearl. We're not going to let that old biddy get me in trouble again. I've had enough of her to last me two lifetimes.*

Gradually the members of the group became acquainted with the strangers on board. Most of them spoke the same language as Abner and his family, but there was one family that did not and Abner did not pay any attention to them. In that family was a grandmother, several adults and a dark haired, blue eyed boy about Reuben's size. One day Abner heard the boy say something to Reuben that sounded like, "Zhe m'appelle Louie."[20]

Reuben looked surprised and answered, "Zhe m'appelle Reuben." Then Louie and Reuben began to talk in the strange language. After they talked a bit, Louie took Reuben's hand and ran toward his grandmother, chattering all of the way.

Abner motioned for Schotzy, and they followed. A small woman with dark hair and piercing blue eyes listened to Louie and then shouted, "Mon Dieu!" She grabbed Reuben, kissed him and began to speak to him very fast in her language.

"She's got a whole row, ain't?" Abner said to Schotzy.

"Ya, and I don't like it one little bit," he replied. "It'll make trouble."

"Why you say that?"

Schotzy shook his head. "I feel it in my bones."

"What fer jabbering do you suppose it is?"

"We could ask Antonio. He probly will know."

"Ya, that's a good idea. I do believe that Antonio can tell us."

---

[20]   zhe m'appelle Louie: I'm called: , or my name is Louie in French

They had just turned to find Antonio when they heard little feet pounding on the deck and a frightened little boy calling, "Schotty! She want me." He wiped his cheek and kept on running until he caught up with them. He made a face and added, "She schmutz[21] me. Don't like. Don't like."

Antonio had been studying the German language since he joined the group several months before and was doing well with it. The boys liked the former priest from another country who had been driven from his home for leaving his church. They knew he spoke several languages and thought that he would be the one to tell about Reuben's ability to speak words in a foreign tongue. It was a big surprise to Schotzy and Abner when Reuben began talking to the other boy in a strange language since he was just beginning to put words together in theirs. When the boys found Antonio, he smiled and asked, "Gentlemen, what can I do for you?"

Schotzy explained what had happened. "I'll be glad to help," Antonio said. "I'll try to speak with the woman to see if I know the language. If I do I'll find out what she wants." When Antonio came back, he looked worried. "I think we should find your grandpa, Abner. We need to explain all of this to him. He'll need to know."

When Abner located Herr Hartzell he found that his father and Cousin Jake were with him; so they came along, too. When the men arrived, Abner pointed with his chin and said, "That boy over there spoke to Reuben and he talked back to him in his language. Then the boy took Reuben to his grandmother. We got Antonio, and he talked to her. Will you tell my grandpa what she said?"

Antonio nodded and replied, "The woman says that Reuben looks just like her brother did at his age. He was a

---

[21]   schmutz: slang for kiss, schmutzy: smeary schmuts rhymes with puts

Huguenot,[22] and was forced to leave France two or three years ago with his family. He hasn't been heard of since. He had a boy about Reuben's age and the boy had a dog. She wants you to give Reuben to her because she's sure he's her nephew. Besides, she says that a French boy should be raised by Frenchmen, not by stupid Krauts."

Herr Hartzell looked at Antonio as if he did not believe what he was hearing. He rubbed his beard, frowned and answered, "Tell her it is not possible. Schotzy saved Reuben's life, and it would break both their hearts if they were separated. Besides we don't know that she really is his aunt. We'll not fight them, but we'll stand firm."

Abner let out a sigh of relief and thought, *Grandpa says we won't fight, but we will stand firm. Now that's a good way to put it.*

While Antonio went to talk to the French woman, Herr Hartzell leaned on the rail and watched the countryside as the boat moved smoothly down the river. Coming toward them was a boat being rowed up the river by men. Abner heard them groan and noticed that their bodies shone with sweat as the muscles of their arms bulged, and their backs bent nearly double. They were chained to the rowing bench, and a man cracking a whip stood in the boat beside them. Sitting in the back of the boat was a heavyset, richly dressed man.

"Grunt, you heretics!"[23] shouted someone on the shore. "You Dunkers deserve what you're getting."

"May God bless you," shouted Abner, thinking again that his papa and grandpa could be among the men who were

---

[22] Huguenot: French protestant
[23] heretic: one who believes differently from the beliefs of the established church

being tortured by having to do such strenuous work. He watched until the boat being rowed was out of sight.

It was a nice day, and he was not sure what he wanted to do next. He was restless, and he did not want to go back to the children knowing he would be teased about Alice. He glanced at his father and saw a strange look on his face. *What have I done now?* he thought, as he tried to think what could have displeased him. *I can't please him, no matter how hard I try. It's always something, and now he's looking at me strangely. I know I'm in for it, but for what? Is he going to talk about the gold coins or me fighting? I'll be glad when I'm grown up and don't have to take orders from anybody. I know I'll have to obey God, but I do hope that being grown up is different.*

Abner started to walk away when his papa called to him, "Son, we need to talk. Come with me." Matthias hobbled toward the front of the boat where they could have some privacy. Abner dragged his feet trying to postpone the discussion as long as possible. When they found two coils of rope, Matthias sat on one and motioned for Abner to sit on the other. He cleared his throat and began, "I know you heard me tell your mother that the men who stole the cow and beat me also stole my money." His voice broke, and Abner looked up in surprise to see tears welling up in his father's eyes. Matthias covered his face until he regained control. "I've worked hard and been proud that my family was well cared for. Now I have to tell you that you're going to have to be sold into bondage. It says in the Bible somewhere that pride goes before a fall. Your grandpa could tell you exactly where, but I can't." He stopped talking, wiped his eyes and then reached over and gave Abner's shoulder a squeeze.

Abner looked at his father in total surprise, and his first thought was, *What is he bawling about?* Then his heart began to sing. *He cares for me, my papa cares for me! I never knew that before, but he really does! He cares for me.* Abner felt as if tears might come to his own eyes; not because he was going to have to be an indentured servant, but because he realized that his father loved him.

"Enough money we don't have to pay for your passage," Matthias continued. "I hope what we have is enough for your mother and me. Your mother is uf gie bindle,[24] and I must be able to take care of her. Houses be dear, and we'll have to have some place to stay when the baby is born. This river trip is costing much more than Jake thought it would. They upped the price." Matthias shook his head in thought and sat quietly looking at a castle with vineyards in front of it and up the hill on both sides. "It wonders me what kind of problems the people have who live there," he said.

When the castle was out of sight he continued, "Another thing, you daresn't say anything to your grandpa or Schotzy about your having to be bound out. If they know about it, they'll want to pay your way, and we can't have that. Schotzy plans on paying Reuben's, Frau Grim's and little Barbara's passage. Besides that he'll have plenty of places to put his money. We can't take from your grandpa. If he knew about it, he would be a bondservant himself before he would let that happen to you. We can't have that either. It would be too hard on him."

Abner took a deep breath, shook his head, and said, "No, I would never want Grandpa to be bound out."

Matthias added, "Jake says being bound out isn't so bad for a boy. You'll be taught a trade, get your food and a place to stay, as well as a new set of clothes every year. When the time is up, you'll receive a new suit and possibly a piece of land. The good thing about it is bondservants have some rights in Pennsylvania. Now Abner, you are not to say anything to anyone about this until the time comes."

---

[24]   uf gie bindle or uf gie bingle: pregnant

Abner's head was reeling with the news. Such a thing had occurred to him, but he really did not think it would happen. *This is bad,* he thought, *especially that I'm not supposed to share it with anyone, not even Grandpa. I don't want to see or talk to anyone. I wish I could walk through the woods and down to the lake at home like I used to when I needed to be alone. I always felt better when I did.* Then he realized that he would never again in his whole life be able to go back to his home and take that favorite walk. He gritted his teeth, clenched his fists and did not cry.

Abner stood up, walked to the rail and leaned on it. As he watched the scenery go by, he thought, *I'll never get tired of seeing the river towns and all of the different kinds of buildings, especially those with pointy round roofs. Some of these towns have been here since Jesus' time or before, and we're going to a place where there are no towns, only wilderness. Everything will have to be built and everything will be new. What a difference!*

There was river traffic, too, to watch. The Brethren group that the Hartzells were part of was not the only one leaving Europe. Going down the Rhine River were many people who had left their homes in search of religious freedom and a better life. William Penn had invited them to settle in Pennsylvania, and that is where they were going. Since there was no war going on right then it was fairly safe to travel, and the Rhine River was the easiest route out of the heart of Europe. Besides passenger boats, there were flat boats that carried freight and logs from the forests upriver to the soggy lowlands of Holland. There the logs would be pounded into the ground and used for foundations for homes and other buildings.

After watching the traffic on the river for a while, Abner decided to see what the rest of the children were up to. He heard laughter, walked around a stack of cargo and saw the girls jumping rope. They were saying:

Down in the meadow where the green grass grows,
There sat Alice as sweet as a rose.
She sang. She sang. She sang so sweet,
Along came Abner and kissed her on the cheek.
How many times did he kiss her?
One, two, three...

Abner felt the heat flow through his body and up to his face. He wasn't sure what to say or do. He did not like to be made fun of, so he turned around and went to the front of the boat again, hoping to find his grandfather. However, he saw his father first who asked, "What's the matter, son? You look..."

"Nothing, Papa, nothing," Abner interrupted. "I was just looking for Grandpa."

"He's chewing the fat with some men about the good old days. Maybe I can help."

"The girls are jumping rope and saying that rhyme about a boy kissing a girl."

"And?"

"They're saying my name and Alice's, and I don't like it. I usually talk about stuff like this to Grandpa, but I can't never find him by himself anymore. Me and Schotzy used to talk about stuff, but if I do now, I'll no doubt blab about my being bound out. Besides, he has Reuben and Minnie, and he don't need me like he used to. I like to talk to Alice, but they're teasing us. I don't know what to do, and I don't have anybody to talk to."

Abner heard his father draw in his breath and make a strange sound. He looked him in the face and saw a kindly smile. "How about me? I could listen." He put his arm around Abner's shoulder and led him back to the spot they had been before.

After they had sat down neither of them said anything for awhile. When Abner looked at his father, he noticed that his father looked as if he could cry. "What is it Papa?"

Matthias shook his head until he regained control and then said, "I've always tried so hard to make sure that you were a good boy, that I think maybe I've been a bad father. It never occurred to me that one day you might not be there, and it never occurred to me to show you how to be a good person, instead of fussing you[25] all the time. Will you forgive me?"

Abner was completely taken aback. A parent apologizing to a child was unheard of. It wasn't in the natural order of things. He blinked. "Sure," he said.

Matthias smiled weakly and said, "Now I feel better. Please come to me whenever you need somebody to talk to." He took a breath and added, "As for the girls singing about you and Alice, remember that if they think it bothers you, they'll do it all the more. Don't let on. We Hartzells are great actors, you know. You can pull it off. And another thing, just remember that wherever you go and whatever you do, Jesus is with you, and the Holy Spirit will guide and comfort you."

"Thanks, Papa," said Abner as he thought, *It's good, Papa's advice. It wonders me what kind of an act I can put on.* He got up and added, "I believe so half I'll go jump some rope if they'll let me." He made his way toward the middle of the boat. The wind had come up, and the river was rough. He nearly lost his footing when a sudden gust took his hat. As he scrambled for it, he fell over Herr Schmitt's anvil and that gave him an idea. As he approached the girls, he could hear that they were still chanting the same rhyme. He tried to jump in but got tangled up in the rope and almost fell on Alice who was jumping. She started to object, but smiled when she saw who it was.

---

[25] fussing you: scolding, punishing, complaining about

"Hey, Alice," he said. "I'd kiss you on the cheek, but your papa is a blacksmith, and I can just see him hammering me flat on his anvil." With that, all of the girls laughed.

Minnie and Alice began to swing the rope for someone else to take a turn when the captain called out. "You young ones can't play there. Some of the passengers are complaining that you make too loud, and it's hard for them to get by. No more rope jumping. On a boat, those are not called ropes, they are called lines. Every line has a purpose and is kept in a special place. Put that one back where you found it and don't touch it from now on."

Late in the morning the captain blew his horn to make an announcement. "We are in luck. See the clock up on that tower? We are just in time for youse to get off and see the famous show that's part of that clock tower. When the big hand gets to the twelve, figures come out and dance around. It's a show you'll want to see. I'll make the boat fast. If youse want off to buy food or stretch your legs, get off and be back in two hours. The little hand is going on twelve and the big hand is at the eight. We'll leave here when the big hand gets to the eight and the little hand is at the two. That's two hours if you don't know. Shops are along that narrow street to the left."

Abner had no money to spend, but he thought he would enjoy looking in the windows and seeing the clock's display. He did not know who he would walk around with and was glad when his parents motioned for him to join them. They strolled a bit and then stopped to watch the noon performance of the clock. At exactly twelve the doors in the tower opened and large colorfully painted figures came out accompanied by music. The first figures were buglers followed by dancing men and women that must have been six feet tall. They were so high up, it was hard to tell how big they were. After the dancers came a figure of a baby, then some children, next older people, and last of all an old man with a scythe, representing death. The figures twirled around, paraded back into the clock, and the doors closed.

"What a show," said Abner. "Just think, if we hadn't been run out of our village, we would never have seen all this exciting stuff."

"I think I could have got along without it," said his mother dryly.

Abner had not expected that the street itself would be so interesting. It was narrow, paved with quarried stone and followed the contour of the river. It was only wide enough for one vehicle and foot traffic. The street and sidewalk were lined with many different kinds of little shops. Mounted on the wall above each shop was a figure showing what was sold there, and each had its own distinctive sign. The goldsmith's was a gold swan; the silversmith's, a silver deer; the bakery, bread and rolls; the confectioner's shop, candy; the toy shop, a tin soldier and the tobacconist, a pipe.

As they passed a bakery, Abner noticed Jake and Trudy inside. Jake saw them too, and came to the door. "You've got to try these little cakes. They're the specialty here. They're copied all over, but these are the best." Matthias hesitated and Jake said, "Come on in and let Abner see the kinds of goodies they have. He'll never get a chance like this again. I'll treat you."

Abner stepped into the shop. "Ummm," he said, "This smells like heaven, and look at all of that good stuff. I never imagined there were this many kinds of schleck."[26] Inside the shop was a very large woman who was buying a torte, sticky buns, little cakes and pastries. Abner stared at her as she reached her hand into her pocketbook and brought out money. She was the first truly fat person he had ever seen. He was thinking, *She sure must stuff a lot of that into her face,*

---

[26]   schleck: good rich food

when his mother grabbed his arm and hissed, "I've told you before not to stare at people."

"Sorry, Mama, that's right, you did tell me before." The other time that Abner's mother had told him not to stare was when Antonio had come to their village. Abner had not been able to take his eyes off the little man because his facial features were different from any he had seen before. He was dressed differently, too. He was a small man with a hooked nose, large dark eyes set far apart, black bushy eyebrows, a bushy mustache, swarthy skin and a beautiful smile with regular teeth. His clothes were much more colorful than people wore where Abner lived. Antonio had come to the Brethren Meetinghouse on the Sunday before the trouble began. He had told Abner's grandfather that he did not speak the native tongue. However, since both knew Latin they were able to communicate. Antonio had been a Catholic priest before becoming a Protestant, and both he and his family had been persecuted. He was the only one to escape with his life. The Brethren had welcomed him, and he had accompanied them when they left their village. He was also a beekeeper and a valuable member of the group who shared honey that he robbed from bee trees, and spent many hours praying for their safety. *I'm traveling all the way across the world, and I will see many different sights,* thought Abner. *I better would break this habit of staring and act as if I've seen everything before.*

"Here are the little cakes I was talking about," said Cousin Jake as he gave them to Trudy, Rachel, Matthias and Abner, and kept one himself. "In Holland and in America they call them cookies. Let me know what you think."

Abner was not one to take a big bite of strange food so he took a little nibble. The taste exploded in his mouth. He wanted to gobble it down but thought better of it. *I want it to last long,* he thought as he smiled. "Thank you, Cousin Jake.

I've never tasted anything better." He looked at his treat and saw that it was a dark brown and bigger than his hand. It was lightly spiced and full of chopped nuts and currants. On it was spread a brown icing like he had never tasted before. "What is that brown icening[27] smeared over the top?" he asked.

"That's chocolate. It comes from a place called South America. Do you like it?"

"Ummm… ya, it's real good," he answered, licking his lips. As he was eating his little cake, he looked out the window and saw his grandpa and Widow Schneider coming into the shop. She was holding tightly onto his arm and gushing, "Oh, Frederick, good it is of you to accompany me on this little outing. I didn't want to go alone. Just for being so nice to me, I'm going to let you buy me one of those brown little cakes. They look delicious."

Abner thought he would choke. There was his beloved grandpa with the widow who had accused Abner of stealing, lying, being sneaky and big feeling.[28] *She's the enemy*, he thought, *and I'll have to protect him from her from now on. I can't let her get her hooks in him.* The widow saw him but pretended that she had not. She took Herr Hartzell's arm and propelled him out of the shop before he saw the rest of his family. "It makes too crowded in here," she said. "I must go to the tobacco shop. We can come back here later."

Evidently, since they said nothing about it, neither Cousin Jake, Trudy, nor Abner's parents saw the widow and Grandpa together. As upset as Abner was, he did not want to spoil their day, so he said nothing either. As they investigated the town, commenting on this and that, they passed a biergarten just as a man with a tremendous belly came out of the doorway.

---

[27] icening: icing, frosting
[28] big feeling: arrogant

"That man must drink a lot of beer," said Abner. "I never saw such a big gut."

"Ya," said Jake, "Look how far out front it is. If he fell, he wouldn't land on his face."

"He must want it out where he can keep an eye on it," added Matthias, as Abner and the men laughed.

Rachel wagged her finger at them and said, "You boys are bad," but she and Trudy were laughing, too.

Further along the street they came upon a man playing a musical instrument that Cousin Jake called a squeeze box. The musician, a short, dark man with a huge mustache, had a monkey with him. It danced around, did a few tricks and then began begging for coins from the people who were watching.

"Look at that little creature," said Trudy. "He's so ugly he's cute."

Abner wanted to give the monkey something, but since he had no money, he decided to give the only thing he had, a piece of his little cake. He broke some off and offered it. Suddenly the owner stopped playing, shook his fist at Abner and cursed him in a strange language. At least it sounded like a curse to Abner.

"Monkeys can get sick if they eat strange food," explained Cousin Jake. "Besides, the owner wants money." He reached into his moneybag and got out a small coin. He showed it to the monkey and then handed it to Abner to give.

Abner looked at the coin thinking, *I sure do wish I could keep this myself, but this is one of those times I have to put on one of those Hartzell acts that Papa was talking about.* He laughed a fake laugh and called for the monkey. It came quickly, grabbed the coin, ran back and gave it to his master who didn't even thank him.

In the crowd he heard someone say, "Who was that fool that gave money to a monkey? He must be rolling in dough."

I only wish, thought Abner. He looked up to see his mother smiling at him kindly, lovingly even, and his heart soared with joy. *She cares about me, too,* he thought. *She really does.* He took her hand, and they walked back toward the boat.

"Ach du Himmel," said Cousin Jake, "I forgot to go to the tobacco shop. I promised Trudy I'd get some of that filthy weed for her mother. I started something when I introduced her to that pipe. She enjoys her smoke, but now have you noticed how she gets all jumpy when she doesn't have it?" After that remark, Abner saw him glance at Trudy to see if she were offended. Trudy nodded and rolled her eyes. *They'll get along all right when they get married*, he thought. *The both of them understand her mother.*

Abner did not want to say that he was sure Widow Schneider got some tobacco herself. It would have become too involved to explain, so he let it go. He was too happy to let anything interfere. He looked at his papa just in time to see his mouth drop open. Abner had to laugh because he was sure that Matthias had just seen Grandpa with the widow. Sure enough, he was right. "Papa," he said, trying not to laugh, "It's not polite to stare at people."

"I do believe she's trying to get her hooks in him," Matthias muttered. "We're gonna have to protect him from her, and it's not gonna be easy."

Rachel looked at him disapprovingly. "Matthias, watch your mouth in front of your son."

"That's all right, Mama," Abner said with a smile. "He said what I was thinking."

CHAPTER FOUR

The walk back to the boat was down a steep incline and before they knew it, they were back in plenty of time to watch the others return and go aboard. Otto Schwartz, Willy Gruver and Seth Kunkle were on the boat already. Abner wondered how Otto had got away from his mother as she always kept her husband and children in a tight pack. As the Schwartzes approached the boat, Frau Schwartz, who usually kept quiet, was yelling, "Enough! No further I'm going. On the boat, I'm not getting. Never! Otto, get off. We're staying here."

"I'm going," Otto yelled back. "I told you. I can't help it that you changed your mind. I'm all worked up about it and I'm going."

When she saw that he would not obey her, she called, "Come and let me give you a good-bye kiss."

"I know your tricks, Mama," he said. "If I get off you'll grab my ear and I won't get away. When the boat goes, I'm going. I'll be a bondservant and take my chances in Pennsylvania."

"Go get him," Frau Schwartz commanded her husband.

Herr Schwartz shrugged his shoulders and then shook his head. "If that's what he wants, let him go," he answered. "He's fifteen years old and big enough and ugly enough to make his way in the world. I'll go aboard and get our things."

"It's umglich," she muttered as she herded the rest of the family up the street without a backward glance. The first thing that Otto did when his parents were gone was to go to the beer barrel and pour a mugful. Abner shook his head. *That doesn't look good,* he thought.

When the French lady came aboard, she had a bag of sweets which she offered to Reuben. "You might as well take them," Schotzy told him. "Sweets are sweets. What's the use of refusing?"

Widow Schneider was still holding onto Grandpa's arm as they walked up the gangplank and stepped onto the boat. Trudy and Cousin Jake had caught up with them and Abner could hear every word that was said. "Herr Hartzell was so kind," she said to her daughter as she smiled coyly and tried to look girlish. "He bought me some little cakes, pastries and sweets and when he saw that only men were in the tobacco shop he insisted on going in and getting some for me." Widow Schneider looked happy but he could not make out the expression on Grandpa's face. *It wonders me if he's one of those famous Hartzell actors, too. I believe so half he is.*

One of the new passengers was a young man of perhaps sixteen, slender build, with reddish brown hair and eyes. Another new passenger was a heavy-set, light complexioned man with a sandy colored mustache, parted in the middle and curled tightly on the ends with wax. He had light blue gray eyes and nearly colorless eyelashes. Nevertheless, he was striking looking, well dressed and taller than most. He wore a large diamond ring on his left hand and he carried himself as though he felt he was an important person. The third new passenger was a bald-headed, middle-aged man carrying metal pipes and a small metal box that looked as if it had been badly burned.

Abner soon learned that the young man was Michael Becker, who had been cheated out of a vineyard that had belonged to his family for generations. "I shall go to America, apprentice myself to someone who grows grapes and makes wine. Then when my bondage is up, I'll be set," he said.

When Martina saw him her eyes lit up. "He's every girl's dream," she sighed.

The second man, Hendryck van Zant, was a businessman from Holland. He said that he bought and sold things throughout Europe. It was obvious from the way he dressed and the ring he wore that he was successful. It took longer to discover that man with the pipes and furnace was Augustus Glassmoyer, a glass blower. They never did learn much more about him. "His breath he saves for blowing glass," Matthias said with a laugh.

Late in the afternoon Trudy walked by where Abner was chatting with some of the passengers. She stopped by the cow and blew her nose. Her eyes were red, and she looked as if she had been crying. Herr van Zant looked at her sympathetically and asked Abner, "Why do you suppose that beautiful young lady is crying?"

"I don't know, sir," he answered. "Sometimes she gets upset with my Cousin Jake. She's going to marry him when we get to Holland."

Herr van Zant smiled broadly and said, "I'm looking for a bride myself and she's a beauty. I think I'll give him a run for his money."

"What do you mean by that?" asked Abner.

"You'll see."

Herr van Zant took out a small coin and offered it to Abner. "For you, if you introduce me to the young lady," he said.

Abner did not feel exactly right about it, but he took the coin anyway and then made his way to where Trudy was standing. "Fraulein Trudy," he said as they drew near, "This here's Herr van Zant. He wants to meet you." Turning to the man from Holland, he said, "Herr van Zant, this here's

Fraulein Trudy Schneider." Pointing to Widow Schneider who was sitting on a coil of rope and smoking her pipe, he added, "That lady over there's her mother."

Herr van Zant glanced at Widow Schneider, but his eyes were only for Trudy. "Such beauty as yours is rare in a woman these days," he said. "It is with great pleasure that I greet you." He took her hand and kissed it. Cousin Jake walked by just in time to see the whole thing. He looked surprised but passed without acknowledging that he had seen anything. Trudy turned red and said, "Thank you. It's not often that a girl gets such a nice compliment." Only then did she pull her hand away.

"That's a nice cow," said Herr van Zant. "Is she yours?"

"No," Trudy replied. "She's Abner's mother's, but I milk her sometimes. She's a little jumpy now. Everything works on her nerves. She doesn't like loud noises or being touched by strangers. Don't stand behind her. You'll wish you hadn't."

"Thank you for warning me, dear lady," said Herr van Zant. "It was a pleasure meeting you." He smiled, bowed and joined the men. *What kind of a smooth talker is he, anyways?* thought Abner.

The boat had not traveled far from the last toll chain before it was stopped again and then again. Sometimes there were several boats ahead of them and they had to wait up to a half of a day until it was their turn to pay. It was plain to see that all of the adults, except Herr van Zant, were becoming very concerned about the time it took and the amount of money that was demanded. At one stop after waiting a particularly long time in line, Abner saw the toll taker staring at Pearl. "Gimme that there dog and I won't charge nothing," he said. "Then youse all can all go through for free."

Abner's heart sank. *I can't get along without her,* he thought. *I don't have darest to talk to anybody for fear of blabbing off my mouth but I can talk to Pearl. Giving her up is too much.* He shook his head. "No, she's my dog and I'm keeping her."

"If I can't have her, youse'll pay double," the man threatened.

Abner shook his head and said firmly, "No, I told you I'm keeping her."

"You're a selfish one, all right," he heard Widow Schneider say.

After that Abner kept Pearl out of sight when they were stopped. Schotzy and Reuben hid their dogs, also. Princess, the cat, was another story. The captain wanted her because she caught the rats and mice on his boat. *We're keeping her, too,* Abner thought. *The captain isn't getting her and neither is anybody else.*

At the first village that the boat stopped at after Herr van Zant met Trudy, he took off and upon his return, he presented her with a bouquet of roses. All of the thorns had been removed and there was a lovely yellow and red cloth wrapped around the stems to keep them fresh.

Trudy, taken by surprise, stammered something Abner could not hear. Herr van Zant looked pleased with himself and it seemed to Abner that all of the people on the boat were suddenly very interested in what was going on. At the next stop Herr van Zant got off, went to the village and came back with a large pouch of tobacco which he presented to Widow Schneider. With a flourish he said, "This is for you, dear lady. May you enjoy every bit of it." He then pulled a small box from his carrying case and presented it to Trudy. "I hope this pleases you, lovely lady." Abner wondered what it was but never did find out. The next few days passed quickly as everyone was watching and wondering what Herr van Zant would bring next.

Before they arrived at the border of Holland, they had to get off the boat, go to a magistrate, and sign the papers for the passengers to become bondservants. After they indicated they were willing to sell themselves into bondage, the William Penn Land Company would pay all the expenses of their journey. When everyone got to America, a broker would buy the right to be the middle man for the group. He would then hold an auction to sell them into bondage for a period of time. Children Abner's age generally were in bondage until they were twenty-one years old. English adults were bound for four years, but a person from the European mainland might work seven years to pay for his passage. It was better than being a slave for life but it was a high price to pay for a trip across the Atlantic Ocean.

As soon as the boat docked Jake called out, "All of youse who are going to be bound out gather here. We'll walk to the rathaus[29] together." He waited until they were assembled and then continued, "When you get there, you will go to a magistrate who will give you a paper to sign. This paper states that you are signing it of your own free will and promise you will work for the person who redeems you for the full time stated on the paper. You will also be asked if you will be loyal to the Englanders' king. He and the government in Pennsylvania want to be sure that you will not turn on him and cause any trouble by trying to turn Pennsylvania into a German state. They also want to keep track of how many of youse are going to any of the British colonies in America. Does everyone understand?"

Abner looked around and saw that among the group were Willy, Otto, Seth, Aunt Edda, Mike Becker, the glassblower and most of the families from his village. Among them was Frau Wentz, the widow of their church elder who had been tied to the back of a horse and dragged to death. She looked so tired and thin he wondered if she would make it. Her son

---

[29]   rathaus: government center

Waldemar and her daughter Violet also looked sickly. Those not in the group were his mother and grandfather, Antonio, the Schmitt family, the Hokes, Widow Schneider and Trudy, Schotzy, Reuben, Minnie, Mary, Frau Grim, little Barbara and the French people. As instructed by his father, he had not said anything to Schotzy or Grandpa about being bound out. However, he knew that they saw him even though he tried to duck down among the crowd. He assumed that his father was going along to keep him company.

As the group was leaving the boat, Abner saw Herr van Zant talking seriously to Trudy. It surprised him so that he stumbled and would have fallen if his father had not grabbed his arm. "There you go gawksing around," he said harshly. "Why don't you look where you're going? You could have fallen in the water."

"Sorry, Papa, but I just wondered what that slick fatso wants with Trudy."

"Calling a person a fatso is not polite. Your mother would not like it at all," scolded his father.

"I know, Papa, but Jake don't like it either. Has he said anything?"

Matthias smiled at his son. "Do you think I'd tell you if he did? Shall we talk about something else?" Nothing came to Abner that seemed worth mentioning. *That's funny*, he thought. *My father wants to talk to me and I can't think of anything to say.*

As they walked the long way up the slope from the river to the town, Matthias pointed down and asked, "Did you take notice of the quarried stone streets?"

"Ya, I did," answered Abner. "Look how worn they are from people walking on them. When we fixed Widow Schneider's steps, grandpa said that those stones had been there for maybe five hundred years. How long ago do you suppose that this street's been paved?"

"It's hard to tell," he answered. "This is an old Roman city that was built around the time of Christ, seventeen hundred years ago. The Romans built good roads and this one was paved with quarried granite. It is hard and holds up for a long time."

The group went through the narrow paved streets, past the half-timbered[30] houses and on up to the government building that stood at the highest spot in the city. Jake was walking fast and everyone was puffing by the time they arrived at the top. Once there, they climbed a great many steps before they reached the huge entryway which had a large round mosaic on the floor. The building was beautiful, made of a cream colored marble with greenish streaks, and yet Abner found it to be disturbing. The mosaic was of animals that were half man and half horse, half man and half goat and other strange creatures. Around a ledge near the ceiling were large white marble statues of Roman gods and goddesses. Abner's eyes grew wide when he saw that none of them were clothed. He was shocked and tried to look away but somehow he couldn't.

"Come along this way," called Cousin Jake. "And try to keep your mind off worldly things." Abner could hear the older boys giggle and snort. *This isn't funny*, thought Abner. *So this is what they mean when they talk about worldly things. I never dreamed there was such stuff. I don't know where to look. If I keep my head down, there they are on the floor and if I look up there they are on the wall. I sure can't walk with my eyes closed.* He kept walking straight ahead as fast as he could.

Cousin Jake led the party up a broad staircase to an office on the third floor and said, "This is the German headquarters of the William Penn Land Company, the company I work for. Here you will sign your names agreeing to work for the

---

[30]   half timbered: houses built of large timbers and stone. Most of the stone is now covered with stucco.

company or anyone who redeems you. If you are fourteen or older you will probably work four years unless you are a skilled worker, in which case you may work two years. If you are less than fourteen years old, you will work until you are twenty-one."

Jake went to the clerk and introduced himself. Abner heard him say something that he did not understand, something about saying and not swearing.[31] *That's strange,* he thought, *Why would anyone swear at the clerk?*

"Now step up one at a time and do what the clerk tells you," Jake said and then walked away to tend to other business.

When it was Abner's turn, a square-faced clerk with a completely bald head and steely gray eyes said, "Put your X here on this line, right here."

"I can write my name," he answered. "I'll write my name instead of writing an X if you don't mind."

"Ya, well, it don't matter to me," said the clerk without cracking a smile. "And I suppose that the man behind you can write his name, too."

"Yah, and he can, for sure," replied Abner proudly. "He's my papa, but he's not going to be a bondservant, just me."

"No, son," put in Matthias. "I have to be one, too."

"All right, step right up," the clerk ordered. "What do you do for a living?"

"I'm a skilled builder and stone mason," noted Matthias. "I understand that if a man is a skilled worker, his time as a bondservant is two years."

"That's true," replied the clerk, "but we also figure that anyone who is your age and does not have money enough for passage probably is not a skilled worker. So we'll put you down for four years just like everyone else. That's the way it works around here. Besides, I can see that you are limping. It

---

[31]   swear: Brethren Church members do not swear an oath since they consider it to be unbiblical.

might be hard to place a cripple. In that case you may have to work longer."

Abner saw that his father was getting upset. He looked for Cousin Jake who was nowhere in sight and said, "I am not a cripple. I am a skilled mason."

"If you are a skilled mason, why are you not working for the king?" snarled the clerk, shoving the paper at Matthias. "Sign here or get out of line. I deal with liars, swindlers and thieves all day long and I do not have time for people like you who pretend to be something they are not."

Matthias took a deep breath and Abner could see that he was doing his best to control his temper. He picked up the quill, dipped it in the ink, shrugged his shoulders as if to say, "What else can I do?" and signed his name.

"Another thing," added the clerk. "Before they will let you into America, you must say that you will be loyal to the King of England. Are you willing to do that?"

"One king is just as good or bad as the next," replied Matthias. He took Abner's hand, and they walked out of the building. There they waited for the rest before going back to the ship. "I hate this," said Matthias, "but I've heard that which does not kill us makes us strong. We must put ourselves in God's hands and see what happens next. I was reading in Psalm 37 and it says that the Lord gives the desires of their hearts to those who delight themselves in Him. Son, we must learn to delight ourselves in the Lord because the desire of my heart is to get my family to Pennsylvania safely, in good health and to be able to take care of them. I may not be able to care for you but I can pray the Lord will. We must pray that we will not be separated so far that we can't see each other often."

The desire of my heart is to be able to stay with my family, thought Abner, but he did not say it. Instead he said, "Let's not think about that now. Look down at the boat and see the river. Isn't it pretty? And look out across to the hills in the distance! Look at that castle way over there. You can see as far as you can see!"

Matthias reached out and ruffled Abner's hair. "You can always see as far as you can see."

All of the future indentured servants walked soberly and quietly down the steps, out of the building and back toward the boat. Abner looked around at the crowd. There was Aunt Edda, his mother's sister, recently widowed and not sure that she wanted to leave her native country and go to America. *I wonder why she decided to go,* he thought. *She's a lot like my mom but a lot different, too. I didn't think I'd like her one little bit, but she and Mom make good company for each other. She has her good points. I guess that's the way relations are. You take them as they come.*

"You have some time before you have to get back to the boat, and more than likely you will never be here again," said Jake. "Why don't you look around? This town is an interesting place and there's much to see. Just amble down and around a little and be back to the boat in time for dinner."[32]

"I always like to look around market and see what they grow and make in a place," said Matthias.

"I really like to go to market, too," added Abner. "Nothing tastes better than fresh food."

They walked around the market and then Matthias asked, "Since we don't have money to buy anything, is it all right with you if we get out of here? We could go that way," he said, pointing toward a large center square nearly covered with tents and open air booths. At one side there was an area with piles of old clothing, blankets, chests, trunks, carrying cases and all kinds of other things.

---

[32]   dinner: noon meal

"Seth would go crazy looking at all of this," said Abner. "He loves old stuff. I like to look at it, too. There must be a story behind everything that's here."

"Ya, das es recht," answered his father. "Most of it has been worn hard. Somebody made it. Somebody used it and now it's here. What happened to the owners?"

"It does give you something to think about," agreed Abner.

"There's a nice chest that we could use but we have no way to get it to the boat and no money to pay for it. I really wish we could get it for your mother."

On the other side of the market they saw Herr Hoke wandering around by himself, looking at things, picking them up and putting them down. "I wonder why Frau Hoke isn't with him," said Abner. "I'm going to wave at him. He sort of looks like a lost dog."

"I'm pretty sure he's not happy about going on this journey," said Matthias. "From what I've heard, Frau Hoke is the one who really wanted to go."

When Herr Hoke saw Abner wave, he joined them, and they walked back to the boat together. As soon as they got there, Abner spotted Schotzy and made his way to him. He had missed his companionship and was eager to get back to the same footing as before. However, Schotzy turned his face away when he saw Abner and did not acknowledge that he was anywhere near. "What's a matter, Schotz? Whyfer are you mad at me?" Abner asked.

Reuben was glad to see him and showed off some new words he had learned by smiling and saying, "Wie gehts,[33] Abner?"

Abner smiled and answered, "Simle gut,[34] Reuben, danke." Schotzy hunched his shoulders and ignored him.

---

[33] wie gehts: a greeting, How are you? pronounced ve gates
[34] simle gut: a response, doing good

Abner reached out and took hold of Schotzy's arm to turn him around. Schotzy shook his hand off and then said angrily, "Your hand, take it off me you big feeling thing and don't ever touch me again or I'll, I'll, I'll…"

Abner was totally surprised. "What's a matter?"

"Don't give me, what's a matter!" Schotzy answered heatedly. "My pappaw was right. I didn't think he was at the time, but he was. You Hartzells are all big feeling."

Abner could feel his neck getting hot. He doubled his fists and shouted, "We are not!"

"Ya, youse are big feeling, and that's because youse think you're better than the rest of us." Schotzy shouted back. "Back in the village, you gave me food and I was glad for it. I got sick and your grandma and grandpa took care of me and nursed me. I was glad for it. I had no clothes. You gave me some of yours and I was glad for them. Now I'm the one who could help youse and youse are too proud to take anything from me. That's proof that you're proud and big feeling." He shouted louder, "Big feeling! Big feeling! Big feeling! You don't talk to me for days and then you go and get bound out. That's what you get for being big feeling. See if I care." He grabbed Reuben by the hand and stomped away.

"Wait," begged Abner. "You don't understand."

"I understand!" Schotzy said as he hunched his shoulders and kept going.

Abner found a spot to sit down and thought, *I'm going on eleven years old, and I am too big to cry. It's not fair. Papa said I daresen't say anything to Schotzy and now he's mad as me.*

Abner's grandpa walked by just then, patted him on the back and said, "What's the matter? You look like you lost your last friend."

"I believe I did. Schotzy's not talking to me. But you are, and that's good. Papa said not to say anything to anybody about my being bound out. Now Schotzy's mad. He says

Hartzells are big feeling not to accept money from him so I wouldn't have to be bound out. Papa said Schotzy would need his money to start a business and you would need your money, too. Papa got himself bound out, too."

"I was afraid that was what he was going to do," said Grandpa. "I figured from the way he was acting that the cook's sons stole his money when they beat him. He said nothing about it to me and I didn't bring it up. I wish he would have confided in me. No doubt we all would have made out better in the long run if he would have allowed me to spend my money or borrowed some from Schotzy to pay for his passage. I would gladly have paid for yours. You know that." Grandpa stroked his beard, sighed a deep sigh and added, "No use crying over spilt milk. What's done is done."

"I know," replied Abner. "Grandpa, it wonders me how all of this came about. Maybe I'm wunnerschnitsich[35] but I think about it all the time. Whyfer couldn't we just stay home, mind our own business and live just like our people did before us?"

"I've thought about that, too," his grandfather replied. "I do believe that we just weren't destined to stay home. We seem to fit into God's great scheme of things to move his people to America so that it will be a godly place. We'll have to wait and see but that seems to me to be the reason. Somebody had to do it and it looks like it's us."

"It's exciting to think of us as being part of God's plan even if I am tired of all of this trouble," said Abner. "Like you say, we'll just have to wait and see."

"Here is a great passage from the Bible that I think about from time to time," said Grandpa. "It's Jeremiah 29:11, 12 and 13. It says, **'For I know the thoughts I think toward you, saith the Lord, thoughts of peace, and not of evil, to give**

---

[35] wunnerschnitzich: overly curious, nosy, rhymes with runner shnit sick

you an expected end. Then ye shall call upon me, and ye shall go and pray unto me, and I will hearken unto you. And ye shall seek me, and find me, when ye shall search for me with all your heart.'God knows the plans He has for you, Abner, and He expects you to seek Him with all of your heart. When you find Him you must obey Him. In that way, you will fulfill God's plans for you."

Abner cocked his head and thought about it. His eyes lit up and then he said with a smile, "That is something, isn't it? To think that God knows my name, thinks about me and has plans for me! What kind of plans do you think he might have for me?"

"I have no idea but when He reveals them to you, you'll know. Just be ready."

"I'll try."

"I bought a book in Frankfort called *The Martyrs' Mirror* that I thought our people should know about. It tells about many, many persons who died for the faith. Elder Wentz's name belongs in a book like this. Who knows, it may be that we, too, will be called upon to give our lives for the faith. In any case, we need to be ready to live for Him or to die for Him."

Abner frowned and said, "I'd rather live for Him than die for Him, that's for sure."

"Of course, you would," Grandpa said with a smile. "But you need to be ready still." Then he added, "Here's another verse you'll like. Psalm 37:4 says, '**Delight yourself in the Lord and He will give you the desires of your heart.**' What do you think about that? Ask the Lord how to delight yourself in Him and it will make your life better as you go along. Besides, it gives you something to look forward to."

"Papa said that very same thing to me this morning. Like they say, 'Great minds run along the same path.' Everyone says I'm just like you and Papa so I must have a great mind, too." Abner laughed and added, "I wish."

"I thought you would like to see *The Martyrs' Mirror.*"

"Not now, Grandpa. I'm not up to talking about dead people. I'm sure they were heroes, but I can't talk about it now. Mom's been keeping Pearl and I must find Princess and take care of her before we get to Die Lorelei. We have to change boats there, and all my things are ready." He had no trouble finding Princess and putting her in her cage. The captain came by, reached in and petted her. "Are you sure you don't want to sell her to me? I'll pay a good price."

Abner shook his head vigorously. "Sorry sir," he said. "She's our cat and we'll need her when we get to America."

The captain patted Abner's back and said, "I admire your spirit. I have a son at home just as big as you but he's a mama baby." The captain sighed, pointed to the right side of the river and said, "See that small castle up there on the side of the hill? That's Burg Katz and down here in the middle of the stream where we must stop to pay toll is Maus[36] Tower. Both of them have good stories but we have time for only one. Which would you rather hear about, Burg Katz or Maus Tower?"

"I like stories," said Abner, scratching his head. "I think I'd rather hear about the Maus Tower, thank you."

"Here's the story: One year the weather all summer was cold and rainy. The crops were very little and the selfish lord of the principality demanded as much as he usually received. That meant he would get all of the grain, even though the peasants would starve if they gave it to him. He didn't care. They had to take all of the grain to him. He put it in that tower in the middle of the river and stayed with it to keep it safe from the people. He could not, however, keep it from

---

[36] maus: mouse

the mice. They swam the river to the grain, ate all of it, and then they ate him. That's how the tower got its name."

"That was awful, but thank you for telling me the story, Captain. There must be many stories along this river."

"Ya, each and every one of these places has many stories. We are coming up on the village of Goar. It was named for Saint Goar, the first Christian missionary to come to this part of the Rhineland." The captain walked away, and Abner returned to the railing to observe the ever moving water. Coming up were large rocks in the stream that made the water turbulent. He was watching the water so intently that he did not see Seth and Willy trying to hold Otto up, nor did he see Otto struggle and fall down. Abner did, however, hear a thump and see him lying on the deck. *I smelled him before I saw him, he's that fersouffa,[37]* thought Abner. *His mother would be ashamed if she saw him now. She always kept her family in line.*

"My mommy I mish," Otto muttered, wiping the tears from his eyes and slobber from his mouth. "My papa, I mish. My brothers, I mish. My sisters, I mish, even. What'sh m'I gonna do?"

He shoulda thought about that before he refused to get off the boat and go with his family, thought Abner. *He's too big to be acting like this.* He shook his head sadly. *I don't hope he turns out like Schotzy's pappaw.*

"Herr Hartzell, you're going to have to talk to Otto," said Willy. "He's at that beer barrel all the time. He's turning out to be a real souffer.[38] He says it makes him forget that he misses his family."

"It wouldn't do any good for me to talk to him now," answered Herr Hartzell. "Put him down over there under the tarp and I'll talk to him when he's sober. Often times this is

---

[37]   fersouffa: drunk
[38]   souffer: drinker, drunkard

what happens when a person is raised very strict and then is on his own. He was never taught self control. That should be one of a parent's main goals, to teach a child right from wrong and how to control himself."

"You're a good man," said Seth, nodding his head. "My dat is a good man, too. My mam said so." Seth was a boy from a village along the river who was hoping to find his father when he got to Pennsylvania. "My mam is a good woman who taught me to behave myself. My dat would have taught me all that stuff if he'd have been home, but he went to Pennsylvania to get a better life for us. My dat is a good man, too. My mam said so. My dat went to Pennsylvania seven years ago when I was five or six and his bound out time has to be up by now. I do believe I'll find him when I get there, don't you? It's not that big a place, is it? Unless he's left already to go back and get us, that is. He's a good man, my dat. My mam said so."

Here he goes again, thought Abner. *He could talk a tin ear on anybody. I sure hope he finds his dat.*

CHAPTER FIVE

The boat pulled alongside a dock, and Captain Garber shouted, "All right, everybody off."

Just as Willy and Seth were trying to get Otto to stand, Jake Altland came by to make sure that everyone in his party was preparing to disembark. "How long has this been going on?" he demanded. "I can't take that boy to Pennsylvania and say that he is a good sober worker with a moral character. It seems to me that I have enough worries trying to get everything taken care of without having a young drunk on my hands. If I see him like this again, I will not take him along."

Then to add to Cousin Jake's troubles along came Herr van Zant. He had a large box of candy which he held out to Trudy. "Dear lady," he said, "Here is a small token of my devotion to one who has added greatly to my enjoyment on this short voyage. I hope to see you again when we get to Holland. Please don't make any unbreakable promises before I see you again."

Jake swirled around and faced Herr van Zant. "I don't know what you are up to, but I do not appreciate your hanging around Fraulein Trudy, giving her flowers and sweets and speaking to her in such a manner," he said in a voice that sounded to Abner as if he were trying very hard to control his temper.

Trudy spoke up and did not even try to control hers. "Herr Altland," she said with fire in her eyes, "I don't recall you ever giving me flowers and sweets."

"Please, Trudy," said Jake. "Don't start in on anything like that. We have to get off this boat right now and down to the next one. If one is there, we don't want to miss it. I just don't have time right now to take this up with you. But if I remember right, you did promise to marry me, and I don't think you should be taking gifts from other men."

"And if I remember right, you haven't paid much attention to me or talked to me in such a nice way," answered Trudy. "You have a list of things to do. You checked off 'Get a wife,' and forgot all about the fact that I am a person, not just something else on a list." She walked away, holding her head high. The passengers picked up as many of their belongings as they could carry and carefully walked down the gangplank to dry land. Then the men went back onboard and began carrying off the heavy things.

When Trudy's chest was carried off, Herr van Zant looked at it with great surprise and then went over and touched it. "It is incredibly beautiful," he said, "and very old. It's inlaid with ivory, mother of pearl and what looks to be gold. It must be worth a fortune. Whose is it?"

"It's Fraulein Trudy's," said Schotzy who was standing near. "I gave it to her. It was in my house behind a door that nobody in my family could get open. After my pappaw died, Herr Hartzell got a ladder, and I crawled in the window. We found that chest and some other old things, and that chest has some good stuff in it. It has a sword with a gold handle, some nice comforts, a wedding dress for Fraulein Trudy, and I don't remember what else."

Herr van Zant looked very interested but didn't say anything. He quickly hurried to a man with a wagon who was waiting to transport cargo from one boat to the next. He spoke to the driver and quickly returned. Rachel was waiting patiently to go back on board to get the cow when he stepped in front of her and walked up the gangplank. She followed him, and they both stood back while the men carried off the rest of the things. When the men were finished, Rachel untied the hobbles from the cow's ankle and began to lead her off. The cow had just stepped onto the gangplank when Herr van Zant came up behind it, gave it a slap and said very loudly, "You are a good old girl."

The startled cow bolted. She fell off the gangplank into the river with Rachel holding tightly to the rope. She fell onto the gangplank, landed on her stomach, and then was pulled into the river. The cow thrashed around and soon was in the main current with Rachel still holding tightly to the rope. Everyone dropped whatever they were carrying and rushed to the bank to watch what was happening. Abner immediately prayed, "Dear God, please save my mother, in the name of Jesus, Amen."

The captain, sizing up the situation, called out, "Let go of the cow, Frau Hartzell. I'm throwing you a line. Grab hold of it and I'll pull you to safety. Let go of the cow! She's as good as lost. No one can save her." He threw the line; Rachel grabbed it, and he began hauling her in just like a big fish.

In the meantime, Matthias rushed back on board and was ready to help Rachel out of the water. He thanked the captain and held his wife until she was steady. "It's good that it's a warm day," he said.

Rachel shivered and said, "That water's cold." Matthias put his arm around her, and they walked unsteadily down the gangplank onto dry land. All of the passengers crowded around, praising God for her rescue, and asking her how she was. "I'm all right," she said, and then all of them went back to where they had dropped their belongings.

"That's odd," said Herr Hoke. "Jake, did you arrange for someone to take our things to the next boat?" Everyone looked in all directions, but there was no sign of Herr van Zant, the wagon that had been waiting, or any of their possessions.

Jake looked stunned. Abner had never seen him with such a look on his face. "I turned my back. I got distracted, and look." He flung his arm in the direction of where their things had been. "I have a suspicion about what happened," he said, shooting a quick look in Trudy's direction. Trudy turned red and looked down at the candy she was still holding. She started to throw it into the river but when he saw her intention, he stopped her and said, "Don't throw it away, you silly woman. Give it to the children."

"So you think I'm silly, do you, Jacob Altland?" she answered angrily. "I may be silly, but I'm not silly enough to marry you. I've never broken a promise before in my whole life, but right now, I'm breaking one. I am not marrying you when we get to Holland, or any other time either."

"Now you *are* being silly," he answered. "Of course, you are. Now let's get going to the next boat and see if by chance our belongings are there."

"What will we do if alls we got is gone?" Abner worried aloud.

"We'll have to depend on our Lord to see us through this," answered his grandfather. "This looks bad, but He'll see us through if we trust Him. Look, Trudy is giving away the sweets. Get some for yourself before they're all."[39] Abner accepted a piece of candy and could have eaten more, but when he reached toward the box again it was empty.

---

[39]   all: a Pennsylvania Dutch idiom meaning all gone

It was over a mile around the rocks and boulders in the river to catch the boat that would take them on the next leg of their journey. The people in the group hurried, hoping against hope for the good news that their belongings would be there. Willy and Seth, the fastest runners, ran ahead to see. They came back with the news that not only were their belongings not there, there was no boat there either.

"What are we going to do now?" Abner asked his papa.

"We'll just sit here until the next boat comes," he said, looking for a comfortable spot for Rachel to sit. It pleased Abner to see how good his papa was looking after his mother. With a worried look on his face, Matthias shook his head. "We can't go back and look for the thieves," he said. "They know that and feel safe."

"That means they have Princess. I'm real glad I held onto Pearl. At least Mama didn't drown. I was praying hard as soon as she fell." He turned to his mother, "How are you doing? Are you all right?"

"I'm all right. My clothes are wet still, but I'm all right," Rachel insisted. "It's good that the sun is out. It won't take long 'til my clothes can make dry."

Matthias reached down and picked a blue wildflower that was near his feet. "I don't have any fancy flowers to give you or any sweets either, but here," he said, handing it to her. She took it and smiled. Abner could tell she was pleased. *It wonders me what Alice would do if I gave her the next pretty flower I see. No doubt she'd be pleased, too. I think I'll do it.*

As they sat waiting for the next boat, a slight breeze came up, and Rachel sneezed. Abner immediately said, "Gezhundheit. I don't hope you make down with a cold, Mama."

Rachel's sister Edda heard her sneeze, too, came over and said, "You have to be uncomfortable. Why don't you and I trade clothes until yours are dry?"

"Right out here if front of everybody?" Rachel objected. "I'm all right."

"The women and girls could form a circle around us. Nobody would look," insisted Edda.

"Thanks, anyways, I'm all right," Rachel answered. Abner saw an annoyed look on his mother's face, and he knew that she would not exchange clothes with anybody. That was because the family money and also Schotzy's gold was sewn onto her skirt, blouse and underclothes. *I wish she could put on something dry,* he thought, *but I know she won't.*

"Come on, Rachel," said Edda. "We haven't done such a thing since…

Abner saw his mother set her jaw stubbornly before she interrupted her sister, "I said I'm all right. Now let it go." Before long she sneezed again.

The next boat did not come that afternoon, or evening, or night. It was not cold, and the night was short, but still, the refugees huddled together to keep warm. "Grandpa, while we're all sitting here, why don't you read a Bible story to us?" asked Abner, and then realized. "Oh, no, he's got your Bible. How can we get along without your Bible? I think we should try to find that fat man and get it back."

"You know we can't go looking for it. God has His reasons."

"But we need it," Abner protested. "Aside from that, it was special because the queen gave it to you."

"It may be that someone else needs it more than I do. If the thief would read it and come to believe, it would be worth it to me to lose it. I remember most of it anyway. I've been reading it every day for more than forty years, and by now I know most of it by heart." He stopped, thought a bit and added, "I know that I'll get another someday."

During the night, Abner heard his mother moan and then felt her get up. He knew that she walked away from the group. The moon was in its last quarter, and it wasn't very bright out, nevertheless, he could see her bend double and knew she was in pain. He got up and went to her. "Mama, what's the matter? Can I help you?"

"I'm all right," she said as she bent over again and moaned. "I guess I hurt myself more than I thought when I fell. You just go get your Aunt Edda and Trudy, and then stay with the rest."

Abner made his way back to the huddled mass, awakened the women as he had been told, and then crawled in beside his father who was immediately wide awake.

"Where's your mother?" he asked in a whisper.

"She's sick, and she asked for Aunt Edda and Fraulein Trudy," Abner whispered. "They just went to her."

"Ach, no! I was afraid that would happen," Matthias whispered as he stood up and went to his wife. Abner sat up for a long while, until he finally dozed off. When he awoke, the sun was coming up with a glorious sunrise, and he could see his mother lying on the grass with his father's shirt over her. He thought she looked very pale and tired. Sitting beside her was his father with a sad look on his face. Aunt Edda and Trudy were curled up sleeping.

"What happened?" Abner asked.

"Your mother lost the baby."

"What do you mean, my mother lost the baby?"

Matthias reached out and pulled him close. "I mean it was born too soon, and it's dead."

Abner put his fist into his mouth to keep from crying out and awakening everyone. *This is more than I can stand,* he thought. *I've lost my home. I've lost Princess. I've lost everything I owned, even the coin Herr van Zant gave me. Everything that was mine except the clothes on my back are gone, and now this. Aside of that, I'm going to be bound out to strangers. I don't see how I can bear it.* Just then Pearl licked his hand. He picked her up, and burying his face in her fur, walked down the river until he saw in the distance a team of horses pulling a boat upstream. *I must get back. They don't need one more thing to worry about.*

Schotzy, Reuben, Minnie and Alice met him before he reached the dock. He could tell that they knew what had happened. Schotzy said, "We're sorry about the baby. Your papa told me that it was a boy." He put his arm around Reuben. "I know you wanted a little brother, too." Abner nodded and couldn't think of anything to say. Schotzy continued, "Your papa also told me that he told you not to say anything to me about your being bound out. I should have known that you couldn't keep your mouth shut about it. I'm sorry I got mad."

"That's all right," said Abner. "We all get mad sometimes."

"I wish I had a way to make some tea for your mom," said Minnie. "I can't believe all of our stuff is gone. Somehow I must figure out how to replace the herbs and medicines that Father Werner gave me. Do you remember what any of the writing said?"

Abner shook his head, "Not good enough to depend on it to make somebody well," he replied.

Alice had not said much, but her eyes were red; and Abner could see that she, too, had been crying. He reached down and picked several small yellow flowers that were growing on the bank. Suddenly he felt very shy as he thrust them at her. She stared at the flowers, smiled a little, turned red and stuttered, "Th-th-thank you."

They quickly walked back to the boat landing. Rachel was still on the ground, but everyone else was milling around, eating bread and cheese that someone had bought in the nearby village. Abner, who usually was in line to eat as soon as there was any food to be had, held back, not sure whether or not he wanted anything. Frau Grim, holding little Barbara, put her arm around him and said, "You really must eat. Each of us must keep as healthy as possible. That is our responsibility to ourselves and to the rest of the travelers. Here, take this bread and cheese. It will give you strength for the day."

"Thank you, Frau Grim, I'll try," he choked. "A lot of people have died that I know and I didn't cry much, and a baby that I didn't even know dies, and I'm very sad."

Frau Grim patted him on the shoulder and spoke to him tenderly. "That baby was part of your family, a hope of something special, and now that hope will never be. You have a right to be sad. In fact, there would be something wrong with you if you weren't."

Abner looked at her gratefully. "It was a good day when we found you in that church and brought you along."

"Ya, it was," she answered. "God's hand was in it. Even when we don't understand His ways or His reasons, we must trust Him."

"What did my papa do with the baby?"

"He went to the church in the village to see if he could be buried there. Poor little thing deserved a proper burial just like everybody else."

Abner faced the church and said, "Goodbye, little brother. I hope to see you in heaven." He waved, then turned around and added, "Here comes my papa, and the boat is here. Off we go again. Sometimes I wake up and wonder where I am or if I will ever stop traveling."

Frau Grim smiled at him with understanding. "I know how you feel," she said.

The man standing at the top of the gangplank saw to it that all of the passengers had disembarked. He paid the men who were driving the horses that pulled the boat upstream, and then turned his attention to the next boatload of people. He shook hands with Cousin Jake, and introduced himself as

Captain Heidler. He stared at the group and then inquired, "How far are you going?"

"We'll get off at the first town after we cross into Holland," answered Cousin Jake.

"Where are your chests? Where are your bedrolls? Where are your belongings?"

"They were all stolen yesterday when we got off the other boat."

"Do you know who stole them?"

"Ya."

"What was his name and what did he look like?"

Jake looked to see if Trudy was close enough to hear his answer, and when he saw that she was not, he said, "He was a fat, greasy-looking, smooth-talking Dutchman with a big diamond ring on his pudgy little finger. He said his name was van Zant."

"That's not his name. He goes by different names," replied the captain. "Vermin like him give the rest of us a bad name. It's a good thing you are not far from Holland because the Mennonites will help you when you get there. They'll find clothes and bedding for you and help you in every way they can. They say that is their Christian mission. You could never have got into trouble at a better place."

"That's good to hear," said Jake. "And now maybe I could ask you a favor? By any chance do you have a blanket we could use? See the lady lying on the grass? She needs to remain lying down for a day or so until her strength returns."

The captain's face changed from a smile to a frown. "She can't come aboard if she's sick. I don't carry no sick people. No one who is with her can come aboard either. I don't know what causes sickness, but if one is sick, others get sick. I know that much. Back off! Raus mitt du."[40]

---

[40] Raus mit du: get out; raus rhymes with mouse

"Captain," said Jake. "She was uf gie bindle, and now she's not. She fell in the water yesterday and spent the night on the ground. She needs a place to rest."

"I've been told a lot of big stories as I've taken people up and down this river, and that is the biggest one I ever heard. Now get off my boat."

Minnie was right behind Jake. "Why are you so mean, mister?" she asked, twisting her hair around her finger nervously. "We're tired, and we're hungry, and we have a long way to go. Why must you be so mean?"

The captain looked down at her with sadness on his face, "Girlie, I'm not mean," he said. "Do you know what would happen if I stopped at a town with a boatload of sick people? The inhabitants of that town would stone me and all of you to death or set my boat on fire. If they set my boat on fire, every one of you would die, because they would not let any of you get out of the water."

"Well then," said Herr Hartzell. "Do you have any blankets we could buy?"

"No, I don't," the captain answered. "Now just get off my boat."

The glassblower stepped up, pointing to himself and Michael Decker. "We're not with them," he said.

The captain lost his patience. "Too bad! How do I know who is telling the truth and who is lying? Get off my boat! Youse are really working on my nerves."

As soon as all of the refugees' feet touched the ground, the captain signaled for the gangplank to be taken up and the boat to be shoved off. He did not even take the time to load the cargo that was stacked along the bank. The French Huguenots were very angry as were the other passengers, but the Brethren stayed calm, saying, "There must be a reason."

"Rachel," said Matthias after he told her that they were not allowed to go. "You must get up and out of the sun. I don't know what will happen next, but I will help you to the outhouse, and then we must hunt some shade. You must look well when the next boat comes or the captain might not let us on that one either. The pastor over in the village said that generally two passenger boats come every day and sometimes more." He took her hand and helped her up.

Rachel looked pale to Abner, and he was glad to hear her say, "It does feel good to get up." She took a few steps and added, "I'm schushlich,[41] but I'll get over it. You're right, we do have to clean ourselves up. We're tired out from not sleeping. We're stinkin' dirty. Our hairs are strublich[42] and our clothes haven't been washed in months. I wish there was something we could do about it."

"You're right," said Jake who had heard what she said. "I'll go to the village and see about getting a comb and some blankets. We better would clean ourselves up. We want to make sure the next captain lets us on board." Turning to Trudy, he said, "Fraulein, would you walk along with me?" Trudy looked surprised and did not answer. "Please," he said softly and held out his hand. "I really want you to. You could pick out things we need that I might not think about." Trudy hesitated a second or two and then stepped toward him. He took her hand, and they headed towards the village.

It wonders me what they'll talk about, thought Abner as he saw them walk away together. *It had me worried when that Dutchman was making up to Trudy. It would be too bad if she and Cousin Jake didn't make up.*

There was a huge willow tree about a quarter of a mile upstream. The entire party moved there and settled under its branches. "This reminds me of the day we ate the whole

---

[41]   schushlich: shaky; having to shuffle one's feet, or unsteady on one's feet; rhymes with push-ly

[42]   strublich: messy hair, windblown

cow and the horse besides," said Martina. "We all had plenty to eat that day."

Michael Becker looked at her with disbelief. "You ate a whole cow and a horse?"

"Not just me by myself," she laughed. "I couldn't eat that much. The animals got hurt by accident, and the men slaughtered them on the spot. We were near a village and we invited all of the people to join us. I never saw anybody eat so much before in my whole life."

"You should have had enough food to last you a week," said Michael.

"Yes, we should have, but we didn't because first of all they were Catholics and they suspected that we weren't. We had to go to their church and pretend. They didn't really believe us and wanted to drown us for our belongings. Then they wouldn't go home until they ate every bit of our food."

"That's just like them Catholics, wanting to steal your stuff and eating your food 'til it was all." said Michael.

"Why are you talking about food?" Alice asked Martina. "You know we're all hungry. I miss the milk. Abner's mom had three cows and now she has none."

"What happened to the rest?" asked Michael as he moved closer to Martina.

"One died in the accident, and we ate her. The other one was stolen. We were staying at a Catholic rectory and the priest, he---"

Michael drew back in distaste and interrupted, "You don't mean to tell me that you stayed in a Catholic rectory with a Catholic priest."

"Yes, we did, and the priest was the nicest man."

"I don't believe it."

"Well, believe it. We were tired and hungry, and it was pouring down rain. We had no place to stay, and he took pity on us and took us in, all of us. He told his cook to prepare lots of good food for us, and when she wasn't there, Frau Grim cooked for us. We really ate and ate. It kept on raining, and we were there several days. The cook was the grouchiest old thing but she really could cook. We didn't know it, but she resented the food we ate. After we left , her sons beat up Abner's papa and stole the second cow."

"I still don't believe the priest didn't have some underhanded reason. He probably told the men to steal the cow," said Michael. "Catholics are not kind to people, and they sure don't just go around feeding strangers. What kind of food did he give you? How many people got sick?"

"Nobody got sick you silly thing," answered Martina. "We had eggs and Johnny cakes and bacon and ham and apple snitz and cheese, and that was just for breakfast."

"You're talking about food again," complained Alice. "Stop it!"

"Come on, Alice," said Abner. "Let's walk back along the bank. I don't want to hear about food either if there's none to eat but I thought I saw something a ways back. Who knows? It's the season for lots of things that are good eating."

"That's a good idea, Abs, but I better would ask my mother." She returned followed by all of the children. "The grownups said to come back as soon as we spy a boat. They said to stay on the path, keep away from the river's edge, don't go too far, and be sure the little ones don't eat anything that would harm them."

CHAPTER SIX

It was pleasant walking along the river in the morning air, and soon the children came upon a raspberry bramble with vines hanging heavy with ripe berries. "Wunderbar!" they shouted and all dived in. It was not long before they were all scratched up; some of their clothes were torn, and their faces and hands were purple. They ate until the ones in easy reach were gone and then they went deeper into the bramble. They were so intent on picking and eating that they did not hear anything coming along the towpath until it stopped beside them. They looked up and saw an old Gypsy cart driven by a strange looking man holding the reins of a beautiful black horse. Whinnying loudly and pawing the ground, the horse frightened the small children who screamed and tore more deeply into the bushes.

"Gypsies steal little children and take alls you got," screamed Freda, Alice and Martina's little sister. "Somebody help, save us. The Gypsies will get us." Reuben and Louie tried to hide behind Schotzy.

"I'm not going to hurt anybody. Tell them to hush," the driver said in a voice Abner was sure he had heard before.

Schotzy recognized it first. "It's my Big Angel," he shouted excitedly as he ran toward him. "Klaus, I'm so glad to see you.

Have you had any trouble? Are you all right? How did you get here? Where's your horse?"

"Hold onto your britches once. I can't answer a dozen questions at a time." Klaus tied the reins onto the cart and stepped down. "Schotzy, my boy," he said as he lifted him up and gave him a hug. He leaned down and picked Reuben up, too. "It is so good to see you two." He set them down and continued, "I never knew I could miss anyone as much as I've missed you."

"Big Angel, how did you get in with the Gypsies?" asked Schotzy.

Klaus did not get a chance to answer because as soon as the adults heard the children screaming, they came running. "It's all right, it's me, Klaus. Don't you recognize me? A Gypsy woman and her husband are in the cart. He's been hurt and can't drive. This horse is strong willed, so keep back from it. The woman can't handle it, and they needed someone to drive so they could catch up with the rest of their caravan. They are being forced to leave this country, and it was too dangerous for the rest to hang back. I thought it would be a good way to disguise myself and catch up with you. Someone stole my horse one night while I was sleeping."

"The Lord does provide," said Herr Hartzell. "The only reason we're here is that we weren't allowed on the boat yesterday. The captain was afraid we were all sick. Now the Lord has arranged for us to meet you. He is so good to us."

"I wouldn't say he was so good to us," said the glassblower sounding disgusted. "I hate all that religious talk. He wasn't watching over us when a thief stole all of our belongings. He wasn't watching after us when the boat captain wouldn't let us onboard and left without us and how about us having to sleep on the ground last night with no blankets?"

"Let's just wait and see," said Herr Hartzell. "You never know what the Lord has in mind." The glassblower snorted and said something under his breath that Abner was unable to hear.

"Klaus," said Herr Hartzell. "Did you see a wagon going the other way carrying bedrolls and other things? Trudy's chest would have been on it, too."

"Ya, and I did. We passed each other early this morning. The driver was proceeding recklessly and nearly forced us into the river. I was busy trying to control this horse and didn't really look at what was on it. Do you want us to go back and get it?"

"No, no indeed," replied Herr Hartzell. "What do you think would happen if you did? Do you think he would give it up without a fight? Just being right here, right now is dangerous enough without you and some of the other men going back for any reason. We must depend on the Lord to take care of us and get us where we're going. I mean it. You men are not to go back."

Everyone remembered another time when the younger men had not followed Herr Hartzell's order and bad things happened as a result. "All right, sir, I promise," said Klaus. "We will not go back."

"Good, I take that as your word."

Klaus spoke to his mother and looked around the group. "Where are Trudy and Jake?"

"They went to the village to see if they could get some blankets, a comb and some food," said Herr Hartzell. "We must make the children clean, and ourselves. Does the Gypsy woman have a bucket to draw water from the river? And do you think she might have a rag, too?"

"I'll see, but I didn't really talk with her. I understood a few of her words, and she must understand some of mine, but mostly we just made motions," answered Klaus. Just then the curtain at the side of the cart opened and out came a fierce looking woman with piercing black eyes, long black hair and few teeth. She spoke angrily in a strange language and flung her arms around as if she were shooing away chickens.

"Antonio," said Abner, motioning to the former priest. "I think you are needed. Klaus doesn't speak her language. Do you?"

"I don't know," he replied. "I'll have to listen." Antonio stood next to Klaus and was a head shorter than the big man. He stood quietly until the woman had vented her fury, and then he nodded sympathetically and spoke quietly. She calmed down slowly and then spoke again. When she was finished, Antonio said to the group, "She does have a bucket and a rag, but we will have to give her something for their use. She says hurry because she doesn't want to stay here long. Also, would some of you men help her husband over to the bushes?" The women and children turned their backs as everyone understood that that meant he needed to relieve himself.

While her husband was out of the cart, the Gypsy woman got in and found a rag and a bucket with a short rope on the bail. She looked around the group, and then her eyes alighted on Rachel. She went back into the cart and found a clean rag. After the water had been drawn from the river, she wet it. While others were washing the children's faces and hands, the Gypsy woman, speaking kindly, washed Rachel's face and hands. After that she took some berry juice and rubbed it lightly on her cheeks. She ran her fingers through her hair, then rinsed out the rag and ran it over her hair several times. She fluffed it up, rebraided it and brought it back into a bun. Abner was astounded that his mother allowed a stranger to touch her; Rachel who was always aloof and reserved. When the Gypsy woman was finished, she smiled and spoke to Antonio who nodded and interpreted.

"She says that her name is Magda," he said. "She wants you to know that she is very sorry that you just lost your child.

She knows that you are grieving, but it is for the best. It is rare for a child under seven years of age survive the ocean voyage. It is just too hard on them. The baby would have died, and you would not have survived either. When you get to America, you will have more children. Don't be sad. Enjoy the son you have for as long as you have him, for he may not live with you when you get to America."

Rachel put out her hand and said, "Thank you." Magda took her hand. The women seemed to understand each other.

Abner had watched the whole process. His mother looked much better now that her hair was freshly braided, and she had some color in her cheeks. *Amazing,* he thought, and then it dawned on him that the Gypsy knew things that no one had told her. *How could she know?* It puzzled him, and he wondered about it for a long time.

Turning to Antonio, Rachel said, "Tell her that if she has something to put raspberries in, everyone will pick until it is full."

In the meantime, the children were cleaned up, and Jake and Trudy returned with their arms full. She had spied her brother from a distance and rushed to greet him. "Why are you dressed in that strange get-up?" she asked, looking him over and laughing.

"It's a long story, Sis, but it's like this, I've joined the Gypsies."

"You have not," she laughed. "I know you better than that."

He laughed, too, and then said, "I'm helping the Gypsies, and they're helping me. I'm staying with them and driving the cart until we get to Holland. My horse was stolen. I was walking along, feeling as if I could be arrested by soldiers any time. I asked God for protection, and came upon these Gypsies. The wife was afraid of their horse, and the husband was in too bad of a shape to drive. I didn't think the authorities would bother me if they thought I was a Gypsy leaving the country. The Gypsies could help me, and I could help them. They are persecuted in this country as much as the Anabaptists are. They shared their bread and cheese with me, and I hope you will share yours with them."

Trudy nodded and said, "Of course." The meal was eaten. Klaus and the Gypsies went on their way, and the rest went back to the boat landing.

"I forgot to get out the comb," said Cousin Jake when everyone was waiting for the boat. "Who wants to be first?" The children scattered like a bunch of chickens when the farmer's wife wants to catch one for dinner.

It was hot. The air was still and heavy, and then the wind picked up. "We must hurry back to the pavilion," said Grandpa. "See that dark cloud? If the storm comes this way, it will make down hard, and we'll all be wet to the skin."

"As hot as it is, I think I'd like getting wet," said Abner. "All of us are covered with sweat."

"Getting wet wouldn't be so bad," said Grandpa. "It's the lightning that comes with these summer storms that is to be feared."

"This kind of weather works on my nerves," said Widow Schneider. "At home when bad storms come, we always crawl under the bed for safety. Now we are out in it. Lightning could kill us you know. We better would get on that boat soon."

There was a small pavilion where the boats landed but nothing that would really protect people from a bad storm. "Where is that boat?" fussed Widow Schneider. "We don't want to get wet." She got out her pipe, but there was no way to light it. She paced up and down the landing while watching for the boat. "Why doesn't it come?"

Abner, seeing the state she was in, tried to keep out of her sight. However, he did not manage to do so. She came around the corner after going to the outhouse, and there he was. She saw Pearl, kicked her, and then demanded, "Why are you looking at me that way, young man? I saw you making faces at me. I know you were talking about me." Her hand shot out; he ducked, but she got hold of his ear and pulled it viciously, breathing hard as she did so.

Rachel, sitting quietly on a bench, saw the whole thing. She stood quickly, walked to where they were and said with a voice shaking with anger, "Frau Schneider, take your hands off my son. He did nothing to cause you to be upset. Before when you said he was bad, I did not take up for him. I'm sorry that I didn't. He's not a bad boy and he's not a disrespectful child. Do not treat him as such. I won't have it." The widow let go of Abner's ear and flounced off in fury.

"Ach, I am fershimmeled,"[43] said Rachel who was suddenly dizzy. She barely made it back to the bench with Abner's help. Her temper gradually cooled, and then she started talking slowly and softly as if it were a great effort. "I have much to be grateful for," she said. "I'm grateful that the Gypsy talked to me about you, and I'm grateful that I saw what just happened. Otherwise, I would not have taken up for you when that woman came to me. I'd have believed you were every bit as bad as she said you were. I always thought that's the way all boys are. My brothers were mean. Even though I never saw you do anything mean, I thought that you probably did mean things, and I just never saw you do them." She put her hand on her head while slowly shaking it back and forth. "I always believed Widow Schneider instead of you although I knew what she was. I'm ashamed of believing her and not you. How could I have been so blind? You're a good boy, and I'm proud of you. Isn't it too bad that I had to lose a child to appreciate what I have?" She reached out, hugged him and

---

[43]   fershimmeled: stressed out, shook up, nervous and shaky

added, "I'll still grieve for the little one, but I'll love you more for having lost him."

Abner snuggled up to his mother even though the day was hot and humid, a real weather breeder.[44] He pulled away quickly as the older boys came around the corner. "Look at the mama-baby," said Otto, pointing his finger at him.

"You wouldn't be calling him a mama-baby if you'd a saw yourself yesterday all slobbering drunk and saying how much you miss yours," laughed Willy. "Abner's all right. Leave him alone." The boys sat down on the ground near Abner, and Willy asked, "Does anyone know a joke?"

"I know one," said Seth. "It's not very funny, and I hope you get it. Sometimes I tell jokes and I think they're funny, and no one laughs, but I like to tell them anyways."

Willy raised an eyebrow, looked at him and said, "We know, Seth. We know. Get on with the story."

"Well, I have to think on it so I get it right." Seth scratched his head and then said, "There were three men talking about the churches they attended. The first one said, 'I'm Reformed.'[45] The second one said, 'I used to be Reformed, but I reformed, and now I'm Lutheran.' The third one said, 'If you really reformed, you'd be Brethren.'" No one laughed.

"Go on," said Willy.

"That was pitiful," said Michael who had joined the group. "Now here is a true story. One day my mom sent me to market with a small crock to get some apple butter just like she had got the week before. The woman who tended the stall was waiting on someone else, so her little girl waited on me. I got the apple butter and paid for it. Then I told her that it was so good and sweet that we couldn't stop fressing[46] it until it was

---

[44]   weather breeder: The kind of weather that brings on a storm.

[45]   Reformed: The German Reformed Church which followed the teachings of Calvin, Zwingli and Hus.

[46]   fress: eat like a pig, gobble down

all. That's why I was back to get more. Then the little girl said, 'Ya, I know it's good, thank you. You're lucky you're getting any cuz we most often eat it all ourselves. We wouldn't have brang no apple butter to market this year, but a rat fell in the big crock, and mom said we migh's well take it and sell it.'"

The boys made gagging sounds; and then Cousin Jake, who had wandered by and heard Michael's story said, "I'll tell one. It's not as bad as the ones I just heard."

"It can't be," laughed Abner. Rachel even chuckled.

"All right, here goes. There was a farmer who didn't talk much. One Sunday he went to church by himself because his wife wasn't so good.[47] When he got home his wife asked him, 'How was the sermon?' and he answered, 'The same.' Then she asked him, 'Was it long?' and he answered, 'Pretty long.' 'Well, what was it about?' The farmer thought hard and finally said, 'Sin.' Then she asked, 'What did he have to say about sin?' and he replied, 'Ach, he was wonderful against it.'"[48] Rachel laughed but the boys did not.

"I changed my mind," said Abner. "It was as bad as the rest. I can tell you something funny that my papa said the other day when we were in the big city. A man with a fat belly came out of the biergarten. When he saw him my papa said, 'It's there so he can look at it.' No, that's not right, he said… What did he say, Mama?" Rachel shook her head. "Anyway, it was funny," he insisted.

The boys looked at Abner, and Willy said, "It's a good thing the boat's coming."

The wind had come up while they were waiting and was pretty strong by the time they got on the boat. The captain looked at each passenger but did not question anyone.

The boat was rocking as all of the passengers quickly made their way under an awning and sat down on benches or on

---

[47] wasn't so good: not feeling well
[48] These are authentic old Pennsylvania Dutch stories.

the deck. There were dark clouds to the northwest that were moving rapidly in their direction. Thunder could be heard in the distance. Before the rain started there was a great flash of lightning, immediately followed by a tremendous clap of thunder. Babies and little ones began to cry. Widow Schneider put her hand to her mouth and turned pale.

"That was close," said Abner's father. "I'm glad we're safe from the lightning and the thunder-boomers." He turned to Abner. "Can you hear the rain? It will soon be making down."

"Ya," he answered. "I can smell it, too. Look at it fast coming towards us on the river! And how hard! Listen! There's hail, too. I'm so glad that we're in out of the weather. If we'd have been out walking, we'd be a bunch of drowneded rats by now."

"Hey, Abs," said Willy with a wicked grin. "Remember when we were back at Frau Grim's house and you sewed your pants on Ascension Day? You know that lightning strikes people who sew on Ascension Day. You're gonna get it now."

There was a flash of lightning followed by thunder that was louder than before. Widow Schneider looked at Abner with pure hatred and said, "That's right he did! If it strikes him, it will kill us all. What Willy said is true. The only way to save the rest of us is to throw him overboard." She started for Abner and then saw that Rachel and Matthias were ready to intervene. She sat back, wringing her hands and looking terrified. Then lightning struck a tree on the bank close to the boat. Widow Schneider screamed one horrendous scream, and then another and another.

"Mother, stop it," commanded Trudy. "We can't have such carrying on." Lightning struck again. Widow Schneider screamed again and again.

"Mother, control yourself," said Trudy. "I said to stop it!" The widow continued to scream. Trudy hesitated and then slapped her.

Widow Schneider pulled herself up short, looked at Trudy with surprise and rage. Then she grabbed her daughter and slapped her again and again until Jake, Matthias and Herr Hoke pulled her off.

"Gertrude Hannah Schneider, why did you do that?" the widow demanded as another lightning bolt shot across the sky a little farther away.

"You always told me to slap a person who had lost control to bring 'em around," Trudy replied, rubbing her cheeks and gasping for breath.

"I have not lost control," shouted Widow Schneider. "I have never lost control in my life and I never will. I've half a mind to never speak to you again as long as you live. You do not deserve a good mother like you have."

Abner looked down the row of people to where his grandfather sat. He saw him with a bowed head, his lips silently moving. Everyone sat quietly until the storm was over, and then the children went out on deck to look for a rainbow. Instead they saw Klaus. "There he is!" shouted Schotzy as he waved wildly from deck. "See you soon, Big Angel!"

The captain raised his sail, and the boat sped across the water at what seemed like a tremendous speed. Abner knew he had never traveled so fast before. The river was wide there with no stops for tolls to slow them down. "If we keep going at this rate, we will be in Holland in the morning," said Cousin Jake.

"Will the soldiers stop us again?" asked Alice fearfully.

"No doubt they will, little girl. Boats and carriages and wagons and people on foot, in other words, everybody gets stopped at borders between countries."

"I don't hope they hurt Abner's papa again," said Alice. "I was so afraid that time."

Cousin Jake looked at her kindly. "Don't you be afraid little one. You just share the blankets that Fraulein Trudy and I got back at the village. Say your prayers and you will sleep like the angel you are."

"Thank you, Herr Altland," she replied. "You're a nice man."

Abner stood by the rail and watched the hills slowly disappear in the distance. Herr Hoke came over and stood beside him. Herr Hoke never said much, but this evening he seemed to want to talk. "Say good-bye to the Fatherland," he said. "We've come a long way, ain't, Neighbor?" He sighed, put his arm around Abner's shoulder and added, "It doesn't seem possible that we'll never see our village again. I remember when you were born, and when you were just a little toodli.[49] You started running almost as soon as you stood up. I can still see you making down the street as fast as your little legs could carry you and your mother chasing after you. You could make fast for a little one. Some of us have the wanderlust[50] and some of us don't. It always seemed to me that you had it and would not stay in the village all of your life like I would. From little on up you liked to wander away down through the woods, across the fields, and around the lake by yourself, the farther the better. But me, I never thought of leaving home. To be going off like this is just more than I can think about. One day at a time, that's all I can handle. Sometimes I don't see how I can handle that much."

"You'll be all right, Herr Hoke," said Abner. "Don't worry."

"I can't help but worry. I inherited my house and my right to use the fields where I grew my crops and grazed my animals. I farmed for the half and I complained about giving

---

[49] toodli: toddler; tood rhymes with stood
[50] wanderlust: desire to travel

the landlord that much. I had it good and didn't even know it. Now I have no home, no land, no animals, hardly any tools or money. I just have no idea of how it's going to work out. My wife and I may have to be bound out for years to people who could treat us like slaves. We're both thirty seven years old. We'll be old before we can even begin to start over. Your grandfather says to depend on the Lord, but for me, it is easier to say than do." He smiled and said, "Thanks for listening. You best turn in now." Herr Hoke stood at the rail looking back long after Abner had gone to sleep.

CHAPTER SEVEN

When he awoke the next morning Abner saw the flattest land he had ever seen. "This land ain't got no shape to it," he said to nobody in particular. "If those windmills weren't there, I don't think there would be anything worth looking at. It wonders me if they keep pumping all the time. I guess I'll find out before we leave here. This place smells different. It has a wet smell like a marsh." He laughed. "I guess that's because we are in a marsh."

"What are you going on about this morning?" asked Schotzy. "When you don't have anybody to talk to, you talk to yourself. Watch out or you'll be as bad as Seth."

"I don't hope," said Abner. "There was a man standing near me, and I thought I was talking to him."

"Yeah, you did! And you just kept running at the mouth not noticing that he was gone," laughed Schotzy. "Here we are in a whole new country, and you haven't changed a bit."

"Ya, well, I'm just gawksing around to see what I can see. Look! There's a stork's nest on top of that pole. There aren't many trees, so I guess they put up a pole for the storks."

"I saw a stork on top of a house," said Schotzy. "The people here believe they bring good luck."

"I remember people back home said they brought babies. I used to believe that, but now I know better." Abner's voice broke, and a feeling of sadness hit him. "Ya, now I know better."

Changing the subject, Schotzy said, "I thought that we would get off the boat as soon as we got to Holland."

"Maybe we aren't even in Holland yet. How can a person tell?"

Willy, who had come by and heard the last part of their conversation broke in, "We are in Holland. You slept right through the border crossing. There was such a backup they opened another line, and we got in close to the front of it. We were glicklich." He looked at Abner and asked, "I know, we aren't supposed to believe in luck, but how else can you explain it?"

Abner rolled his eyes and answered. "Do you mean to tell me that after all of my grandpa's teaching, you still don't know? Well, don't expect me to tell you." He shook his head and then said, "The scenery is interesting but I'm more interested in food. Have you seen anyone giving out food?"

"No," said Willy. "It's nearly time to get off the boat, so I don't think we'll get any for awhile."

"One thing's for sure," said Abner. "Since none of our people have any possessions, it won't take much time to disembark."

As they stepped ashore everyone was asking, "What do we do now?" They should not have worried because a group from a religious sect called the Mennonites were there to meet them. It was the mission of the Mennonites in Holland to meet the boats and care for refugees who had been treated badly in the countries of their origin. Abner had never seen a sweeter face than that of Frau Veldt who was there to greet them. She reminded him of his grandmother. She took them to the Mennonite mission for breakfast and provided them with places to stay. In no time at all everyone was settled.

She also told them that there was work to tide them over until they could continue their journey.

"That was a miracle if I ever saw one," Abner said to his parents when they were settled in a small room with featherbeds and plenty of down filled comforts.

Matthias nodded and said to his wife, "Rachel, you stay here and rest at least until tomorrow. Abner and I must go and see about the jobs the lady was talking about."

When they arrived at the meeting room, Frau Veldt told them what to expect. "There are two kinds of jobs available today for the men and boys," she said. "One is at the duck processing plant, and the other is at the tulip farm. One is to the right, and one is to the left. Take this coin and flip it. If it comes up heads, you go right. If it comes up tails, you go left. Your jobs are waiting for you. The women and girls will spin, weave, sew, mend, care for the babies or do some other work around here. Even little children can help. The Bible says if you don't work, you don't eat." She smiled at each one as they went out the door.

Abner flipped the coin, and it came up tails. He and his father went out the door, turned left and walked several blocks. "I can hear those ducks already," said Abner. "They make loud."

Ahead of them was a large shed, and inside it were crates filled with ducks. Beyond the crates was a chopping block. One man was chopping off heads. Two people were picking the feathers and down off the birds. A man was singeing[51] them. Two women were washing them. Two people were gutting them. Two others were giving them a final wash. Abner caught a whiff of the ducks and made a face. "Ach, they stink." he said. "What job is mine?"

The foreman led them to their workplace and said something that they did not understand. He picked up a

---

[51]   singeing: burning off the fuzz

freshly killed bird, showed them how to pick, and then showed them another bird with torn skin and shook his head.

Before he even began to work, Abner said again, "They stink, ain't?"

Matthias nodded his head and said, "Ya, Abner. They smell as bad for us as they do for you. There's no use going on about it." Without saying more, he began picking.

The glassblower came in and he was given the job of singeing. When Willy, Seth and Michael arrived, they had to gut the birds.

On the way in, Seth stopped to chat. "Otto was with us," he said. "When he saw he was expected to clean ducks, he said it was women's work and he kept on going. I told him he better would work, and he said I didn't need to think that I could boss him around. So I don't know where he went, maybe the other way. He said he believed he could do better by himself. I don't think he can, do you? It seems like a dumkopf[52] thing to me, not doing what we're told, beins we're in a strange country and all." The foreman walked toward Seth and said something he did not understand. Next, the foreman stuck out his tongue and made a cutting motion. Seth understood that, but he looked hurt. "I just wanted youse to know about Otto." The foreman gave him a dirty look, and Seth stopped talking for a while.

It was a long day. Abner's nose would itch, and he would try to scratch it. Down would get on his face, and then it would itch all the more. He had been on the move all spring and most of the summer. Standing still was hard, and his legs began to twitch. In order for the feathers and down to come off easily, the ducks had to be picked while they were still warm and dry. That meant that sometimes blood was still dripping from their necks when the pickers got them. Abner

---

[52]   dumkopf: literally dumb head, stupid

ended up with blood on his hands, arms, feet, legs and all over his clothes. Flies buzzed around his head and around the birds. "I wouldn't care if I never saw another duck in my whole life," he said, adding, "Ach, they stink."

"It could be worse," said his father. "You could be gutting them."

Abner glanced toward the older boys, chuckled at what he saw, and knew his father was right. "It's good we got here first."

When the ones who worked with the ducks got back to their lodgings, no one wanted to be near them, they smelled so bad. "You must go around back, strip your clothes off and soak them in cold water," said Frau Veldt.

"But we got nothing else to put on," protested Abner.

Frau Veldt pointed to a pile of clothing. "Find something that comes close to fitting you. Then wash out your own clothes and hang them out to dry. By the time you have washed yourselves and your clothes, your supper will be ready."

Abner wanted to know what the girls had done all day, but he was too tired to ask. He went to sleep at the supper table, and his papa carried him up to bed.

The next day there were no ducks to dress so everyone in the group turned to the right. Schotzy was with them, as well as Reuben and the French boy, Louie. They walked to a farm where they dug tulip bulbs from a long field. There was a windmill with arms that continually turned with a squealing, scratching, screeching sound, pumping water from the ground into a canal. The boys spent the day bending over, digging up bulbs, shaking off the dirt, putting them into crates and carrying them to the shed, while the foreman yelled at everyone to work harder, work faster, be more careful, not to cut bulbs with the shovel and to be sure to get them all.

"I thought I was tired yesterday, but today was worse," Abner said to his father as they walked back to the Mennonite home. "Whyfer did that man holler at us all the time? He even hollered at the little ones. It wonders me whatfer work we'll do tomorrow. I hope it's not this again, but I don't hope it's picking ducks either."

"You remember the saying about beggars can't be choosers?" asked Matthias. "Think about it. Besides, tulips don't stink."

Abner turned to his best friend and said, "You're not a beggar, Schotzy. Why are you working? You wouldn't have to."

"Well, what would I do if I didn't? Yesterday I felt terrible, playing all day with my dog and Reuben. The ladies looked at me like I was a lazy bum. It's better I work."

"I guess you're right. What did the girls do?"

"Some of them sewed," said Schotzy. "A lady showed Martina how to set up a loom, and she started to weave a blanket. Another lady showed Alice how to spin. Poor Alice. It's harder than you think to spin an even thread. She spun until her finger started to bleed. They told her she should have complained sooner that her fingers hurt. But you know Alice, she never complains about anything."

"You're right, Alice doesn't complain," said Abner. He had never noticed. "She'll get the hang of it before long, I'm sure," he added. "How about Minnie? What did she do?"

"She worked in the garden. She pulled weeds and planted spinach and lettuce. Even planting it this late, they'll get a crop. Rich people in England buy greens that are grown here, and these people like their greens, too. The lady talked to her about the herbs that were growing and about the other plants."

"That should have pleased her," said Abner. "What did the women do?"

"They sewed on comforters that they fill with duck down," said Schotzy. "Trudy and Frau Hoke got the job of washing the down and the feathers. Wet feathers don't smell like roses."

"You don't have to tell me about not smelling like roses," said Abner. "Did you see me when I got home the other night?

"Ya," laughed Schotzy. "I did my best not to get downwind of you."

"Seth and Willy were worse."

"You're right, they were."

"What about the rest of the women?" asked Abner. "What did they do?"

"Your mother was determined to work as hard as the rest, but she turned pale and nearly fainted, so Frau Veldt told her to rest. I hope she'll be all right. I heard the women talking about the ocean voyage. It sounds like we ain't seen nothin' yet. They said the same as the Gypsy said, that no babies live through it. Lots of people die, especially women who are going to have a baby. Us men are tougher. We make it."

"It wonders me what Frau Grim will do about little Barbara. Did you hear her say?"

"No," Schotzy said with a worried look on his face. "My mother died when I was just little, and I don't remember her at all," he said. "Frau Grim is the closest thing to being a mother to me that I have ever known. I hate to think of her not going with us, and I hate to think of anything happening to little Barbara."

The next day was Sunday. The Brethren group went to church with their hosts in the morning. There was a light lunch at noon, and Herr Hartzell called his people together outside in the backyard for an afternoon service. He began by asking, "How many of you know what God said to Joshua after Moses had died?"[53]

---

[53]   Joshua 1:2-9

Abner thought he knew, but he was not sure, so he did not answer. Neither did anyone else. Grandpa did not waste time waiting for someone to reply but simply said, "I don't have my Bible, but I know He said to be strong and of great courage because He would not fail the people nor forsake them. He said to remember the words of His book and meditate on them day and night. What do you think meditate means?" He again answered his own question. "It means to think about it. God also told Joshua to tell the people not to turn from His words to the right or to the left, but to stay on the straight path so that they would prosper wherever they went. The same applies to us today. God will protect us, but we must do what the Good Book says." He stopped, looked around and then began to pray, "Our Father in Heaven, let our actions today and from this day forward be pleasing in your sight, in Jesus' name, Amen."

Herr Hartzell stood quietly, then looked around and said with a nervous chuckle, "I've never done this before, and I want to do it right." He closed his eyes for a moment and added, "If there is anyone here who believes that Jesus Christ is the son of God and feels ready to be baptized, he or she should come forward. If anyone does make that decision, we will then go to the nearest pond and have a baptism. Let us sing *Fairest Lord Jesus* while those who are ready come forward."

Abner gulped. He had said he wanted to be baptized, but was he ready? He listened to the others sing while he stood on one foot and then the other. A little voice in his head said, *This is what you've wanted, now do it.* Another little voice said, *No, you're too young to know what it's all about.* Then the first voice came back, loud and clear, *Now is the right time. You will never be ready by yourself, but Jesus will help you.* At those words, he went forward. He was followed by Frau Grim, Aunt

Edda, Antonio, Seth, Herr and Frau Bollinger, Herr and Frau Rohrbaugh.

For the baptism Frau Veldt provided long white shirts for the men and boys and white robes for the women. Everyone walked about a quarter of a mile to the pond. It was a warm day, perfect for a baptism. Abner and his grandfather stepped into the water first and waded to a spot that seemed to be deep enough. "Grandson, don't be afraid," Grandpa whispered. "I've never done this before but I won't drop you. I do believe I'll do it right."

"Sure you will," Abner whispered back.

Herr Hartzell spoke to the ones who desired to be baptized, "Before I baptize you, I must ask each one of you three questions. If you can answer 'I do,' to all of them, I will baptize you. The questions are, 'Dost thou believe that Jesus Christ is the Son of God and that he brought from heaven a saving gospel? Dost thou willingly renounce Satan with all his pernicious ways and all the sinful pleasures of this world? Dost thou covenant with God in Christ Jesus to be faithful until death?'"

Abner came first. When asked the questions he looked his grandfather in the eye and answered, "Ya, I do."

"Abner Frederick Hartzell, I now baptize you in the name of the Father," he said. He then placed one hand over Abner's nose and with the other hand lifted him off his feet and plunged him face down until he was completely under the water. Next he said, "I baptize you in the name of the Son," and plunged him again. For the third plunging he said, "I baptize you in the name of the Holy Spirit." When the ceremony was complete, his grandfather shook his hand and said, "I welcome you into the body of Christ."

Abner got out of the water. Antonio went in. Herr Hartzell repeated the ceremony until he had baptized everyone who had gone forward. When he was finished, Rachel rushed to her sister and embraced her. "Edda," she said, "I'm so glad." After Rachel kissed her sister and welcomed her into the body of Christ, she went to Abner. "I knew you were growing in your knowledge and love of the Lord, so I was not surprised to see you go forward to be baptized. But Edda! Now that was a surprise. How good it was to see her accept Jesus as her Lord. I've been praying, but you're never sure. Bless you, son. Now let us congratulate the rest and wish them the best." *This is what I wanted for a long time,* thought Abner. *I believe it will be easier to be good now that I belong to Jesus.*

When all of the Brethren were congregated in the large meeting room, Herr Hartzell said, "Believers should keep their eyes on our Lord Jesus to learn His ways as He has shown us by His own example. In this way, we learn the mind of our Master even in the smallest things. We should look only to His perfect example and His words to show us the way to live holy lives in obedience to His commands. To show us that in His kingdom the servants are the greatest, Jesus washed the apostles' feet on the night before he was betrayed. We will now follow His example by washing each other's feet."

The men washed the men's feet, and the women washed the women's feet. When everyone's feet had been washed, Herr Hartzell prayed a special prayer for the new members of the body of Christ asking God to bless them and prepare them for whatever lay ahead. Then the group celebrated by having a love feast.

On the morning following the baptism service, Herr Hartzell, Matthias, and Herr Hoke were sent off on a construction job. Herr Schmitt went to work for a blacksmith. Antonio went to remove bees from someone's chimney and to harvest the honey. For the boys, it was back to the ducks. Abner and Schotzy picked while Reuben and Louie helped them.

It was no different from the time before, except that Abner now was the senior member of the picking team. "You don't look so hogged up today as you did the first day," said Schotzy. "You must be getting the hang of it. Look at me. I must look like a murderer."

"You'll catch on pretty soon," said Abner. "I sure wouldn't want to do this for a living but it isn't as hard a job as bending over, picking up tulip bulbs, putting them into boxes, and lugging them to the end of the row. They tell me that in a few weeks the bulbs will be replanted. That's all bending over and planting instead of digging out. I don't get it why they take them up if they just go ahead and replant them."

"They sell flowers in the spring and bulbs in the fall," said Schotzy. "They know what they're doing." He put his finger to his lips, spit away the down that stuck to his lips, and then motioned with his head that the foreman of the job was heading their way.

He did not know much of their language, but he did know, "Too much talk. Knock off the blabbermauling."[54]

When things got slow late in the afternoon, Seth took a duck's foot, found the ligaments that controlled the toes and sneaked up behind Abner and Schotzy. "Quack, quack!" he hollered, and the boys jumped.

"Haw, haw, haw," came a loud laugh. "I got here just in time." There was a dark man coming towards them, laughing so hard that he could hardly stand. It was Klaus. "Ach du lieber," he said when he finally stopped laughing. "I needed that laugh."

Reuben dropped the duck he was picking and ran to him. "They told me that you are an expert picker by now, Reuben, and you would show me how to do a good clean job," Klaus

---

[54]   blabbermauling: running at the mouth

said as he lifted the little fellow above his head. "How are my boys doing?"

"We're just about experts, but we were just told that we run at the mouth too much," said Schotzy, trying to keep his voice down. "I'm so glad you are here and safe, Big Angel. I'd like to hug you, but if I did, I'd have you covered with feathers and down and blood and guts."

"It looks like I already am," Klaus said as he put Reuben down and hugged Schotzy.

As they walked back to the mission, Schotzy, who had been looking closely at Klaus, asked, "What did you do to yourself that you look so dark?"

"The Gypsy made a schmutzy[55] out of black walnut hulls and something else. She rubbed it on my hair, my face, my neck and my hands. It will wear off, but I might look a little streaked for a while. She didn't want any trouble getting across the border, and she figured I would look more like a Gypsy if I was dark. She was right. I had no trouble at all."

"I don't care what you look like," said Schotzy. "I'm so glad you found us."

"Me, too. I missed all of you and also my sister. Did she get married yet?"

"No," said Abner. "And there don't seem to be any plans for it either. Herr van Zant stole her chest and wedding dress. Maybe that's the reason."

"How about you, Abs, did you get baptized yet?" asked Klaus.

"Ya, yesterday. At first I thought I was not ready, but something told me to go ahead and do it. I don't feel much different."

"They say that it's not how you feel that counts, it's what the Bible says," said Klaus. "I was baptized as a baby, but not since I've been grown up. The believer's baptism makes

---

[55]   schmutzy or schmutzich: a mixture that can be smeared

sense to me. If I'd have been here, I may have gone along with you."

"Me and Minnie were talking about it," said Schotzy. "We don't know if we're gonna get rebaptized and belong to your church, or not. We don't know enough about what's in the Bible. Besides, we think maybe we should be older when we join."

"Well, little friend, how old are you?" asked Klaus.

"What day is it?"

Klaus pursed his lips and squinted his eyes as he thought hard. "As far as I can figure, it must be July 22."

"Rats!" said Schotzy. "I missed my birthday."

"What day was it?" asked Abner.

"I was ten on July 20."

"We can pull your ears[56] anyhow," said Abner, reaching for one. "We need to celebrate."

"You're not pulling my ears. It's not my birthday," said Schotzy covering both of them with his hands.

"I can so," said Abner as he started to wrestle with his friend.

"No, no, no," said Klaus pushing Abner away with his big right hand. "It's not his birthday. If he doesn't want you to, you can't pull his ears until it comes around again."

"All right, be that way," Abner said with a put on scowl. Then he broke into a big smile and said, "Happy Birthday. I'll get you good next time."

"You'll have to catch me first."

Klaus had stopped at the Mennonite mission before he went to see the boys, so the rest of the group knew that he had caught up with them and was safe in Holland.

At supper that night, there was rejoicing that everyone was together again. Herr Hartzell offered a prayer of

___

[56] Pennsylvania Dutch birthday custom is that however old one is, one's ears get pulled that many times.

thanksgiving, and then everyone had a good supper which included Antonio's honey. When they were finished eating, Cousin Jake stood and said, "I have an announcement to make."

He's going to tell us when he and Trudy are getting married, thought Abner. *That's nice. I like weddings.*

"Trudy and I have decided not to get married now," said Jake. "You have all heard that all of the babies and most of the women who are expecting them do not survive the ocean voyage to America. I do not want to take the risk that it would happen to Trudy. We'll get married when we get to Pennsylvania, if she is willing to marry me still when she knows me better. Does anyone else have anything to say?"

Looking as if she were about to cry, Frau Grim stood and glanced around at the group. "I have something to say, too," she said. "You are the nicest people I have ever met in my whole life. You are truly my family." She choked up and could not speak. When she regained control she continued, "It breaks my heart to say this, but I'm going to stay here until Barbara is old enough to travel. I cannot risk her life by going with you now." She sat down and wiped her eyes with her apron. Reuben ran to her and put his arms around her. He wanted to say something, but words would not come. She handed Barbara to Martina, and he crawled onto her lap just as he had done the first time he saw her. Schotzy hugged her, too, but found no words to say.

Just then Frau Veldt came from the kitchen and announced, "Every morning we sent out so many to work, and that many came back for supper and stayed the night, but one less than that many reported for work each day. Can anyone explain how this happened?"

No one spoke, but everyone turned and looked at Otto. His face became fiery red, but he sat in his chair without saying anything. Finally Jake stood, looked at him hard and asked, "Otto, have you been going to work?"

"Yes, sir, I have," he answered.

"All right, I'll put it this way," said Cousin Jake. "Did you go and work where you were sent?" Otto squirmed and continued to look down. "I am not your mama, and I am not your papa," scolded Jake. "I do not have to put up with this kind of behavior. You have one and only one more chance. You stay sober and do exactly as you are told, or you will not go along with the rest of us to Pennsylvania. Do you understand?"

Otto stood up. "I thought if I got away from my mama once, nobody would boss me around," he replied angrily. "I'm not a baby, and youse want to boss me around more than she did. I'm fifteen years old now, and I don't have to take it." He turned away from the table and walked out of the house. Herr Hartzell followed closely behind.

"Otto," he called to him. "Think. What will happen to you if you walk out now? Where will you go? What if you get sick? You had better think this over."

"Herr Hartzell, you just don't understand," he said. "You never had people bossing you around all the time like I've been bossed around."

"Is that what you really think?" asked Herr Hartzell. "That I've never been bossed around? You have never heard my story, have you?" Otto shook his head. "I was bound out when I was eight years old. My parents sent me off to be the whipping boy for the son of the king and he was one spoiled prince. If he was bad, I got whipped. If I was bad, I got whipped. If he didn't do as he was told, I got whipped. If I didn't do as I was told, I got whipped. What do you think of that?"

Otto hung his head and did not respond.

"I've watched you in church, in the neighborhood back home, and during the times I was teaching lessons. You don't pay attention, and you don't have much self control. You think your mother was strict with you, but she wasn't. You are free to walk away from here if you want, or you can go back in the mission and apologize to Herr Altland and to our hostess for taking advantage of their goodness. The choice is yours."

Otto placed his hands on his hips, thrust his jaw forward and did not answer.

"Do you remember the name of the place your parents are?"

"No, but I could find it," replied Otto. "It was the place with the big clock and the people came out. I can find them if I want." He looked at his fingernails and then said, "Like I said, I'm fifteen years old, and I can take care of myself." He squared his shoulders, turned his back and walked toward the town.

Abner saw the disappointed look on his grandfather's face when he returned. "That one thinks he knows a lot more than he does," he said. "He's to be pitied. He has a hard road ahead of him."

The group had been working and staying at the Mennonite mission for two weeks when Frau Veldt said, "We usually don't keep people here as long as you have stayed. We made an exception for you because everything had been stolen from you, but you can stay only a few more days. By then the ladies should have one comforter made for each of you and some clothing for the ones who need it most. I don't think it will be a hardship for you to leave because ships sail for England several times a week."

The next morning Cousin Jake went to check on sailing schedules, and the rest returned to work. "Just think," said Abner towards the end of the day. "Not long and then in our whole lives, we won't ever have to pick another duck."

"You don't know that for sure," said Schotzy. "I'll bet you the time will come when you have to pick ducks, and when you do, you'll think of me." Schotzy laughed and slapped Abner on the back leaving a hand-shaped imprint of down. "How do you get down off of a horse? You don't get down off a horse, you get down off of Abner." He tried to wipe the down off Abner's back, but just managed to smear it around. Abner could see the foreman looking at them, but Schotzy was in a silly mood and did not seem to care.

"I don't even know how to get up on a duck, so how can I get down from a duck?" Schotzy asked. Abner, Reuben and Louie laughed and the foreman headed their way. "Settle!" he said.

The workday was finally over. The boys washed their hands and left the duck slaughter house forever. When they got back to the mission, there was a horse and cart out front. Standing beside it was Herr van Zant. "It wonders me what that fat thief wants," Abner said to Schotzy.

"Not so loud. He'll hear you."

"I don't care," said Abner. "That's what he is, a thief, and he knows it." He nodded to the man.

Herr van Zant, looking very uncomfortable, said, "Is this where you're staying? I need to talk to your grandfather and return some things to him."

"I'll see if he's back from work. Can I tell him what you want?"

"No."

Abner could feel hatred and anger building inside himself until he could hold it no longer. "You're a lowdown stinkin' thief," he said. "And you made my mama's baby die. That was my little brother. My mama hasn't been good ever since. How could you come around here after you did a rotten thing like that?"

Herr van Zant put his hands over his face. "I'm truly sorry," he said.

Abner stared at him and asked, "Are you being false, or do you mean it? Saying you're sorry isn't enough. Everything you say or do has consequences. You need to think before you do something or say something. Didn't anybody ever tell you that?"

Abner was so angry he could have torn into the man like he and Minnie tore into the soldier when he was beating his father on the boat. "Easy, Abner, easy," said Schotzy, taking hold of his arm, and then turning to Reuben he said, "Go get Herr Hartzell as fast as you can. I must stay here with Abner."

"Don't worry," said Herr van Zant. "I'm not going to hurt him, and I'm not going to go away." He looked at the ground and said no more.

The boys eyed him suspiciously and remained quiet also. Schotzy turned his back on Herr van Zant and said to Abner, "I'm proud of you. I remember the day I first heard your grandpa say to you that words and actions have consequences. I had never heard that before. It was after you told the magistrate off about letting me go hungry all winter. I'll never forget that as long as I live."

"I was scared that I would be punished after I said it. That was just before all of the trouble started. Now it really wonders me why Herr van Zant came and found us. I guess we'll find out. Here comes Grandpa."

Schotzy let go of Abner's arm and whispered, "I'm proud of you that you didn't lose your temper."

"Thanks. It wasn't easy."

Grandpa did not tell the boys to leave, so they stayed and listened.

"Your grandson told me about the baby," said Herr van Zant. "I can't make it up to Frau Hartzell, but I am sorry."

"Being sorry isn't enough," said Herr Hartzell. "Everything you do has consequences."

"Ya, I know. Abner just said it. My papa also told me that a long time ago, too, but I wouldn't listen. Now it's too late. I can't go back and show him I'm sorry, but I can show you that I am." Herr Hartzell said nothing and neither did the boys. They wanted to hear everything the thief had to say.

Herr van Zant rubbed his hands together nervously and began talking. "As I was going through your things to sell them," he said, "I came upon your Bible. I had not touched a Bible since I dropped out of seminary." He stopped, took a deep breath and added, "I just made a vow to be honest, and I'm breaking it already. I was thrown out of seminary."

They waited for him to continue. "When I saw that it was inscribed to Frederick Hartzell, and it was from a queen, I knew I had something precious. I was excited about how much money I could get for it. Then I wondered how a humble man like you could have known a queen and been given such a valuable book. Suddenly, I was ashamed that I had taken what must be your most precious possession. In fact, I was more ashamed than I ever imagined I could be. God got hold of me, and I cried out to Him for forgiveness. Suddenly His power came over me, and He gave me a vision of hell. He let me know that I would have no more chances. I would be there very soon if I didn't change right then. I fell to my knees and cried out for forgiveness and mercy."

"Praise God," said Herr Hartzell.

"I've brought back everything I took from you and your people, and then some. On the boat I heard your grandson tell his mother that he and his papa saw a nice chest that she would like. I got a nice one for her. I also got good blankets to replace the worn ones I took. I'm returning the anvil to the blacksmith. I bought some tools that are better than the ones he had. I bought more leather for shoes as well as shoe tacks and different sized laths so the cobbler can make more kinds of shoes. There is a new set of equipment for the glass blower because his was pretty much worn out. I also have treats for the children." He smiled at the boys, but they did not return his smile. He looked around uncomfortably and added, "Here's money for the cow." He reached into the cart, got the Bible and gave it to Herr Hartzell who took it carefully, but still did not say anything. Next, Herr van Zant brought out a birdcage with a cat in it.

"Princess," said Abner, as he reached for his pet. He got her out of the cage and held her tight. "Are you all right, old girl?" he asked tenderly as he let her down to take a stretch.

"Did Fraulein Trudy get married yet?" asked Herr van Zant.

"No, not yet," answered Herr Hartzell.

"That's good," said Herr van Zant. "She's a lovely lady, and she deserves better than Jake." He nodded his head, looked at the boys and added, "Ya, I know. She deserves better than me, too." No one said anything to that remark either.

"I must go find my mother," he continued. "I know she's been praying for me for many years. I hope she's still living. My father isn't, that I know. It's too late to make amends to him. He tried to raise me right. May God bless his soul and bless all of you. You're good people. You can have the cart and horse. Goodbye." He tipped his hat, turned to leave and began walking down the road. After he had taken about a dozen steps, he turned back. "When I was looking for you, I saw the boy who left his parents and then was at the beer. He was begging on the street. I thought you would like to know."

"Thank you for telling me, but there is nothing I can do about him," said Herr Hartzell. "He left us of his own free will. We're leaving here tomorrow, and he is not going along. If the Lord puts it on your heart, watch out for him. After things get bad enough for him, he may listen to you."

Supper that night was a combination of a joyous and a sad affair. Herr Schmitt was overjoyed to get his anvil and the new tools. Grandpa was pleased with the return of his Bible. Abner held onto Princess as if he would never let her go, but he petted Pearl once in a while so she would not get jealous. Minnie beamed when she saw her portfolio with its leaves and notes from Father Werner. Trudy got the wedding dress out of her trunk and showed it off. Everyone was pleased to see the return of the things that had been stolen, as well as the chest for Rachel and the new blankets. The treat Herr van Zant mentioned was sweets for each child and a large basket of peaches to be shared by all.

Even with all of the enjoyment, there was the unspoken knowledge that they would leave soon, and Frau Grim and little Barbara would stay behind. *How can we be so happy and so sad at the same time?* thought Abner. *It doesn't make sense.* He took Barbara on his knee, bounced her up and down saying, "Reite, reite allua reite."[57] Barbara laughed, reached for him and said, "Da da." He held her close and kissed her.

As if she could read his mind, Frau Grim spoke to him, Schotzy and Reuben. "You boys have been like sons to me. I love you so very much." Abner kept holding Barbara until Martina took her. He could see that it was all Martina could do to keep from crying. Reuben crawled onto Frau Grim's lap, put his arms around her neck and said, "Love you."

Frau Grim wiped her eyes and ran her hands over his soft wavy hair. Then she did something surprising. She took his hand, brought it over his head and said, "See if you can touch your ear." He reached around and he touched it. When she made sure his arm was all the way over his head, she said, "You're wondering why I wanted to see if he could touch his

---

[57]   reite, reite, allua, reite: ride, ride the horsy, ride

ear. I've been trying to remember this old saying and I finally did. It's, 'If a child can reach over his head and touch his ear, he's at least seven years old.' I was worried about Reuben being old enough to survive the trip, and he is. He's just not going to be a big person when he grows up. The other thing is, the French lady says that her nephew is five going on six years old. Reuben can't be her nephew if he's seven. She has no claim on him."

Schotzy jumped for joy. "I wasn't really worried, mind you, but I feel much better about both things that you just figgered out." He kissed Frau Grim on the cheek.

"You'll be all grown up when I see you again," she said with a sad smile.

Schotzy whispered something in her ear, and she objected, "But that's too much. I don't need that much. Frau Veldt got me a job as a nanny with a rich family. They have a boy five years old and a girl three. I can keep Barbara with me. I'll be all right."

Schotzy shook his head. "You must keep it."

Frau Grim appealed to Herr Hartzell, "Tell him it's too much."

He took her hand and said, "You're a very special person and whatever he gave, I am sure you deserve. You can have the horse and cart, too. Auf Weidersehn,[58] dear friend."

---

[58]   Auf Weidersehn: goodbye

CHAPTER EIGHT

Well outfitted with comforts, pillows and new clothes, the refugees left the mission early the next morning, each carrying a lunch. "We will never forget the kindness of you Mennonites," said Herr Hartzell as the refugees were leaving the mission. "If there is ever anything that we can do for you, you may be certain that we will do it. You can ask us any time from now until the Lord comes again."[59]

Everyone in the party climbed aboard a boat bound for Rotterdam where they would catch a ship for England. The children immediately began counting the windmills.

"Tell us about windmills, Cousin Jake," said Abner. "What are they there for?"

"Mostly they pump water out of the land so it can be farmed," he said. "They came up with the idea about five hundred years ago. Someone had gone on a crusade to the Holy Land, the place where Jesus was born. While this person was there, he saw windmills pumping water out of the ground to water the earth. This person, whoever he

---

[59] It took more than two hundred years, but the American Anabaptists were able to repay the kindness of the Dutch Mennonites following World War II. They provided 40% of the relief that was sent.

was, changed the idea around to pumping the water out of the ground so that the the earth would be dry enough to grow things. Then someone else said that if people put up the earthen walls around the marshes they could have more land to grow things on. So they did that. It took many years to wash the salt out of the ground but now it will grow good crops. The earthen walls are called dikes, and they hold the water back from the rivers and the sea. It rains a lot here, so there is almost always too much water. That's why the windmills run whenever the wind blows. If they didn't, the ground would be too wet to grow anything."

Abner looked at his cousin with admiration. "How do you know all this stuff?"

Cousin Jake pointed to his head and said, "There's a whole bunch of weird stuff in there that I may never use, but it comes out once in a while." He laughed and continued, "Did you know people can send messages with windmills. They have prearranged signals that mean certain things depending on where the sails or arms are and the way they are tilted. They use those signals in time of trouble or war. Would you like to know what these people say if someone is ferhuddled?"[60] Abner nodded. "They say he got knocked on the head by a windmill."

As the refugees approached Rotterdam, the river traffic became very heavy. "This is interesting, watching all of them boats," said Abner.

"Not all of them are boats, you know. Some of them are ships," said Cousin Jake.

"Is that right?" said Abner. "What's the difference?"

"Boats float on top of the water and ships displace water."

---

[60]   ferhuddled: mixed up, confused, bewildered

"I don't know what you are talking about when you say displace water."

"See that ship over there?" Jake asked as he pointed to an old wooden ship that sat high in the water. "It's empty or nearly so. See the line halfway up the side of the ship? When the ship is loaded it will be down in the water to that line. That's because it will be heavy and push the water out of the way. The ship weighs the same as the amount of water it displaces. That's what displace means. Don't ever get on a ship if the load line is below water level. The ship will weigh more than the water it displaces and will probably sink."

"I'll remember that," said Abner. "We're going to England first and then to Pennsylvania, and we don't want to sink on the way."

"Das es recht," said Jake. "We want to get there all right. Also, ships have decks below and boats don't."

"The houses here don't look much different from the ones up the river," said Abner, "but the place smells different."

"That's the sea air that you are getting a sniff of. You'll breathe a lot of it before you get where you're going. Look to your left, and you can see the open sea and then a little further, see that tall pole sticking up there? I do believe that's the mast of the ship we're going to sail on. Tell everyone to eat lunch and then be ready to disembark as soon as we land. We must hurry. The wind is blowing hard, and the captain will go the second the tide turns. We want to be on that ship."

"What has the tide got to do with it?"

"When the tide turns, it will carry a ship with it and give it an extra boost," said Cousin Jake. "Now go tell them like I said."

Abner ran around the deck yelling loudly, "Cousin Jake says to be ready to get off this boat as soon as we land. Whenever the tide turns, that there boat over there is going to go, and we want to be on it."

Everyone except Widow Schneider got up and began getting ready to leave the boat. The widow, however, sat quietly, smoking her pipe.

Trudy, seeing that her mother was not preparing to disembark, said, "How can I help you, Mama?" Widow Schneider put her nose in the air and ignored her daughter.

"Mother, why are you acting like this? Can't you see that the ship is right there? We need to get on it as quickly as possible." The widow turned her head and would not look at Trudy.

"Ach du lieber, Mama," said Trudy, plainly disgusted. "Stop acting like a child. I told you a dozen times that I'm sorry about what happened."

Trudy reached down to pick up some of her mother's things, and the widow pushed her away. Turning to Frau Hoke who was standing near, the widow said, "Tell that woman that I am not speaking to her, and I will not do what she or that Hartzell snot tell me still."

Schotzy, seeing what was going on, ran to get Herr Hartzell. Abner was watching, and when his grandpa came into sight, the widow seemed to turn into a different person. She smiled and said, "Frederick, so nice it is of you to come and help me get my things together. I could use some assistance. Help me off the bench. I'll be ready in plenty of time."

That old biddy, thought Abner. *How can anyone be so false? I'm sure my grandpa can see right through her, at least I hope so.*

When the boat was close to the ship, Abner looked up, and gasped, "It is so big! I never saw anything so big before."

"You're a hick," hissed Widow Schneider. "Gawksin' at the ship just like a hick."

Abner started to say something back, but thought better of it. *It's no use wasting my breath on such as her,* he thought.

However, he did toss his head and give her an impudent look which he knew he should not do.

It is not an easy task to hurry up the steep gangway while carrying a bedroll with all of one's belongings wrapped inside, but the refugees managed. They were barely on board when the captain called out for the anchor to be lifted and the sails to be unfurled. All of the passengers who had come down the Rhine River stood along the rail waving goodbye to anyone who might be looking. There was a lurch, the ship creaked, and they left the mainland of Europe forever.

"Everyone must go below," shouted the captain. *I don't want to go below,* thought Abner. *I want to smell the sea. I want to look at the water. I want to watch the land disappearing. I want to know how the sailors handle the ship.*

"Move along everyone, move along," a sailor called out. "You heard the captain."

Abner walked as best as he could on the rolling ship toward the open hatch. He looked down. *I see we must crawl down a ladder,* he thought. *Some of the ladies aren't going to like that.* He swung around and had started down when the smell of the place hit him. It was a mixture of tar, vomit, unwashed bodies, old fish, spilled beer, pickled fish, urine, and what smelled like the leavings of some goats that had been on previous trips. Abner coughed. *This is the worst,* he thought. *If this doesn't kill us, nothing ever will. I don't hope that when we go across the ocean we aren't in a hole such as this.*

"Everyone should find a spot and stay there until we land, no matter how long it takes to get where we are going," called out a short sailor with the dirtiest uniform imaginable. "Them's the captain's orders. He don't want no movin' about or carryin' on down here except for youse to use the slop bucket."

"Where's my chair to sit on?" asked Widow Schneider. "A body needs something to sit on."

"Sit on something you brought along, ma'am," replied the sailor. "That's what everybody else is going to do."

"Well, I never heard of such a thing," she said with a huff. She turned to Jake and demanded, "Did you know that we would not have anything to sit on? It was your idea for us to leave home. Now here we are, with nothing to sit on. I'm going to go talk to the captain. Who does he think he is, treating people like this?"

Jake answered softly, "I'm sorry, Mother Schneider, but I did not know it would be like this. When I went to America ten years ago, there weren't nearly as many people taking the trip. Now there are many more people who want to go. The ship owners tell the captains to fill up the vessel, to pack them in. I'll see if I can arrange your belongings so that they will be comfortable for you to sit on." Abner watched him and knew that he was trying his best, but he got no thanks from her.

"When you're done fooling with that," said Widow Schneider, "go awhile and get fire for my pipe onc't."

Jake nodded courteously and said, "Ya, as soon as I can."

Everyone got settled below with considerable complaining. Widow Schneider did not calm down until Cousin Jake found time to go to the galley. He brought back a coal, lit her pipe and waited to see if there was anything else she wanted. *Oh, no,* thought Abner. *I thought this place smelled as bad as it could get, but I was wrong. There is no getting away from it. Maybe if I breathe just a little I'll be all right.* He tried that a while, but it did not work. The rolling of the ship and the smells combined with the lunch that he had eaten quickly before boarding the ship made Abner sick.

"Where's a bucket?" he asked anyone who might be listening. "I have to kuttz!"[61] He looked around and found

---

[61]   kuttz: vomit; sounds like cuts

one just in time. His mother pulled a rag from her bedroll and wiped his mouth.

"I need a drink of water." he said when he was finally finished retching.

"Don't drink much," she said. "You need to leave[62] your stomach rest. If you don't, you'll just throw it up again."

"I'd make you some mint tea, if I had any hot water," said Minnie. 'That would make you feel better." Abner thanked her, and then returned to his spot and sat down.

The next person at the bucket was Herr Hoke. "Ach, watch out, it's gonna go both ways.[63] I've never been so sick." He bent over and held his stomach. "I wish I'd never left home," he said.

Frau Wentz, who seemed to be more frail every day, ate very little and kept none of it down. Her little ones cried much of the time, and she got little sleep. "I just don't know what to do," she said. "Waldemar and Violet don't look so good, and they miss their papa so."

Abner could not get comfortable. He stayed still a few minutes and then began to move his legs, then his arms, then his whole body. He stood and stretched. He ran in place. He sat down again and tried to make his bedroll comfortable. It could not be done. Nothing worked.

"Quit rutching[64] around so much," said the stranger who was next to him. "Ain't you got no rest in your britches? You keep it up and I'll let you have a good one. You're working on my nerves."

"Sorry," Abner said as he tried to stay still. "How long do you think it will take to get to England?"

"How should I know?" asked the stranger crossly as he turned his back and closed his eyes.

Abner could not see high waves and their white caps, but he could feel the action of the sea. So could everyone else. The further from land, the rougher it became. *I'll never get used to this,* Abner thought as the ship creaked, groaned,

---

[62]   leave: let is often used for leave, and the other way around.
[63]   go both ways: vomiting and diarrhea at the same time
[64]   rutching: wiggling, moving nervously

shook and complained. *I may have been the first to get sick, but I'm not the only one.* Nearly everyone was sick sooner or later. Five days later when the ship got to England, all of the refugees were very glad to get off.

"What a fast passage we made," said the captain, rubbing his hands together. "It was just about as fast as we've ever traveled. Sometimes it takes three weeks."

Three weeks! thought Abner. *How could anyone stand it to be on that stinking bucket for three weeks?* What he did not know was that soon he would embark on a voyage that would take three months.

When the ship docked and he got up into the light and out of the foul smelling hold, Abner took a deep breath of air and thought nothing had ever smelled so good. Some people thought fresh air was bad, but he did not believe it. He saw that the English coast was rocky and beautiful, and the harbor was calm. He, along with his dog, and the rest of the passengers walked down the gangway and onto British soil. His legs felt funny, and he thought, *I've never heard of such a thing. This country rocks like the ship did when we first got on it.*

"What's the matter Abs?" called Cousin Jake. "You still got your sea legs?"

"Whatcha mean?"

"I mean does it feel strange to walk on dry land?"

"Ya," replied Abner. "Whyfer do I feel so doppy?"[65]

Jake chuckled. "Your body had to get used to the movement of the ship," he said. "Sailors call that getting your sea legs. Now you have to get used to the land again."

Abner laughed at himself. "I hope it happens fast. I don't hope people think I've been drinking too much beer."

---

[65]   doppy or doppich: clumsy, awkward

Schotzy, accompanied by Herr Hartzell, came running up to him. "Hey, Abs, we're gonna see about buying supplies for the houses we're going to build. You goin?"

"Ya. I'd like that. Where you goin?"

"There's supposed to be a shop up that hill that sells what we maybe could want," said Schotzy. Turning to Cousin Jake, he said, "Herr Altland, we need help. Would you make yourself along and talk to the Englishers for us?"

"Why not? It will give me practice in English. I want to buy materials for Trudy's and my house. If I go in with you, we can no doubt get a better price because of the larger order."

"Well, sure," answered Schotzy. "You help me, and I help you."

"This will be a big surprise for Trudy," said Jake. He smiled in anticipation of Trudy's reaction. "Won't she be pleased when I tell her that I bought windowpanes and hardware for our house!"

It was a bright clear day with the wind blowing off the sea. Abner stopped halfway up the hill to get his breath. "Good idea," said Herr Hartzell. "I'm out of breath, too. My legs aren't as strong as they used to be."

As they rested, Abner asked, "Where's Reuben?"

"He wanted to stay behind with Louie and play on the beach."

"Oops, I forgot about Princess. I hope my parents have her."

"They do," replied Grandpa.

Abner began to pant as they made their way up the steep street that wound its way from the water to the main part of the town. "Whew, this is too much," he said. By the time they got to the top, he was out of breath. Pearl, his nearly grown German Shepherd, was panting, too. He wondered why he should feel as he did, forgetting that for five days he had hardly slept and kept very little food down.

First they came upon a shop with a cutout of a glassblower hanging above the door. The proprietor, a stocky man with a shiny bald head and ruddy face, asked what he could do for them. Cousin Jake, speaking in halting English, said, "It's fast to forget a foreign tongue, but the words I'll try and make right. Window panes we need, a double gross or more."

The shopkeeper looked pleased with the order. He dipped his quill into the ink and began to write with a flourish. First he wrote the date on the paper, July 20, 1735.

"Why did the man write July 20?" asked Schotzy. "That can't be right."

"I learned about this last time I was in England," said Cousin Jake. "On the mainland everyone goes by the new calendar, but here they go by the old one still. Someone who studies these things discovered that there weren't enough minutes accounted for on the old calendar. Because of this the calendar dates were several days behind from where they should have been. The pope put out an order, but because the pope said it, the English would not change. In their eyes anything the pope said had to be wrong."

"What is the date in Pennsylvania?" asked Schotzy.

"The same as here," answered Jake. "Pennsylvania belongs to England so it follows the old calendar."

"So in this country and in Pennsylvania the date today is July 20," said Abner. It suddenly dawned on him that according to the calendar used in England, it was Schotzy's birthday. He shouted, "Happy Birthday!" His hand shot out and he grabbed Schotzy's ear. He began to pull, counting, "One, two, three, four... gotcha," he laughed.

Schotzy tried to get away and before either of them knew it, they were wrestling on the floor.

"Enough!" said Herr Hartzell. "Get up Abner, and behave."

"Sorry, Grandpa, but in this country it's Schotzy's birthday."

The shopkeeper looked at them in astonishment and then said, "Please start over. What do you want and how many?"

"At least two gross of windows like so," said Jake showing the size with his hands. "Two gross," he repeated holding up two fingers, "or as many as you can get together for us by the time our ship leaves for America. How much want you now?"

The shopkeeper did not understand. Jake thought hard and then rephrased his question. "What cost it?"

The shopkeeper smiled at the language and the chance to make such a good sale. Abner stuck his nose as close as he could to the paper and saw 288 plus. He wondered what it stood for. He was surprised to discover that it was the double gross of small window panes. Grandpa and Jake looked the numbers over. So did Schotzy. They came up with a final figure, and Jake told the shopkeeper he would have to go to the bank. All through the dealings, Grandpa and Jake kept their faces straight, not letting their feelings show.

They passed the hardware store on the way to the bank and decided to stop in since the bank was farther up the street. Grandpa and Cousin Jake inquired about buying enough hardware to put in four good sized houses, including brass door latches, latch plates, hinges and locks. The men discussed how many doors and how many windows would be in the houses. They wanted to be sure they got enough of everything that would be needed. They also wanted to know the cost. Jake wrote it all down on a paper. Schotzy listened closely while Abner kept the dogs.

When they got to the bank they found that dogs were not allowed in, so Abner stayed outside. When Schotzy came out, he was jumping with excitement. "It's too good to be true," he said, then looked around to see if anyone was watching or listening. "All that stuff we looked at will take only five of them. Can you imagine that? We can get enough for four houses and a lot more stuff, like a barrel or two of nails and a present for Minnie."

Abner looked at Schotzy standing there excited and full of joy. He tried to appear happy for his friend, but suddenly he felt nothing but envy. *This isn't right,* he thought. *Schotzy is rich, and I don't even have one single pfennig. I promised You, Father, that I would always help anyone who needed help. How can I help anyone if I have no money? Herr van Zant didn't even give me back the coin he gave me. I didn't know what it was, but it was something.* He forced a smile on his face and said, "That's just great, Schotz, just great."

Still excited about his fortune Schotzy said, "Herr Altland and I are going on into the town and see what else we can see. You goin'?"

"I don't think so. I'm ge-pooped.[66] That climb the hill up took it out of me. I'll go back with Grandpa. Maybe we'll find a place to sit along the water."

Half way down they were met by Willy who was bursting with news. "You seem full of yourself," said Herr Hartzell. "Where are you headed?"

"I just came up to tell you something," he said. "You missed some big ruckus. Fraulein Trudy went around looking for Herr Altland, and when she couldn't find him, she was mad enough to chew nails. She said that he told her they would go over town together and buy things for their house. Then she found her mother and started talking to her, but the old biddy wouldn't listen. Fraulein Trudy really got mad then. She really carried on. She yelled at her mother and told her that she was not going to marry Jake, I mean Herr Altland. Widow Schneider put her fingers in her ears and said, 'I'm

---

[66]   ge-pooped: tired, can also mean soiled by diarrhea or a dirty diaper

not listening! Then Trudy said, 'You better would listen because I'm going to be a redemptioner, and you are going to be a redemptioner like me. We have to sell ourselves into bondage because I have no money at all. I know that you don't have enough to pay your way and neither does Klaus.' The old lady still stuck her nose up in the air and didn't talk to Trudy. What do you think?"

Willy likes to gossip, that's what I think, but I'm not going to say nothing. So Abner kept quiet. His grandpa did not say anything either.

"I'm going over town and see what's up there," Willy continued. "Seth didn't feel like going along since he had no money to spend. I said, come along, we can still look, but he said he'd ruther walk along the shore and watch the little kids play. He wants to watch the ships come in and go out. Good luck to him, I'd ruther see what's in the town."

"Willy, I was just thinking," said Herr Hartzell. "It's all right for you to go into town since it's morning, but don't speak to strangers, and be sure to stay on the main streets. Find Jake and Schotzy and stick with them. A place like this where ships come in is not a safe place for a lad by himself. There are men who kidnap boys like yourself and ship them off to be sailors. Didn't your father ever tell you anything like that?"

"Naw, my father never ever told me nothing. You saw how he acts. He just sits with his face in his hands and never says nothing. I'll be careful, don't worry."

"What I said to Willy goes for you, too, Abner. I wouldn't want anything to happen to you."

Abner took his grandfather's hand, and they walked back down to the shore looking at the houses that were very different from the ones back home. "These houses have that coarse grass for roofs," said Abner. "It's a wonder they don't catch on fire."

"That roofing material is called thatch. No doubt they do catch afire unless people are careful and don't let their fireplaces get too hot. They have to have their chimneys cleaned pretty often, too. Even so, it seems to me that lightning could set them on fire pretty easily."

"I wonder what kind of roofs we'll have in America," said Abner.

"We'll just have to wait and see. Jake said he believes there may be slate in the area where we're going. Otherwise, we'll probably have wooden shingles and have to make them ourselves. Slate shingles are fireproof, last longer and are much heavier than wooden ones. Slate is costlier, but if we used it, the houses would be finished faster than they would be if we have to make our own wooden ones."

"There's lots to think about when you build a house. I wish I was going to be there when you do it."

Herr Hartzell looked at Abner as if he did not comprehend what he had just said. Then it dawned on him. "Ach, Grandson," he said. "I forgot that you are going to be bound out and aren't going to be with us. I totally forgot." He turned his face away. What had begun as a lovely day suddenly seemed cold. "Let's go see if we can find something to eat," he said, changing the subject. They made their way along the waterfront looking for an eating place until they saw a little pub ahead that had a sculptured fish out front. Just before they got there, Grandpa grabbed Abner's arm and propelled him into the pub as fast as he could.

"Pretend nothing happened."

"What? What happened?"

"I said to pretend that nothing…." Just then Grandpa turned rapidly and ducked his head as Widow Schneider walked by.

"I get it," laughed Abner. "I'll protect you, Grandpa, I promise. She kicked Pearl. Did you know that? If she gets too friendly with you, Pearl and I will figure out how to fix her."

Grandpa's eyes twinkled, and he said, "I imagine you could, but please don't. It's hard to lose your life mate. Your grandmother has been gone only a few months, and I miss her terribly. The widow's husband has been gone a long time, and no doubt she would like another."

"I pity the one she gets," said Abner. "And I don't hope it's you."

Herr Hartzell laughed hard, the first hard laugh that Abner had heard from him since Grandma died. "I better wouldn't say anything," he said as he patted Abner's back and then went to the counter to order their dinner.

Abner sat at a table in the back of the pub while his grandfather waited for two portions of fried fish, bread, butter and pickles. When Abner bit into the crisp white fried fish his face lit up, and he could not help saying, "Wunderbar! I never fressed anything better. This is good, ain't so?"

As they ate their dinner, they saw Widow Schneider walking back toward the pier. Under her arm was a large package. "I don't hope that's tobacco," said Abner, "but if she's got none she goes ferdudst. I hate that stuff. How about you, Grandpa?"

Herr Hartzell made a face. "I don't like it either," he said. "I bought her some onc't, but no more."

"Ya," said Abner with a chuckle. "She can just put that in her pipe and smoke it."

They ate slowly, watching the people go by. After a while, they saw Jake, Schotzy and Willy go by and then turn around and come in. Jake had a bouquet of flowers and a bag with something in it. He laid them on a table and went to order the food. Willy crept close, nodded his head toward the flowers and whispered, "I told him about Trudy being mad, and he bought them for her. There's sweets in the toot." Abner and

Grandpa kept on eating. "I think it will take more than that to get Trudy over her mad," continued Willy. "And another thing, did you see that greistlich man that was in the town where Minnie came from? He's here, and he's looking for her. He said that she belongs to him. He claims that her step-father gave her to him. He wants to go on the ship with us to Pennsylvania."

Abner looked at Willy, not quite understanding what he had just said. "What do you mean, her step-father gave Minnie to him? Can he do that, Grandpa?"

"I don't know, but I don't think so."

"Minnie won't hold still for it, that's for sure," Abner said as he gulped down his last bite and stood to leave. "We better would find her and tell her."

"Sit back down," said Grandpa. "I'm not finished, and it won't do any good to get Minnie all fussed up. Like I said, we are in England, and the laws here are different. Sit down."

"But she's afraid of him, and he has a powwow spell on her," persisted Abner.

"You don't believe in that superstition, do you?" asked his grandfather. "I often heard you say you didn't believe in superstition."

"I don't, but you shoulda saw that man. He's so ugly he'd scare anybody." Abner shivered just thinking about him. Pearl growled softly, and Abner reached down to give her a pat. When he looked up, he saw Widow Schneider come in the door. She spied Herr Hartzell and made her way directly to him. Pearl bristled, growled and showed her teeth.

The widow backed away from the dog, ignored Abner and smiled at Herr Hartzell. "Frederick," she said in a sweet gentle voice. "Would you be so kind as to…?"

Herr Hartzell stood quickly and said, "I'm sorry Frau Schneider, but it's not possible." He turned his back on her and strode out the door with Abner and Pearl close behind.

Pearl stopped, showed her teeth and gave one final growl. Grandpa walked rapidly toward the wharf with Abner at a trot to keep up. When they had gone some distance his grandfather slowed down and said, "Some things have to be cut off the sooner the better. It makes it easier if people catch on quick."

"I understand," said Abner, "but you know how hateful she's been to me ever since she thought I took her lucky pfennig. I proved to her that she was wrong and I didn't do it. Then she got more hateful than ever. I don't hope she gets as ugly to you."

"I wouldn't count on it." Their conversation was cut off because Minnie, Mary and Alice were coming towards them. The girls were full of the sights they had seen.

"Herr Hartzell," said Minnie excitedly. "You'll never guess who I saw!"

"I know who you saw," said Abner. "Herr Flickinger."

Minnie stared at him. Then she turned so pale that her freckles seemed to stand out on her face. Her knees buckled, and she sat down hard on the street. She covered her face and stayed there for a while. When she tried to get up, the girls took her hands and helped her.

"I thought you said that you aren't afraid of him," said Abner when she had regained her composure.

"I'm not. I never was," Minnie answered hotly. "It just took me by surprise, that's all. Where is he? I don't hope he knows I'm here."

"He knows all right, Willy told him."

Minnie turned to Herr Hartzell. "I'm not afraid of that man," she said. "It's that he's nothing but trouble. He's evil. He casts spells on people. If you or Cousin Jake or anybody else gets in his way, he'll cast a bad one on whoever it is. He wants me back, and he'll do everything he can to get me back. He won't hurt me, but I'm afraid of what he might do to other people. We must not let him go on the ship with us. Do you know where Cousin Jake is? I need to talk to him."

"We saw him back aways at a pub getting something to eat. Just go along this street until you come to a place with a statue of a fish out front. You'll find him there."

Minnie, followed by the girls, walked quickly in the direction of the pub. When they were nearly out of sight, Abner said, "They didn't tell us who they saw. It wonders me who it was."

As they walked along the shoreline, the wind was brisk and they could see white caps on the waves out on the ocean. They came upon a bench in a place that was sheltered from the wind and sat down. The afternoon sun felt good. "Minnie says she's not afraid, but I believe so half she is," said Abner. "What do you think, Grandpa?"

"I hope she isn't," he answered. "But if she is, she would hate to admit it."

"Do you think we can keep that man from getting on the ship with us?"

"I don't see how," said Grandpa. "If he pays his fare, he can go the same as we can. Let's talk about something else."

CHAPTER NINE

Abner turned toward the ocean and held his hand above his eyes to shade them. "I do believe it is the sails of a ship out there. I hope it's ours. It would be good if we didn't have to wait here long. Those sheds we have to stay in don't look to me like they would hold up in a storm."

"The sooner we leave here, the sooner we'll get to Pennsylvania," answered Grandpa nodding his head. "It's nearly August now by our calendar. If we could leave here soon, we should be able to get there by late October or early November."

"That would mean that we got there by Hallowe'en," said Abner. "I hope so. I always like to go around with my hollowed out turnip with a light in it. I never played any mean tricks, but I know that Willy, Otto and Max did." He sighed a deep sigh. "Those three will never go Hallowe'ening together again."

Herr Hartzell sighed, too. "Many things have happened in the last few months," he said. "Elder Wentz and Max were killed. Your grandmother died. Schotzy's grandfather died. Some of the little children died. We were forced to leave home, and we've been traveling ever since. I'll be glad to get some place, settle down and stay there."

"Me, too," said Abner. He would have liked to have talked to his grandfather about being bound out and not being with the rest of the family but he was hesitant. Since his father had not asked Grandpa for the money for their passage, it was as if Abner knew that Matthias would not like the idea of sharing how he felt with Grandpa. Abner sighed again. He looked out to sea, and it seemed to him that the ship was closer.

There is something I've wanted to ask Grandpa about ever since I was baptized, he thought. *I guess I better would do it now since this is the first time I've had him to myself for a long time. But what will he think of me when I tell him?* He shrugged his shoulders. *I may as well get it over with.* He took a deep breath and said, "Grandpa, I thought that after I was baptized I wouldn't do bad things or think bad thoughts, but I do. It's worse now than it was before. When I saw Schotzy with all that money, I wanted it so bad. Well, not his money, but some of my own. I know that's coveting, and I know that's wrong. I'm glad he has it, but I don't even have one pfennig to buy my mother a present. And another thing, back in the pub I really wanted to sic Pearl on Widow Schneider. I've been teaching her every day, and she obeys me. She would have gone after that woman if I would have given the word. It was all I could do to keep from it."

Herr Hartzell laid his hand on Abner's shoulder and said, "Grandson, I am prouder of you than I ever have been in my life. You controlled yourself, and I didn't. I should have answered Widow Schneider kindly or at least politely. The way I acted will bring trouble. I knew it, but I still did it anyway." He shook his head, stroked his chin and looked out to sea in deep thought. Abner sat very still as he always did when his grandfather was thinking.

After what seemed to Abner to be a long time, his grandfather spoke. "In the letter to the Romans in the Bible, St. Paul says that he has the very same problem. Does that surprise you?"

Abner nodded, "Ya, and it does."

"The reason we have the problem is that we are all sinners."

Abner, looking perplexed asked, "Well then, how does anybody get to heaven?"

"That's a good question," replied his grandfather. "Jesus came to earth and lived without ever committing one sin. He was a perfect person. When He died on the cross, He was a perfect sacrifice, and all of our sins were nailed to the cross with Him. When He bled, His blood covered them all. That means that every sin that was ever committed or ever will be committed was laid on Him to make us right with God. It says in **Isaiah 53:4, 5, 6 'Surely he hath borne our griefs and carried our sorrows: yet we did not esteem him stricken, smitten of God and afflicted. But he was wounded for our transgressions, he was bruised for our iniquities: the chastisement of our peace was upon him; and with his stripes we are healed. All we like sheep have gone astray; we have turned every one to his own way; and the Lord hath laid on him the iniquity of us all.'** Iniquity means sin. Jesus paid for our sins with His blood. When Jesus died, the curtain of the Holy of Holies in the temple in Jerusalem was torn from the top to the bottom. That means that we Christians can approach God, ask for forgiveness in Jesus' name, and we will be forgiven. Jesus is in heaven interceding for us. He is between us and God asking Him to answer our prayers."

"Whew," said Abner. "That's good to know."

"You're right, it is good to know. And there's more. He sent His Holy Spirit and with the Spirit's help we can learn to obey God, to control ourselves and to forgive others. God promised that."

Abner looked relieved. "I'm glad you cleared that up for me."

"When it comes to self control we should remember that how another person acts should have no bearing on how we act. We should act in all situations as Jesus would act, using the Bible as our guide."

Abner squeezed his grandfather's hand. "Thanks for telling me. It makes me feel better, but then again I think so half that I shouldn't feel better. I went off this morning without asking my parents' permission to go. Now I'm in trouble. I better would find them and confess, but it is so nice sitting here in the sun, I hate to move."

He looked up the street and saw a man who looked familiar, yet something about him was different. *This must be the person that the girls saw, but who could it be?* He was tall, broad shouldered and dressed in dark clothing. *I don't know any tall man who would wear clothes like that except the magistrate from our village, but he doesn't walk like that. The magistrate stumps along, but this man makes nice.* "He turned to his grandpa and asked, "Who is that man coming towards us? He looks like I should know who he is, but I don't."

Pearl sat up, pulled on her leash, yapped happily and wagged her tail. "Who is it, girl?" Pearl continued to bark and jump wildly. Abner stood, shaded his eyes and then shouted, "It's Father Werner!" He and his dog ran in the priest's direction. "What are you doing here?" he demanded. "You belong back in your village with your people."

Father Werner gave Abner a hug while walking toward Herr Hartzell. "You're surprised to see me, aren't you?" he said as the two men shook hands.

"I am, indeed," said Herr Hartzell. "How did this come about?"

"The cook, her family and their bunch succeeded in running me off. I didn't realize how deeply they resented my taking care of refugees and had been in contact with the bishop long already. He came to visit the day after you left. I had recognized your cow and was taking it from them just as he arrived. They denied that they stole the cow and said that I wasted the church's money and goods on heretics. Then the cook said that I was a heretic. She had heard me say that I believed much the same as you do, meaning that I believed that when it came between believing the Bible and what the pope said, a person should believe the Bible. I did say that." Father Werner shook his head and sat down on the bench as if he were very weary. "I tried to do my best for my people and my best for the suffering ones who came to my doorstep. Jesus said to practice hospitality. I was sure that was what God wanted me to do, and now look what happened!"

Abner looked at his grandfather and saw the loving concern on his face. "Just exactly what did happen?" Herr Hartzell asked.

"The higher ups are deciding if I can still be a priest. That's why I am not dressed as one. I've been transferred to Baltimore, Maryland. From there, I'll be sent to a mission near the Pennsylvania border to work with our people and the Conewago Indians."

"That won't be far from where we're going to settle," said Abner excitedly. "Cousin Jake told us that William Penn's people wanted us to settle near the Maryland border to keep the Marylanders off his land grant."

"That's interesting," said Father Werner. "They told me that Pennsylvanians are moving into Maryland territory.[67] That's one reason they're sending me there."

---

[67] The Maryland, Pennsylvania border was supposed to be along the 40th parallel, but when William Penn discovered that his only port was about fifteen miles south of the parallel, he claimed land further south. This led to trouble between the colonies that was finally settled when the Mason-Dixon line was surveyed.

"There are always two sides to a story," said Herr Hartzell. "Have you been here long?"

"I got here several days ago. We had a slow trip across from Rotterdam. You left my village several days before I did, where have you been?"

"Mennonites in Holland took care of us for nearly three weeks," said Herr Hartzell. "Everyone did some assigned kind of work while we were there. They tried to find jobs for us that fit our abilities. They were happy to learn that Antonio worked with bees. He went around getting them out of people's chimneys and houses. He brought a nice crock of honey along."

"My jobs were picking ducks and picking up tulip bulbs," said Abner.

"They put you to work, did they? That's good, and how was your trip?"

"We had some exciting adventures on the riverboats."

"There are all kinds of people on the different boats and ships," said Father Werner. "One who stood out on the ship I came on was an unusual man who was looking for a Minnie Ness. Do you suppose that's our Minnie?"

"Ya, that's our Minnie," said Abner. "She hates that man. She acts like she is not afraid of anything in this world, but she's afraid of him. He taught her how to powwow, and she says he has power over her. He wants her to be his slave. We must protect her from him."

His grandfather looked at Abner with astonishment. "How do you know that?"

"She told us."

"Well, be sure to point this man out to me if you see him."

"Just look for the ugliest, most greistlich man you ever saw in your life, and that's him," said Abner.

Father Werner nodded. "Abner's not far from wrong in his description," he said. "I don't trust that man. I was going to wait for the ship that goes to Baltimore, but I'll take the one you go on. It won't be any trouble getting passage from Philadelphia to Baltimore. That way I'll be with friends, and I can help watch out for Minnie. We don't need to tell her, but that's what I think we should do."

"I appreciate that, Father Werner," said Herr Hartzell. "I really do. We'll pray, and I'm sure she'll be all right, but I do believe that there's a good chance there'll be trouble aboard our ship. I'm sure I can use all the help I can get." He smiled at the priest who had become his friend.

"Since I'm not dressed as a priest, I don't know what to have people call me. Perhaps I should have them call me Herr Fritz," said Father Werner.

"That's a good idea," said Abner, "Beins Schotzy named his dog Werner in your honor."

Father Werner burst out laughing. "I have never been so honored in my life. I have not laughed for so long I thought I had forgotten how," he said.

Herr Hartzell, patted him on the back. "I know the feeling," he said. "Now we had better get on back to where the ship will land. I imagine it will be in port several days until it gets unloaded, reloaded, and all of its business attended to. Still we need to be sure our names are on the roster so we can go. We never know when another ship will bring more people who want to go to America."

Abner, Herr Hartzell and Father Werner had just stood up and started down the hill when Willy caught up with them. He was so intent on telling his news that he did not notice Father Werner. "I told Jake, I mean Herr Altland, that Trudy was mad, and he bought her some flowers and sweets."

"You told us that already," said Abner.

Willy ignored him and went on. "But I don't think it will help. She was really steaming when I left. I want to see it when he gives them to her. It will be a good show." He rubbed his hands together in anticipation. "Come on, Abs."

"That's all right," said Abner, not letting on anything about Father Werner. "I'm going to stay with my grandpa and Herr Fritz."

"Right," Willy said, and ran on down the hill.

Abner looked at Father Werner and said, "I really can't call you Herr Fritz. It doesn't seem right. I'm going to keep on calling you Father Werner if you don't mind. It's better. That's who you are, and that's what I think we should keep on calling you."

"Thank you, Abner," he said. "I appreciate that. You're growing up and so is your dog. She's a beauty. Is she as good a pet as you thought she'd be?"

"Ach, ya! She's a good puppy dog, all right. Alsatians are the best."

They made their way slowly down to the water, enjoying the beautiful view and the sea breeze while watching the ship come in. "That's a nice air," said Abner. "We better would breathe it while we can. It won't smell so good on the ship if it's anything like the other one. I'm looking forward to getting to Pennsylvania, but I sure don't like to think about getting on another stinkin' ship."

"I'm not looking forward to it either," said Father Werner. "I've been told that you never know how the voyage is going to be. Sometimes it's real bad, and sometimes not so bad. A couple of years back, one of my parishioners inherited a large estate, worth a lot of money. He was surprised to get it because his cousin was in line ahead of him. However, the cousin had gone to America, and when he received word that he should come back, he refused. He sent word that he would not cross the Atlantic Ocean again even if they made him king. Isn't that something? He gave up that big, beautiful estate because he would not get on another ship and come back across the ocean. I hope our crossing is better than his was." They walked on a little farther, and then he said, "I wish you would catch me up on the news. What is this about Trudy and Jake?"

"Jake has a lot on his mind, and he forgets about Trudy's feelings," said Herr Hartzell. "Could be he's too old to get married and set in his ways, but I don't think so. I'm sure he cares for her, and she for him. It seems to me that she wants him to pay a little more attention to her."

"I'm sure it will work out," said Father Werner.

Abner saw his parents at the foot of the hill. They were sitting on a bench just looking at the water. Princess was sleeping on Rachel's lap. *Now I'm in for it,* he thought. *I know I should have let them know that I was going along with Schotzy.*

He could not believe it when they turned and smiled at him. "I hope you had a grand day with your grandpa," said Rachel. "We saw you run to catch up with him so we knew where you were. We just sat here all day and rested in the sun. We tied a string around Princess's neck and kept her with us. What a nice day we had. It was like we were young again."

Well, if that don't beat all, thought Abner. *I'm not in trouble after all!*

When Jake arrived he immediately sought out Trudy. He smiled as he held the flowers out to her. She looked at the flowers and then at him. She thought a bit and said coldly, "Herr Altland, did someone suggest to you that you bring me flowers?" She took them, looked at them and added sarcastically, "And I suppose you have sweets, too! How very thoughtful and original of you to do such a thing, beins you're such a busy man." She turned away from him and began handing the flowers to the girls who were standing around. "Aren't these lovely? It is good to have a man who appreciates beauty."

Jake stood quietly waiting to see what Trudy would do next. She returned to him, took the sweets and began passing them around to the boys. Next, she looked at Jake seriously and said, "I need to speak to you in private." She walked along the waterfront, and he followed her. After they had talked for a while, they found Widow Schneider and spoke with her. Abner wondered what was being said. When the conversation was finished, each of the three walked away in a different direction. *I hope they get this straightened out,* thought Abner. *I don't like this at all. And there's Willy, looking disappointed that there wasn't another big fuss.*

The big ship was about to land and there were more exciting things to think about than other people's problems. It was a thrill just to look at all those sails. "What is this big boat called?" Abner asked Herr Hoke who was standing beside him.

"It's *The Augusta Margaret,*" he replied. "I cannot imagine staying on that thing for five or six months."

"Who said we could be on it for five or six months?' questioned Abner." I heard everybody say two and a half to three months."

"It all depends on the wind. People always hope it will take the shorter time, but it could take much longer," replied Herr Hoke. "The problem is, though, that the faster we go the rougher the water. The rougher the water, the sicker we get. The better the weather, the longer it takes. Then we get sick from rotten food and spoiled water. We can't win. Just so we get there before winter sets in, but we probably won't."

"Like Grandpa says, 'What doesn't kill us makes us strong.'"

"That's my problem, little fella," said Herr Hoke. "I'm afraid it will kill me. A lot of people die on these trips across the ocean, lots and lots of them. I'm not afraid to die, it's just that I don't want to be buried at sea and have the fishes eat me. I want a place in the ground that's my own. I don't want to get on another ship. I was on one ship already, and it nearly did me in."

"Have you talked to Grandpa about it?"

"No, you seem to be the only one I can talk to. My wife is always busy or hanging around with the women laughing and gassing,[68] and I can't get her alone to talk to her. She tells me not to grex and moan,[69] but she wasn't sick like me on that other rocking, creaking, stinking ship. Your grandfather is always busy or hanging around with the men, and it's not something I can talk about with just anyone." Herr Hoke squeezed Abner's shoulder and added tenderly, "You're the closest I ever had to a son. If anything happens to me, I want you to have my tools and things. My wife knows about it."

Abner smiled at him encouragingly, "Herr Hoke, nothing's going to happen to you," he said.

Herr Hoke shrugged his shoulders and then reached inside his shirt and pulled out a small bag that hung around his neck. He untied it, took out a few coins and gave them to Abner, saying, "A boy needs some money." He retied the bag, replaced it carefully inside his shirt and said, "Thanks for listening."

Abner was so surprised he did not even thank him. He looked in his hand and counted twelve pfennig. "Twelve! That's a lot. Are you sure? That's enough to buy a lot of things."

"Like I said, 'A boy needs some money.' I'm just glad that I can give them to you. I wish it were more." Herr Hoke smiled at him kindly and then walked away into the evening dusk. Abner never saw him again.

---

[68] gassing: passing the time in idle chatter
[69] grex and moan: complain

"Hey Abs," called out Schotzy as he came down the hill toward the ship. "Where's your grandpa? I got something for him."

"He's around here somewheres," answered Abner.

Schotzy seemed to be excited. "I got him a present, and I want to give it to him."

"In that case, I'll help you find him," said Abner just as both boys spotted him.

Schotzy rushed up to Herr Hartzell and handed him a small package. He was so excited he could not stand still. "You have been so good to me I wanted to buy you a present. I never bought anybody a present before. Here it is. Open it up. I want to see if you like it."

Abner watched his grandpa unwrap a small square box. He fumbled around and finally got it open. Inside was a gold watch. "The man told me they make the best gold watches here in England," said Schotzy. "I hope you like it." Herr Hartzell looked at it in shock and surprise. "Whatsa matter?" Schotzy asked. "Don'tcha like it?"

"Ach, ya, I like it! I often thought I would like to have a gold watch," Herr Hartzell said, choking up with emotion. "I never thought I'd get one. I thought when we took you in, we were making a sacrifice. I never thought you would turn out to be such a blessing. This watch is a much nicer one than I ever imagined having. Thank you very much. It was a good day when you joined our family. I truly appreciate it."

The next few days were busy ones. Food had to be purchased for the voyage and brought on board the ship. It was a tremendous job, and all of the men in the party were busy hauling and loading for several days. The last things to be brought aboard were barrels filled with beer and barrels filled with water. Abner saw that Cousin Jake's and Schotzy's order was safely stowed away, as was his mother's chest from Herr van Zant. It was filled with clothing and blankets.

The morning of the day the ship was scheduled to leave, Abner, Herr Hartzell, Father Werner, Matthias and Klaus were standing around with their bedrolls, chests and other belongings, waiting for the women to get ready to go aboard the ship. While they were watching others go aboard, Klaus said, "Take notice of that there young woman by the gangplank, the one with the dark red hair. She's nice. I'd like to know that redhead."

"She's English. You couldn't even talk to her," said Matthias.

"Ya, but I can make motions," laughed Klaus. "Maybe Jake would teach me some English. Somebody on the ship must speak English. I'll get acquainted with her one way or the other before we set foot in Pennsylvania."

"Listen at him!" laughed Matthias. "You sound like a determined man."

"Das es recht," Klaus nodded and pursed his lips.

"Well then, wait for a chance to take her arm when she may be in danger of falling," said Matthias. "Or better still, make yourself into a hero and rescue her from a bad villain."

"Speaking of bad villains, here comes Herr Flickinger," said Abner. "Have any of youse ever seen him before? He's the tall one with the one shoulder higher than the other and the one leg shorter than the other. That's him, walking crooked."

Herr Flickinger, who seemed to know that Abner was talking about him, looked at him with eyes blazing and full of hatred. Then his eyes passed over the rest and settled on Herr Hartzell as if challenging him. "Whew!" said Abner who suddenly felt weak in the knees.

Grandpa said, "Father God, protect us in Jesus' name." Herr Flickinger dropped his eye and continued up the gangplank.

"Ach du lieber, my mother is with him," said Klaus. "There goes big trouble, if you ask me."

The others nodded and didn't say anything.

"It wonders me where he'll be on the ship," said Abner. "Minnie thinks he has lots of money, so maybe he'll have a cabin. I hope so. Then he won't be down below with us. I wouldn't want to have to look at that greistlich creature all the way across the ocean."

"Abner, mind your mouth," said his father. "The man can't help how he looks. Let's talk about something else."

"Has anyone seen Herr Hoke?" asked Klaus. "Do you think he'll show up for the sailing?"

"I'm sure he will," said Matthias. "Frau Hoke isn't worried."

"Maybe she's not worried, but I have my doubts," said Abner.

"Why do you say that?" asked his father.

"He told me he was afraid he would die if he had to get on another ship. You know he was sicker than anybody else all of the way from Rotterdam. He gave me some money and said I was to have his belongings."

"Why didn't you say something about it before?" asked Matthias.

"I didn't think he was going to run off. Should we go hunt him?"

"If he wants to go along he will," said Herr Hartzell. "It wouldn't do any good for us to go looking for him and risk having the ship go without us. Besides, if he thinks he is going to die and we convince him to go anyway, we would feel terrible if he did die. It's best for him to make up his own mind."

"It wonders me what Frau Hoke will say," said Abner. "He said that he never wanted to leave home. She's the one who insisted."

"The ship hasn't gone without him yet," said Matthias.

"No, but we'll see," answered Abner. "Look, there's Martina with that Michael Becker. She thinks he is so gutgucklich.[70] I can't see it myself."

"He's all right," said Klaus, "except he doesn't like Catholics."

"He was robbed of his inheritance by his Catholic uncle," said Matthias. "Michael took him to court, and a Catholic magistrate sided with the uncle. Still, that doesn't mean he should hate all of them."

"He does though," said Abner, smiling at Father Werner. "We couldn't tell him you're a nice person. He wouldn't listen. Michael is a stubborn bonehead, if you ask me."

"Just so nobody ever says that about you," said Matthias with a twinkle in his eye. "Here comes Minnie and the rest of the girls. We better would call her over so she doesn't meet that man when she's by herself."

"I'll call her," said Abner. "Hey, Min, where are Schotzy and Reuben?"

"They wanted to give their dogs a good run before they took them on board the ship," she answered. "They knew it would be a long time until the dogs would get to exercise again. They let them off their leashes, and Rufus ran off. They went looking for him and Reuben is afraid they'll never see his little dog again. Trudy is with them."

"Do they know that the ship will leave when the tide begins to go out whether everyone who wants to go is on board or not?" said Father Werner.

"I guess they do," said Minnie. "That's the way it was on the other ship. How long will it be until we leave?"

"Not long," said Matthias. "I hope the women will be soon ready. Times like this work on a man's nerves."

---

[70] gutgucklich: good looking; gut rhymes with foot; guck rhymes with look; lich sounds like lick

"The women will be here, don't worry about them," said Klaus. "What we need to do, Matt, is hunt for my sister and the boys, and we better would get a move on."

"You're right, let's go."

"Go, and may God go with you," said Herr Hartzell.

"Where did you see them last?" asked Klaus.

"Up the hill and down the hill up and over that way," Minnie said, pointing north. The two men took off running.

While they were gone, the women brought the children and their personal belongings out of the sheds and boarded the ship, all but Frau Hoke. "Where's Herr Hoke?" she asked. No one answered. She said more loudly, "Does anyone know where my husband is?"

Abner stepped forward and said, "I'm sorry to tell you, Neighbor Lady, but I think he's run off and is not going to Pennsylvania."

"But he was the one who wanted to go. I always wanted to stay home."

"He was wonderful sick on the boat that came here from Rotterdam," said Abner. "He was afraid that he would die if he got on this one."

"Why didn't he say something to me?" asked Frau Hoke trying not to cry. "I could wring his neck, he makes me so mad. That's like him not saying anything. I must go find him. I told Herr Altland that I'm not going without him. We've been married nearly twenty years. What would I do without him?" She clenched her jaws in thought and then turned to Abner. "If we're not back by the time the ship leaves, you may have our things."

"Frau Hoke, I'm concerned about you," said Herr Hartzell. "How can you find him? You can't even speak the language."

"I don't know how I'll find him, but I will. Please pray for us." She kissed Abner on the cheek, something she had never done before, picked up her bedroll and began walking up the hill toward the town. "Auf Wierdersehn," she called back.

"She was always a good neighbor lady," said Abner. "I'll miss her."

It was plain to see that the sailors were readying the ship for departure. They began loosening the ropes, and Abner saw the first sails unfurl. Everyone who was waiting on the wharf hurried on board. Cousin Jake came around checking to see if everyone he was responsible for was there. "I've not seen Trudy, Matthias, Klaus, Schotzy or Reuben. Where are they? Has anyone seen them? The sailors are making ready to pull up the gangplank."

"No, no, no!" shouted Abner in a panic. "Tell the sailors not to do that! They went looking for Reuben's dog. I mean Trudy and the boys went looking for Rufus. My papa and Klaus went looking for the boys and Trudy."

Cousin Jake pulled on his hair and said, "That woman of mine! I can't get off and try and find her. I have responsibilities here. There's nothing I can do." He clenched his fists and then said, "Herr Hartzell, pray! They have to get back in time."

Abner closed his eyes to pray. He knew that his grandfather and Father Werner were praying, too. When he opened his eyes, he saw that the pretty red haired lady was standing beside him. He heard her say something which he supposed was English, and was surprised when Father Werner answered her in the same language.

Nearly everyone on the ship was hanging over the rail watching to see what would happen. Just as the sailors were going to pull up the gangplank, Minnie ran out onto it and yelled at them. "Wait, they'll soon be here," she shouted. She stood there without moving until the sailors took hold of her arms and began to drag her onto the ship. She struggled and then pointed up the hill towards the town. "Look up to the top of the hill! There's Uncle Matthias carrying Reuben.

Klaus is carrying Schotzy and Fraulein Trudy is carrying Rufus. The men are running, and she is coming as fast as she can."

The sailors did not understand what she was saying, but they looked up to where she pointed. Just then Klaus put Schotzy down, turned around and ran back up the hill. He picked up his sister and carried her to the ship. Matthias and Reuben made it first, followed by Schotzy and his dog, then Klaus, Trudy and Rufus. As soon as they were onboard, the gangplank was lifted, the anchor hauled in and the rest of the big white sails unfurled. The ship jumped in the water and made a fast start across the Atlantic Ocean.

CHAPTER TEN

Abner, Schotzy, Reuben and their dogs were walking on the main deck toward the hatch that would take them to their quarters below. "You had us worried," Abner said to Schotzy. "What happened?"

"A man had a girl dog just like Rufus. When Rufus saw her, he ran toward her as fast as he could. Then the man claimed that Rufus belonged to him. A policeman came along, and believed the man. They wouldn't have given Rufus up if Klaus and your papa had not come for us. Ach, what if we would have missed the ship? I don't even want to think about it. What do people do in a country where they can't speak the language?"

"It would be hard. It will be hard on the Hokes," he repeated.

"Why do you say that?" asked Schotzy.

"Herr Hoke has been gone a couple days," answered Abner. "Frau Hoke went looking for him just before we sailed, and neither one of them came back. Since they aren't on the ship, they'll have to figure out how to get food and a place to sleep. I hope they find each other. It wonders me how they'll make out, but I have my doubts that we'll ever find out."

"Just about everybody was sick on the trip from the mainland to England," said Schotzy, "but not sick enough to stay here and not go on to Pennsylvania."

"Herr Hoke was sure he would die if he got on another ship," said Abner. "As full as this ship is, it looks like there are lots of people who weren't afraid to get on it."

"Your cousin says ships are much fuller these days than they used to be," said Schotzy. "We better would go below and find our places to sleep before they're all taken."

"I'm not anxious to go below as bad as that other ship stank," said Abner. "But I guess we better would. Wait. I need a drink of water."

On the way to the water barrel, Schotzy shouted excitedly, "Look! Out to your left. There is a whole bunch of dolphins, and they are catching flying fish for their dinner!" Watching them was so interesting that they almost forgot to go down and find their places to sleep.

"As much as I don't want to, I guess we better would go on down," said Abner as he headed for the hatch.

"Did you forget you wanted a drink?" asked Schotzy.

"Ya, I guess I'm getting forgetful in my old age," said Abner and went back to the water barrel.

A sailor who spoke their language was standing there. "You can't have a drink just any old time you want one," he said. "Water is given out at certain times a day. That is the only time you can have it. Depending on what kind of ticket you bought, you may have to share your water with your dogs." He gave water to them and their dogs anyway, and the boys were grateful. "This could get me in trouble, you know," he said.

"Thank you," aid Schotzy. "What's your name if we need you?"

"I'm Karl Wildasin. Just call me Karl."

As they began to descend the ladder that would take them to the lower decks, another sailor yelled at them but they did not understand. He came close to them, shouted in their faces as loud as he could and pointed to the dogs, "No, no, no."

"He must be talking about the dogs. What do you think is the matter?" asked Abner.

Father Werner who was behind them, chatted with the sailor. He then turned to the boys and said, "Your dogs have to be caged or tied with a very short rope. If they bark much, bite anybody or cause any trouble, they will be thrown overboard. Unless, of course, you see that the one who makes the decision receives extra money that no one else knows about. It's called a bribe."

As they descended the ladder, the first thing Abner noticed was that this ship did not smell as bad as the other but it did have an odor that he could not place immediately. He sniffed several times and then asked, "What do I smell?" He did not get an answer because Schotzy had spotted Klaus and the rest of their party and was making his way toward them.

"Where have you been?" asked Rachel. "People are crowding in, and it's been hard holding a place for you. Put your things down and make yourself comfortable. Isn't it a blessing that this ship doesn't smell like the other?" She turned to Matthias and asked, "Husband, what do I smell? I can't place it."

"It's tobacco. These ships take people to America and bring back tobacco. This area was stacked as full of it as could be. There's big money in the tobacco trade."

"Speaking of tobacco," Rachel continued. "Where's Trudy's mother?"

"She's over there," said Matthias, pointing with his chin. "See the man with the strange eyes? Don't let him see you staring at him. He could be dangerous. How her mother took up with him, I'll never know."

"This ship is much bigger than the last one we were on," said Abner. "I hope Widow Schneider is far enough away from us that the smoke doesn't get to us."

"Even if she would be far enough, I don't think she's the only smoker down here," said Matthias. "Here, let me help you with those dogs. Did you say they had to be tied with a short leash?"

When all the Brethren, except Widow Schneider, were grouped together, Herr Hartzell said, "This seems to be a good time for a short lesson and prayer. We will be this close together on this ship for at least three months and possibly more. It will be hard not to work on each other's nerves, not to make each other angry, and not to turn against each other in many ways. It will be hard work to bear with each other, to bite your tongue, to forgive each other, to be good to each other, to pray for each other and to be content. We cannot do this by ourselves, but there is a source of help that is always available. In Philippians 4:12, the Apostle Paul says that he has learned to be content in all circumstances because 'I can do all things through Him who gives me strength.' Who does he mean when he says, 'through Him who gives me strength?'"

"I don't know for sure," said Minnie, "but I do believe that it must be Jesus."

"Very good, Minnie," said Herr Hartzell. "You catch on fast. Jesus and the Holy Spirit are right here with us on this ship. Jesus promised to be in our midst. He also promised that He would put the Holy Spirit in our hearts if you believe in Him. They, Jesus and the Holy Spirit, will help you control yourselves. It would be very difficult if not impossible, to do it alone, but with their help you can do all things. That is one of God's promises. So while we are on this ship, I want you, each of you, to pray each day for each person in our group. I want you to be kind and to speak kindly to each other. There is to be no loud or crude language and no tricks. I want you to be polite to everyone on the ship, not just those in our group. Make sure that you do not take advantage of anyone on the ship. Take your turns, and if someone wants to go ahead of you in line, let them. We are Christians, and we are here representing Jesus Christ to the rest of the passengers and crew. They know that we are a group of people who have been driven from our homes and out of our country because we do not worship the way the government and churches of our country want us to worship. As I said, the other passengers and crew will be watching us. This is not going to be an easy thing. There are evil people on board who will tempt you and try to get you in trouble, but remember, 'Greater is He that is in me and you, than he who is in the world.'[71] It will be for God's glory when we conduct ourselves in such a manner."

Herr Hartzell looked around the group and then asked Jake if he had anything to say. "You covered about everything, sir," he answered.

Herr Hartzell smiled. "We want to get to Pennsylvania safely, quickly and in good health," he said, "Let us pray." He closed his eyes and bowed his head, "Father in Heaven, You have protected us and brought us this far. We thank you for that and for the many things you have done for us and continue to do for us. We now ask You to keep your ministering angels around us to protect us as we go across this big, wide ocean. We ask You to help us control ourselves and to be content under all conditions, in Jesus' name we pray, Amen."

Father Werner, who had set his things next to them, listened closely to what Herr Hartzell, said, "That was very

---

[71] I John 4:4

well put," he said. "I could not have said it better myself, and I've had years of study under learned professors. How did you, a laborer, learn so much?"

Abner was proud of his grandfather when he answered, "Thank you for the compliment. I may be a common laborer, but I've had years of study under the greatest teacher of them all, the Holy Spirit. Jesus said before He ascended to Heaven that He would send a Helper who would teach us all things. I've read the Bible almost every day for forty years, and the Holy Spirit has taught me every day. I've learned much and there is much more in the Bible for me to learn."

"We Catholics have been taught that it is dangerous for common people to read the Bible because they get wrong ideas and thereby condemn themselves to eternal damnation. However, everything you have said since I met you has been correct as I understand it. This is interesting. Could my church possibly be wrong?"

Herr Hartzell raised his left eyebrow and stroked his beard as he did when he was thinking. However, he did not have the chance to respond to Father Werner's question because the ship's bell rang, signaling that it was time for supper. Antonio, a former Catholic priest, cocked his head and generally kept his distance from Father Werner. It was not as if he disliked him, it was more like he had nothing to say to him.

Herr Hartzell asked God's blessing on the food, and then everyone got his or her dish and spoon and lined up for the evening meal. Abner felt hungry but was apprehensive about eating. "I haven't been sick so far today," he said to his mother. "I don't think I'll eat much just in case I can't keep it down."

"Don't worry about eating too much, young man," said a stranger standing behind him. "They won't give you too much. You can depend on that."

As Abner waited to get his food, he could hear complaints from those who had already received theirs. "Are these rocks or what?" "They'll break me pegs."[72] "Whatfer slop is this?" and "Where are the pigs?" "Do they really expect us to fress this?"

When the members of the Brethren group received their food, they ate without saying anything. Abner gulped, blinked his eyes and thought, *The biscuit is hard, but I can handle it. What wonders me is whatfer stuff this is and how anyone could prepare it? It looks sort of like oatmeal, but there is more to it than that. I think I'll call it mystery mush.* He turned to Schotzy and whispered, "This is genuine mystery mush. There is something different in it that I've never tasted before. It really wonders me what it is. It really isn't all that bad, but it feels different in my mouth."

After he had eaten most of it he looked in his bowl closely and asked his mother, "Mama, what are those black spots in this stuff?"

It's pepper," she answered.

"It doesn't look like pepper to me," he said.

"It's pepper."

"Look at it close, Mama. I think I see little tiny wings and legs in there."

"Hush, it's pepper."

"Mama, would you lie to me?"

"Abner Frederick Hartzell," she said, somewhat exasperated. "I said to hush. Look at it this way. You are going to have to eat this all the way across the ocean or else starve to death. Wouldn't you rather it would be pepper? Now hush up about it."

Everyone was standing around when Father Werner went over to where Klaus and the boys were and began to talk. "I have news for you, Big Angel, as Schotzy calls you. The beautiful red-haired girl that you mentioned this morning wants to meet you."

---

[72]   pegs: English slang for teeth

"You're trying to make a fool out of me," laughed Klaus. "You may be a priest, but I don't believe you for a minute."

"I'm serious," replied Father Werner, holding up his right hand. "Would I lie to you after just hearing Herr Hartzell's lesson? I couldn't possibly. I might enjoy having some fun with you, but lie? Never!"

"Well then, what is it about?"

"I didn't mention it this morning, but I do speak English a little. I was standing on the deck praying for you and the others to get back before the ship left, when the lady came and stood between Abner and me. Everyone got excited when you and Matt came tearing down the hill with the boys. We were all rooting for you. She spoke English, so I spoke English back to her. When she saw you rescue the boys and Trudy, she asked if you were a reliable person. I assured her that you are honest, reliable and unmarried." Father Werner's eyes twinkled. "She is a maid. Her mistress is married to a gentleman whose family does not approve of her and is trying to get the marriage annulled. He is sending her to Pennsylvania where she will be safe from them. She had a bodyguard, but she paid him yesterday, and he did not show up today. She needs another bodyguard and wonders if you would be available for the job."

"Would I be available for the job?" Klaus laughed and slapped his knee. "Would I be available for the job?" he repeated. "Lead me to her. I was ready five minutes ago." Klaus smoothed down his hair, and then getting serious he asked, "What do I say to her?"

Abner smiled and thought, *Klaus is funny when he's all worked up. I never saw him like this before.*

"Don't you want to know the terms of the employment?" asked Father Werner.

"Ya, sure," said Klaus, somewhat embarrassed. "I need to know that."

"The mistress wants you to be stationed outside her door at all times and to be with her when she walks on deck. That means you sleep outside her door. You may have a little time off every day if you arrange for someone to guard her at that time. You will eat with her and the maid at the captain's table. She does not believe in the hired help being treated the way the upper class English treat people who work for them. She may have been a maid in the family's home or perhaps her father is a tradesman. Whatever the situation, her family is socially far beneath her husband's family."

"What's her name and how much will she pay me?" asked Klaus, who had settled down somewhat.

"I thought it was the redhead's name you were interested in," teased Father Werner.

Klaus blushed and said, "I am. I am."

"The maid's name is Elisabeth Winslow. You do not need to know your employer's name.[73] Just say, 'Yes, ma'am,' or 'No ma'am,' or 'May I help you, ma'am?' If I mentioned her name and the word got out, people would talk about her all of the time. Besides that, the ones looking for her might be on this ship and they would find her. She will pay for your passage and pay you what she considers to be fair when we get to Philadelphia. If your services are satisfactory, she will

---

[73]   There is a legend in the upper region of the Susquehanna River that says William Penn's grandson married a lowborn woman. The Penns who were upperclass, were totally against the marriage. They sent the grandson to France while they planned to kidnap the bride, put her in a convent, and arrange an annulment. The grandson managed to escape and return to England where he made plans for his wife to go to Pennsylvania. He would follow and meet her upstream from Selingsgrove. Just before her husband arrived, she supposedly was injured in an Indian attack. When he arrived, she died in his arms.

want you to accompany her and her maid far inland, up the Susquehanna River to where her husband will meet her."

"Since I don't know her language, how will I know what she wants?"

"I will be available to help you any way I can," said Father Werner. "And I will help you learn English if you want me to."

"I would appreciate it very much," said Klaus with a smile. "Look at me, I have a job, and I have a chance to meet the most beautiful woman in the world. It sure beats being an unemployed army deserter, with no money and no chance to find a wife." He looked up toward heaven and said, "Thank you, Lord!"

While Klaus and Father Werner were talking, others who were standing around moved closer and closer to them in order to hear what was being said. *Them people are just plain schnuppisch,*[74] thought Abner as someone pushed against him.

Just then there was a loud scream, and suddenly everyone looked in the other direction. They were surprised to see Minnie attacking an elderly man who stood crooked and could not see straight. It was Herr Flickinger.

"Stop her," Widow Schneider said.

"What is the matter with that girl?" asked Frau Bentzel.

"That's the way the young act these days," said Frau Rohrbaugh.

"The old man came up from behind and took around her neck.[75] That's why she screamed and is acting that way," said Frau Bollinger.

Herr Flickinger grabbed Minnie's arms and held her tight. "You belong to me," he said roughly. "Your mama sent word that you were mine. Mine in more ways than one. Don't

---

[74]   schnuppisch: snoopy

[75]   took around her neck: put his arm around her neck

you understand that? Why did you run away? We had good times together."

By that time Matthias, Cousin Jake, Klaus, Father Werner and a couple of other men took hold of Herr Flickinger. "Let her go. She is my niece and my ward as well," said Cousin Jake angrily. "If you ever touch her or come near her again, you will have me and these other men to answer to. We will not tolerate having you come near her. If you want to find out what it's like to be fish food, just try it."

Breathing hard from trying to pull away, Herr Flickinger said, "You muscle boys might think you have the upper hand, but I have powers the likes of which you have never seen or even heard of. Youse have tangled with Adolph Flickinger and youse will live to regret it. Or maybe you won't *live* to regret it," he added ominously. They let him go, and he limped proudly back to his spot beside Widow Schneider.

When things had settled down, Herr Hartzell called his group together. They sat down to hear his message, and others sitting nearby listened to what he had to say. "Jesus said to turn the other cheek," he said. "That means that we do nothing to Herr Flickinger except pray for him and treat him respectfully. Do you hear me? There are several places in the Bible that tell us that it is not up to us to seek revenge. God will take care of it. Now let us pray for peace, harmony and protection on this ship."

As he began to pray loud enough for everyone on the deck to hear, Herr Flickinger began to sing a raucous song at the top of his lungs. Since it was a well known song many of the passengers began to sing along, until no one could hear Herr Hartzell's prayer. When anyone looked in Herr Flickinger's direction, he looked back with a smirk as if to say, "I will do as I please, and there is nothing you can do about it."

The next morning the men who had taken hold of Herr Flickinger were vomiting. Each had a high fever, stomach cramps and diarrhea.

Herr Hartzell said to these men, "I want you to know there is faith healing and casting out of demons which some people call powwowing, and there is the calling forth of evil spirits and casting spells which is also called powwowing. They are totally opposite, and yet they are called by the same name. It's confusing. Today we will claim the Lord's power of faith healing and the casting out of demons. Jesus said that whatever He did, we can do also. I have no doubt that these men are under a hex inflicted on them by Herr Flickinger. That means demonic oppression. Now listen carefully, it says in the Bible that every knee shall bow and every tongue confess that Jesus Christ is Lord. That includes demons. Now, all of you who believe that there is more power in the name of Jesus than anything else in heaven or on earth, lay hands on the sick ones while I pray."

The Brethren group crowded around and touched the men. "We call this the laying on of hands," said Herr Hartzell, and he began to pray. "Father in Heaven, in the name of Jesus, we call on You right now to honor Your promise to cast out demons in Your dear Son's name. We thank You for that power. Now, you foul demons under the strongman spirit of infirmity who have taken up residence in these men, come out of them." He raised his voice, "Come out! Come out! I say in the mighty name of Jesus. You cannot stay, and you know it. I bind you up, and I cast you out. Go and don't come back."

In a totally different voice he prayed, "We praise You, Father God, who sent Your son into the world to free us from the bondage of sickness and sin. We praise You, Jesus, who said that whatever You did, we can do also. We praise You,

Holy Spirit who told me what to say. Thank you, Father, in Jesus' name, Amen."

The men who were sick immediately got up and were fine in no time.

Herr Flickinger, upon hearing the prayer and seeing the healing, began to curse at the top of his lungs. He turned purple, frothed at the mouth and then fell to the deck. He lay quietly for a while. Widow Schneider went to him and tried to help him, but he said, "Get away!" Then he called, "Minnie, come to me. Everything I have is yours. Come to me."

"I don't want to go near him," whispered Minnie. "He's bad."

"Come to me little maidel.[76] Think of all I taught you," Herr Flickinger said in a persuasive voice. "Think of the good times we had together. You mustn't be afraid to come to me. Now come."

"I'm not afraid," she said. "But I'm not gonna do it."

"You know that the God you now worship is not as strong as the one I taught you about," continued Herr Flickinger. "So come."

"He is so," she answered.

"Then prove it and show me that you are not afraid. Alls I want is for you to bring me some beer."

"Old Flick, I don't trust you."

"You mean you don't trust your God to protect you from what you think I might do to you. Minnie, liebling,[77] I would never hurt you. You know that. Just come. Bring me a mug of beer and look into my eyes. You will be better off with me than you ever were or will be with anyone else. Now come."

Suddenly there was fear among the people who heard the conversation. "It's best not to mess with that old devil dog," said Frau Bentzel.

----

76   maidel: girl or unmarried woman
77   liebling: little love, darling

"Ach, you're right," answered Frau Bollinger. "You never know what will happen. Just thinking about it gives me goose bumps."

Herr Hartzell looked at them as if he could not believe that they had said that. "But you just saw how those men were healed in the name of Jesus," he said. "Why should you be afraid?"

"You just never can tell," replied Frau Bentzel. "I ain't gonna take no chances."

"Me neither," added Frau Schmitt. "You just never can tell." Abner heard what had been said and saw others nod their heads in agreement. *That doesn't make much sense to me,* he thought. *They believe in the power of Jesus' name, but aren't going to take any chances. Now that's not what I would call a lot of faith. And yet, I sort of feel the same myself.*

Suddenly Herr Flickinger shouted, "Minnie, I told you to come here right now. Get over here with some beer, or you'll be sorry."

Herr Hartzell had been thinking and praying silently, but when he heard the shout, he called softly to Minnie. "I think you best go to him and take him the beer. Show him that you are not afraid of him."

"I'm not afraid of him," said Minnie with a shiver. "But he might do something to me."

"When you become a believer in Jesus, He gives you a new spirit," said Herr Hartzell. "And as it says in Second Timothy 1:7, **'He has not given you a spirit of fear, but of power and love and sound mind.'** It says, not fear, but boldness; not fear, but power and love; not fear but a sound mind.' You do not need to be afraid of him. Face your fear, cast it away and take him some beer."

"I can't."

When Herr Flickinger realized that Minnie would not do as he asked he yelled at Widow Schneider, "Gerty, get me some beer." She immediately got up and got it for him.

The ship headed southwest and sailed in that direction for a number of days in order to catch the trade winds. As they got farther south, most days were pleasant with a warm sea breeze but others were downright hot. The *Augusta Margaret* put into port in the Canary Islands to take on fresh water and rum. Jake asked the captain if he could go ashore and buy some milk for the children and he came back with a big bucketful. "This really hits the spot," said Abner. "I never knew how good milk could taste. Thank you, Cousin Jake, I'll plant a cabbage in your garden sometime."[78]

The captain did not allow any of the indentured passengers off the ship for fear they would not return. For the most part the passengers were required to stay below, but occasionally they were allowed up on the main deck. One day Karl came down and told them they could go up and see whales jumping and having a good time in the water. There were dozens of them, and the refugees found it hard to believe that such huge animals even existed much less jump out of the water and flip around like they did. "Jonah would have had a wild ride in one of those," said Abner with a smile.

Breakfast each morning was one quarter of an apple until they were gone, a hard biscuit and some more of the cooked mush made of whatever the cook put in it. "This food is interesting," said Rachel. "Every time it's different, and every day it's the same still."

"The cook puts in whatever strikes him," said Matthias. "I just hope he doesn't put in the floor sweepings, but I wouldn't be surprised." He looked fondly at his wife and added, "I am so hungry for some of your cooking. You make the best

---

[78]   I'll plant a cabbage in your garden sometime.: I'll do something nice for you sometime.

apple strudel that I ever ate. You do wonders with chicken and vegetables and roast beef."

Rachel was beaming with the compliment, but Abner said, "Let's not talk about good food. On this trip I've eaten food I never thought I could gag down. I remember that not long after we left home, someone gave me a dodger[79] that was better than this biscuit, and I didn't want to eat it. I was going to give it a pitch, and Grandpa told me to eat it and be glad I had it. He was rough, and I wasn't used to that from him. I didn't think I could eat it, but I did. I've eaten worse since." Then he asked, "Do you remember the parsnips?"

Rachel looked at Matthias and said, "I don't remember any parsnips, do you?"

He made a face and said, "Ya, I do. We were at Frau Grim's house. We stayed there several days because it was raining and soldiers were looking for us. Her rich daughter-in-law came to see how she was. Frau Grim's stepson was going to throw her out with nothing to go on, and his wife brought Frau Grim a big basket of parsnips. Nothing else but parsnips! It was Ascension Day, and no shops were open. The Bollingers, the Rohrbaughs and the Lutzes came to the door, and Frau Grim took them in. There was a good supper prepared for us, and we were ready to eat just as they arrived. They were starved so we left them eat first, and they ate everything, except the parsnips."

"What did you eat?" asked Rachel.

"Parsnips."

"Ho, ho, ho," she laughed. "How about you, Son?"

"Ya, me, too. And Grandpa."

"I wish I had been there to see it," said Rachel. "That would have been too good to miss. Youse Hartzells are such sneaks when it comes to parsnips."

---

[79] dodger: hard blah tasting biscuit

"Grandpa told me to take a bite of parsnips and a gulp of milk and make it come out even," said Abner. "I managed to get them down that way. Papa and Grandpa ate theirs without a fuss. We were all proud of each other. Schotzy and Reuben both ate them and were glad for them."

The man who always complained about the food chimed in, "Parsnips could not possibly taste as bad as this stuff. Ya, we have a remarkable cook," he said sarcastically. "Some days it tastes more like pig slop. Some days it tastes less like pig slop, but it always tastes like pig slop."

Another man added, "I wouldn't even give my little wutzies[80] such as this."

"I should tell them it would taste worse without the pepper," Abner whispered to his mother.

Ignoring him and the men, Rachel said, "We must eat and then redd up."[81]

"It wonders me why we don't redd up as soon as we get out of our bedrolls," said Schotzy. "My grandma always said you darsesn't make your bed as soon as you got out of it because it was bad luck. You had to throw back the covers and let out the night air that was bad for you. You didn't have darest[82] to make the bed until it was stone cold. Since you aren't superstitious, why don't you make your bed right away?"

"Washing your covers is hard work," said Rachel. "First, you have to haul in the water, heat it in the fireplace, and cut up your soap in the water so it dissolves. Then you carry the hot water out to the tubs. That's just to get started. Before you put the bedding in the water, you must check to see if there are any greasy spots, dirty spots or bloody spots that

---

[80] wutzies: little pigs; wutz: pig or hog; rhymes with puts
[81] redd up: clean and straighten up and area
[82] You didn't have darest: You would not dare. an idiom, darest is one syllable

should have soap rubbed into them first. Only then is it time to put the bedding in the hot water, and it's usually so gall durn hot it scalds your hands. It's got to be hot to get the sheets and comforters clean. You have to scrub the sheets and comforters, slosh them up and down in the water with a stick, wring them out by hand and you're not done yet. They have to be rinsed in cold water, wrung out again and hung out on a line or bushes to dry. Now can you understand why housewives want to keep the bedding fresh as long as possible? We usually washed it twice't a year in spring and fall. Bedding stays fresh longer if it gets aired out daily and hung out the window for a good airing onc't a week."

Rachel turned to Abner, "Remember how we used to hang the covers out the balcony window to air out? That was one job I didn't like, but I'd be glad to do it now."

"I didn't know you didn't like hanging the covers out, Mama," said Abner.

"I didn't like washing them either, but there was no use complaining about it," said Rachel, casting her eyes in the direction of the men who always complained. "Nobody would listen anyway. Why should I waste my breath?"

Abner and his mother cleaned and straightened their area and then sat down. Michael Becker and Martina came and sat down beside them. "I want to know about Schotzy's birthday and the calendar," said Michael.

"I'm not sure I have time," kidded Abner. "I have a lot of places to go and things to do, but, beins it's you, I'll tell you. This is how it is: You know how easy it is to lose track of time when you're traveling. When Schotzy's birthday came around, we were in Holland. You know how it was. We were picking ducks and working with tulips and being on the boat and getting to Holland. He wasn't keeping track of the days and missed it. When he found out the date, it was July 22. His birthday was July 20. He had missed it by two days."

"Get on with the story," said Michael. "What has Schotzy's birthday got to do with the calendar? You haven't got to it yet."

"Have a little patience," said Abner. "Where are you going in such a hurry?"

"I just want to know," said Michael. "I like to know things. You always go around the barn[83] when you tell a story."

"All right, I'll tell you. I had missed pulling Schotzy's ears on his birthday so I started to pull them anyway, but Klaus wouldn't let me. He said you only have darest to pull them on a person's birthday, and then only how many times as how old he is. When the birthday is past, you aren't allowed to do it. So I didn't get to pull his ears.

"Then when we were up in the town in England, the shopkeeper wrote down that the date was July 20. I was surprised and asked Cousin Jake how that could be. He told me how it came about. When the old calendar that had the months and leap days like we have now was put into effect by Julius Caesar before Jesus was born, it was off by just about one day every hundred years. You would think that wouldn't matter, but after more than a thousand years, it was like ten days off. Pope Gregory XIII was told about it by men who study these things. They proposed skipping some days so the calendar and seasons would match. The pope then said that was the thing to do and ordered it done. All of mainland Europe went along with the idea. It's funny but some people carried on because they thought the days were stolen from them. Since the English were not about to do anything the pope said, they did not go along with him and his new calendar. That's why the dates are different."

---

[83]   go around the barn: drag out a story, put in unnecessary details

"Good for the English," said Michael. "I wouldn't do what the pope said to do either. What about in Pennsylvania? What calendar do they follow?"

"It's an English colony, and so it does whatever the English do," answered Abner.

"That's good," said Michael. "Thank you for telling me. I'm glad we aren't following the pope's orders."

"You're as bad as the English," said Martina. "You wouldn't do what the pope says even if it was the sensible thing to do." She shook her head. "You're impossible."

Michael flushed and said, "Well, if that's the way you feel about me, I can find plenty of other girls on this ship who won't argue with me."

"I'm not arguing with you, silly," said Martina. "I just meant that the pope cannot always be wrong. He must come out with good ideas sometimes."

Michael flared up in anger. "You are always pushing them blasted Catholics in my face," he shouted. "You know how I hate 'em. If the pope says it, I'm against it, and I don't believe it! There is no good in one single one of them there Catholics. They're all rotten. Since you are such a Catholic lover, underneath your skin you are probably just as bad as they are. I don't have to listen to you any more." He turned around and strode away.

Martina's mouth dropped open in surprise, and a tear ran down her cheek. "All I said was…"

"Martina, dear," said Rachel. "You are better off that he has gone. You wouldn't want to be hooked up with such a bonehead, would you? Keep your head up and don't let him know he's hurt you. You are a beautiful young woman, and there are plenty more fish in the sea than were ever caught out."[84]

---

[84]   plenty more fish in the sea than ever were caught out: lots more men and boys to be had

"But all I said was…"

"My grandpa always says it's better not to hang around hotheads," said Abner. "He says it's somewhere in the Bible."

The winds slowed and the ship was amidst a spot where there was a lot of seaweed. Karl, the sailor who brought them food and whatever news there might be, told them that some times ships were becalmed around there and just stayed at the same place for a long time. The *Augusta Margaret* kept moving but not much. Karl also told them that this was the place where there were lots of eels to be seen. One day he and some other sailors got on a lifeboat and went fishing. They caught several bucketsful of eels, and they were served for supper. It was a grand feast for everyone who liked eels, but they were one thing that Abner could not eat. He tried, but it was not possible.

As the weeks went slowly by and the days got shorter, people began getting restless and uneasy, all except Herr Flickinger. He changed his tactics and began to sing little songs that entertained the children. He told them stories and how to plant their crops according to the phases of the moon. "You always should plant onions when the horns of the moon are down," he said. "But crops like peas and beans do best if planted when the horns of the moon are up. Hogs should be slaughtered when the moon is getting bigger, and roofs should be put on then too, so they don't curl up. It's very bad luck if anyone breaks a mirror. You will, in fact, have seven years' bad luck if you do. Here is something else to remember, if you dream of someone wearing black, someone will die."

One day Herr Flickinger reached behind Waldemar Wentz's ear and found a half pfennig. "Mama, Mama," he cried as he ran to his mother. "How could he find money behind my ear?"

"It was no doubt planted in the dirt," Frau Wentz replied.

Minnie told her sister Mary to keep away from Herr Flickinger, but she went anyway. Mary would repeat Herr Flickinger's superstitious sayings, and it would make Minnie livid. Every time Minnie saw Mary near him, she would go to her as fast as she could amidst the crowd, grab her by the arm, swat her on the bottom and pull her away. "I told you to keep away from him," Minnie would yell, but Mary would return every chance she got.

"Why don't you mind?" Minnie shouted one day when she had pulled her away more times than she had kept count.

"He likes me, and he told me a secret," Mary said. "He said that I'll always have good luck if I put my right foot down first when I get out of bed, and I should always step out with my right foot when I go any place. He gives me apple snitz to eat and sometimes raisins. One day he'll find money behind my ear like he did Wally's, and when he does he'll let me keep it. He told me he would. I never had any money before."

"Don't you understand that he is bad, bad, bad?" asked Minnie, exasperated that her sister was so stubborn. "If you don't stop hanging around from him, you'll be sorry. Don't you remember that I rescued you and you should mind me?"

"Even if you did rescue me, you're not my boss," replied Mary. "I don't care what you say, I still like him. He told me how to get rid of warts. You have to go to a neighbor's house and steal her dishrag. You bury it under a tree and by the time the rag is rotten, the warts will be gone."

"Now he's telling you to steal. Can't you see he's bad? If you ever got to know him like I do, you wouldn't like him," said Minnie. "Now I'm warning you, keep away from him, or I will tie you up like a dog."

"You ain't got no rope," replied Mary tossing her head. She sat down on the deck beside Minnie and Trudy and waited for her sister to be distracted by something else. Before long she was back at Herr Flickinger's knee, getting him water and listening to his stories.

CHAPTER ELEVEN

One day after they had been on the ship about two months, Abner, Schotzy and Reuben saw that Minnie and Trudy were sitting together. The boys moved over and sat beside them. After a bit Alice and Martina came closer joined in on the conversation. Abner could tell that Trudy was very unhappy. It had been weeks since she and Jake broke up. Both of them seemed to be miserable, but she would not give in and speak to him. Over Trudy's shoulder Abner could see Jake approaching them. There was room on the deck amongst the group, and he sat down beside Trudy. When she saw him, she tried to get up, but he took hold of her arm and would not let her go.

Trudy turned to Minnie, "Tell Herr Altland to let go of me, or I'll scream," she said.

"Trudy," ordered Jake. "Stop acting like your mother and listen to me."

Trudy reached over with her free hand and slapped him hard. "I am not like my mother," she said angrily.

"Really?" replied Jake patiently. "You could have fooled me. In fact, you are so much like your mother that I now know why the good Lord did not let me marry you in Holland. When I met you for the first time, I thought you were the perfect woman. I'm thirty-five years old, and you are the first girl I ever asked to marry me. I wanted someone just like you and I never found one until that day up in Rittendorf when Abner introduced us. The strange thing was that I asked you the first day I saw you." He shook his head as if not believing that he had been so rash. "In my whole life I had never asked anyone to become my wife, but asking you seemed so right."

Trudy looked down at her arm where Jake was holding it and then up to his face where there was a red handprint. She started to say something and then decided not to.

"Trudy, look at me and know that I want to marry you still," said Jake. "I won't though, unless you change some of your ways. The first way you must change is this business of not speaking to me when there is a misunderstanding between us. We had no definite arrangement to go shopping together the first day off the ship in England. I thought you wanted to rest or go with the women. Schotzy asked me to go along as a translator when he purchased materials for houses in Pennsylvania. I saw this as a good opportunity for me to save money for our house by putting in with him. By going in together, we got a much better price on everything we bought. I was thinking how pleased you would be to hear about the great bargains we got, and what a nice house I would be able to build for you."

"I thought you said we would go together to get things for our house when we got there," said Trudy.

"I did, but not the first day," said Jake. "When you saw how steep the hill was to the town, you said you didn't know if you wanted to climb it right away."

"Oh," said Trudy.

"Then when I heard that you were angry, I felt like the child who, seeing beautiful peach blossoms wanted to give them to her mother because she loved her so much. She picked the blossoms without knowing they were the peach crop. Her mother, not realizing the blossoms represented her child's love, became angry, scolded the child and threw the blossoms on the ground."

Trudy reached up to touch the red spot on his face. Tears were running down her face. "I'm sorry," she sobbed.

He loosened his grip on her arm and continued, "Another thing I will not put up with is being compared to other men. That fat thief bought you flowers, sweets and who knows what all. I bought us the highest quality hardware for our house. I'll pick flowers for you from our garden when we get one. I'll buy flowers for you sometime but I don't care to spend the money at a time when we need to hold onto it. Do you understand and agree that is a wise thing to do?"

Trudy looked up at Jake with love in her eyes. She nodded her head and said, "Ya, I agree that's wisdom."

Jake took Trudy's hand and said, "This is the way my dat was. He used to bring my mom the first strawberry or the first peach of the season. He would come into the house and say, 'Come, Annie, I want you to see this brand new hummy.[85] It's worth dropping whatever you are doing just to see it.' I always thought that his ways were dear. You don't really know me yet. You will find that I will have some nice ways about me, too, if you give me a chance."

Through her tears Trudy said, "I know you have nice ways. I think maybe I have some, too. I can't be just like my mother, can I? I don't want to be like her." She hesitated, thought a bit, started to say something, and stopped. She took a breath, let it out and then said, "I'm thinking it, I may as well say it. Since you got up nerve enough to talk about it, you may as well spill your guts and get it all out. What else is there about me that you can't stand?"

Jake's eyes popped open, and his eye brows shot up in surprise. He, too, hesitated and then said, "You asked, so

---

[85]   hummy: calf

don't get mad when I tell you. You get upset when I don't hang around you all of the time. Schwiesshart,[86] I love you so much I cannot concentrate when I'm near you. I cannot work when you're around. All I can think about is you. It is my job to get you, and the rest of the group, safely off this ship and to the wilderness of Pennsylvania where we can claim our land and build our homes. I daresn't make mistakes. People's lives depend on my having good judgment. Do you understand? You are my Hepzibah,[87] the one in whom I take delight. My Beulah, my bride. I don't think that you have an idea how lovely you are or how much I love you. When we are married and can be together in our own home, it will be different. In the meantime, you will just have to put up with it. It's my job." He stopped, looked at her as if he really wanted to kiss her and said, "That is, if you are speaking to me now and if you will marry me after what I've just said."

"I thought that you got to know me better and discovered that you really didn't like being around me much," said Trudy. "My mother always told me I wasn't pretty. Then for the last few years she said I was too old for anyone to ever want me. I've been so unhappy. I guess I didn't know how to act any differently. Will you forgive me? I'll try to see things your way and be a perfect wife."

"I'm not asking for perfect," said Jake. "All I'm asking is that you love me, care for me, and don't act like your mother."

September passed into October, and it was hurricane season. Even though the passengers had never heard of hurricanes, they were about to find out about them because their ship was in the path of a major storm. The crew of the *Augusta Margaret* worked to get ready for it, and Herr Hartzell reminded the people to pray. The sailors brought a triple portion of food down and then closed the hatches. Everyone

---

[86]   schwiesshart: sweetheart: pronononounced shwees hart
[87]   Isaiah 62:4

below deck was locked in. It was dark down there because the candle inside the pierced tin lantern had been put out as a safety measure to keep the ship from catching afire. The wind came up and tossed the ship violently back and forth. It creaked and groaned as it rolled with the combined forces of the wind and waves. Rain lashed the vessel and began to come in through the cracks. The dogs whimpered, and the children clung to their mothers as the storm grew worse.

Abner, who had not been sick on this leg of the journey, became violently ill. "I think I'm going to die," he said after he had thrown up everything he had in his stomach and continued to heave. "I'm not afraid to die," he groaned. "Let me die, God." There was nothing that could be done for him or anyone else. The storm became worse, and the noise was horrendous. Cargo broke loose, rolled and slid around in the hold beneath them. Anything on the open deck that was not lashed down extremely well, broke loose, rolled around and ended up in the ocean. After a series of particularly deep rolls, everyone and everything slid back and forth from one side of the ship to the other. Then the hatch broke open, and water began pouring in. It was not long before the passengers, as well as most of their bedding and belongings were wet.

"We're going to die! We're going to die," cried someone.

"I don't care if we do," muttered Abner. "How much more miserable can we get?"

"The food is all," said Willy. "We've been down here in the dark for days. How long does a storm like this go on?"

Herr Hartzell looked at his watch. "I've been keeping track," he said, "and it has been five, going on six days. I think we'll be out of it soon. It sounds like the wind is letting up." He was right. The captain had maneuvered the ship out of the path of the storm, and the ship continued on its way north towards Philadelphia.

After the storm passed, Klaus came down to see how they were. He looked around the dimly lighted deck and said, "It's beautiful out in the sun this morning, so different from what it has been. Wasn't that storm something? I could feel your prayers. The captain said he was surprised this ship could take such a battering. I wish I could talk good enough to him to say your prayers saved us." As his eyes got used to the dim light, he glanced around and said, "This place looks like the pigs were at it, and it smells worse. I wonder if the captain would let youse bring your bedding up on deck to dry out. I'll ask about it when I go back up. Now tell me, how did everybody come through the ordeal? Was everybody sick?"

Schotzy spoke up, "Just about everybody got sick, especially Abner. He was begging to die."

"Poor Abner, are you better now?" He nodded, and Klaus asked, "Was anybody hurt?"

"We all rolled back and forth, back and forth all over the place," answered Schotzy. "We were all banged up some, but no one was hurt bad. What about you? Where were you during the storm? I was worried about you beins you have to stay outside the lady's door."

"I was all right. My lady let me inside the cabin, or else I would have been blown overboard."

Just then he spotted his sister beside Jake. "I heard that the storm blew us far from our regular track. In fact, the sailors say that the captain himself doesn't know where we are, except that we are far north of where we were," he said. "What news do you have for me, I hope."

"We have our differences settled," said Jake. "We've discovered that neither of us is perfect and have decided that is a good basis for any marriage. We'll get married as soon as we can after the voyage is over and everyone and everything is taken care of."

"I'm glad to hear that you two have kissed and made up. I could have told you that Trudy wasn't perfect, but you wouldn't have believed me," he teased. "And I have some news for you, too," he added with a grin. "Elisabeth Winslow, also known as Betsy, is going to marry me."

"What?" sputtered Jake. "How can you do that? You don't even know the girl, and you don't speak her language."

"You've got a lot to talk about, telling me I don't even know the girl. I've seen her every day for more than two months. How about yourself? When it's the right person, you know."

"When will we get to meet her?" asked Trudy.

"I don't know for sure. I'll have to see if you can come up tomorrow."

Schotzy who heard the news rushed to Klaus' side. "What do you mean you're getting married," he asked. "You never asked me if it was all right."

"I never asked my mother either," Klaus replied. "And speaking of Mother, I see her looking at me. I better would go to her and pretty quick." Turning to Trudy he said, "I gather she's still not speaking to you."

"Whatever gave you that idea?" asked Trudy with mock surprise.

Klaus then made his way to his mother. "Greetings, dear Mother," he said. "I came down to see if you're all right. This is the first chance I've had to get down here since the storm came up."

"It's a wonder you came to see me at all," replied Widow Schneider. "You had to stop and visit with those other people first. Go get me a light for my pipe. I haven't had a smoke since the storm began."

"Aren't you going to say, 'Nice to see you, son,' or 'How are you?' Even 'Good to see you made it through the storm,' would be nice. I came down to see you and tell you some news. I'm sorry, but I do not have time to go hunt up a light for you. I have to get back shortly. I do have to stay on the job most of the time. Now tell me how did you come through the storm?"

"I've half a mind not to talk to you either," Widow Schneider replied. "A lot you care about me. When I think how I carried you in my belly for nine months and changed your diaper and gave you the best years of my life, and you won't even do one little thing for me. You are an ungrateful son if I ever saw one!"

"Mother, don't give me that 'I carried you in my belly' stuff. It was worn out years ago. I came down to see how you are, and if there is anything I can do for you or bring you next time I come down. I also wanted you to know that I'm getting married as soon as we get to Pennsylvania. I have to get back now. I've been gone too long."

Widow Schneider seethed with anger and looked around for someone to take it out on. Princess, who was free to roam wherever she wished on the ship, found Widow Schneider's leg and rubbed against it. "What got against me?" she screamed. When she saw that it was Princess, she said very loudly, "That witch of a cat has no place on a ship. Everyone knows that taking a cat from its home is bad luck, and having a cat on a ship is worse luck. We've had nothing but bad luck since we left home. It's the cat's fault, and someone should throw it overboard."

"That's right," called out Herr Flickinger. "A pfennig for anyone who will see if the cat can swim." The passengers gasped at the idea. Some were horrified while others were thrilled at the idea of getting money for little effort. Several young men dived for Princess, but she evaded them.

Abner, still weak from being sick for five days, ran toward the cat, stumbling over people who were in his path. "Come kitty, kitty, come. Come here, Princess," he called. He grabbed her and confronted Widow Schneider. Shaking from anger and exhaustion, he said, "How could you say such a thing, you hateful old biddy? You know Princess is a good cat. Nearly every day she catches a mouse or rat and brings it to Grandpa before she eats it. The rats would have been chewing on all of us and the food onboard if she hadn't done that." He turned to the young men who wanted the reward and yelled at them, "Don't you dare hurt my cat."

Matthias was on his feet in a shot. He ran to Abner and shook him until his teeth rattled and then swatted him on the bottom. "Don't you ever speak to an older person in such a disrespectful manner. Have you no shame? We've talked to you about self-control, and we thought you were doing better. Now look how you have disgraced your mother and me. Take the cat, put her in the cage and go sit down." Turning to Widow Schneider, he said, "We apologize."

"If you are really sorry, throw the cat overboard," she answered.

"I can't do that," Matthias replied.

"That proves to me that you are not really sorry, Matthias Hartzell. All of you Hartzells are hypocrites, big feeling hypocrites, and all of you are going to be sorry before this trip is over. You are going to be sorry that you ever tangled with me."

Late in the afternoon a seagull flew in through the open hatch and began flying wildly around, banging into the bulkhead until its head was bleeding. Nearly everyone stood up and swatted at it. The children jumped up and down waving their arms and screaming. The frightful racket made the poor bird more agitated. "Herr Flickinger told me that when a bird flies into a house or place like this, someone is going to die," said Mary in a loud voice.

"Hush," said Minnie. "Hush and sit down."

Just then the gull crashed against a rafter and dropped to the deck fluttering. It landed in front of a woman who was expecting a baby, and then it thrashed around until it was dead.

"This is terrible bad luck," said Widow Schneider. "Something bad is bound to happen."

The captain did not send word for the passengers to bring their bedding up to dry in the sun. Everyone had been in their damp clothes and slept in their damp bedding for several days, and it began to take its toll. Almost everyone began to cough, sneeze, wheeze and wipe their noses. Frau Wentz had difficulty breathing. She never complained, but died quietly without a struggle. Herr Hartzell took her death hard. He asked Trudy to prepare her body for burial instead of simply having her wrapped in her blanket and buried at sea. "She was a martyr just as her husband was," he said. "Her heart was broken when he died."

Frau Bentzel immediately began mothering the Wentz children. "They will help take the place of my little boy who died not long after we left home." she said.

The next night an old man died, and then little Violet Wentz. "She and her mother weren't meant for this world," said Frau Bentzel. "I feel as if I've lost another child." She took Waldemar Wentz onto her lap and cuddled him close. "Stay well," she whispered. "Stay well."

The pregnant woman tried to give birth but did not have strength to deliver the baby. Sailors came down with handkerchiefs over their faces and carried the bodies away. Herr Hartzell held a service for each before they were cast into the ocean. Abner watched as his Grandpa served as chaplain. *That's a hard job*, he thought.

One morning Karl came down with pieces of dried codfish and passed them around to everyone and said, "The captain doesn't want all of you to die. That's why he is giving you better food. He makes his money on the number of people he is able to sell in Philadelphia. He musta forgot to have you air out your bedding after the storm. He has a lot on his mind, ya know. I don't think he knows where we are. That storm musta blew us to kingdom come. It ruined a lot of our food, too."

Abner sniffed the fish and licked it. It was very salty. Then he tried to bite into it, but it was too hard. "You have to suck on it awhile boy, or else pound it with a hammer," said Karl. "That will soften it up."

When Herr Schmitt heard that, he went to his anvil, got his hammer down off a shelf and said, "Line up, kinder,[88] and we'll soon have some food for you. I never thought when I learned to be a blacksmith that I would be preparing food for a crowd on my anvil." He laughed and began pounding the fish. After the children were taken care of, the grown-ups brought their pieces of fish to be pounded, all except Frau Schneider and Herr Flickinger who did not care to join the crowd.

Seeing that they weren't going to have theirs taken care of, Jake went to the widow and said, "Mother Schneider, I will take your fish to be pounded and get you a light for your pipe. Which would you prefer for me to do first?"

She looked at Herr Flickinger and back to Jake. "Will you get his pounded soft also?"

"I'd be glad to." She handed Jake the fish. "I need something to drink, too."

No sound of a thank you from her, thought Abner. *I must remember to thank people when they do something for me. It sure is ugly when you don't.* Then he said to his mother, "I wonder if I should have eaten the fish beins it's so salty and all. I'm really thirsty, and I might be sick again."

"You have to have water, or you *will* get sick again," she said.

---

[88] kinder: children; rhymes with cinder

After awhile Karl came down again with a bucket full of something to drink. "The water barrels were knocked over in the storm and some of them came apart," he said. "This watered down beer is all we have to drink."

"Ach," said Abner to his grandfather. "Now I'll get a beer belly and talk funny."

"A little beer won't hurt you," Herr Hartzell said. "In fact, it may kill the bugs that were in the water. It's when you overdo anything that you get in trouble. We strive for moderation in all things. That means neither too much nor too little."

Father Werner who was nearby, looked at Herr Hartzell with admiration. "What amazes me about you is the way you turn every little thing into a life lesson. You are the best teacher I have ever encountered."

"Thank you. Coming from you that is a real compliment."

After everyone had their drink, the captain came down to look the people over. He spoke and Karl translated. "The captain does not speak your language, but this is what he had to say: 'I've been told that your bedding is damp. We don't want you to get sick, so you may take it up on the deck and drape it over whatever you can find to dry it out. There may not be enough room for all, but do the best you can. The rest you will just have to lay out on the deck.'" Karl pointed to Jake. "The captain says for you to take care of it."

There was a scramble to get things together and up on deck first. "Easy does it," Jake called out. "You'll get your chance. You need to help each other take the bedding up the ladder and out through the hatch." Even though the children were not needed to help and were probably in the way, he let them go up into the sun. "Don't cause any fuss or make a racket," he said, "or no doubt you'll be sent right back down."

Abner blinked when he got outside. The sun was bright in a clear blue sky. The air was fresh and had a wonderful smell. *It is so good to be out*, he thought. *The sun is warm and comforting. I wish I could just lie down and get warm all the way through.*

"Let's go find Klaus," said Schotzy, taking Reuben's hand. "It wonders me where he stays. He must be around here some place." Before long they saw him out walking with the mysterious lady. She was covered from head to toe in a heavy brown material. Her hat, which was large with a heavy veil, completely obscured her face. The boys rushed to Klaus as soon as they saw him, but his face remained frozen. He shook his head, telling them not to come close. The lady said something, and Klaus relaxed.

"She says it is all right for me to talk to you," said Klaus. "How are you doin'?"

"Gut,"[89] said Schotzy. "Can we see where your cabin is?"

"We'll walk around that way," said Klaus. "Just follow us. Where is Father Werner? He has been a great help in helping us understand each other. In fact, he's such a good teacher that I'm getting through to Betsy most of the time. English is hard, but a person can do what he has to do if he makes up his mind to it."

"I'm proud of you Klaus," said Shotzy. "I know my Big Angel can do anything."

"Thanks," said Klaus, "but I asked where Father Werner is."

"He's up here somewheres," said Abner. "We're bound to run into him one way or the other."

When the mystery lady saw the women hanging the bedding over the railing she asked if there had been a problem. The boys nodded their heads. "Wet." They tried to explain, but she did not understand. They got to the back of the ship and began walking into the wind. The contrast with the other side was striking. In no time Abner was chilled to the bone and began to sneeze. "It's hard to believe it's the

---

[89]   gut: good, rhymes with fruit

same day, as cold as it is on this side," he said. "I gotta get outa this wind."

"Right here is my lady's cabin," said Klaus. She says since you are cold you can come in."

The cabin, which was as neat as could be, had a lower bunk and an upper bunk as well as two chairs. Standing beside one of the chairs was the beautiful red haired lady. As the boys crowded in, Klaus said, "I want you to meet Miss Betsy, the lady I am going to marry when we get to Pennsylvania. No one in this world is luckier than I."

"How do you do?" said the boys.

"Klaus has been my Big Angel ever since I met him," said Schotzy. "I hope he can keep on being my Big Angel after you are married."

"My Big Angel, too," replied Miss Betsy, pointing to herself.

"And me," said Reuben.

"It's close quarters in here," said Klaus. "I think you boys must go outside."

His employer shook her head vigorously and said, "Wait." She took off her hat and the boys stared. She was without doubt the most beautiful woman that Abner had ever seen, more beautiful even than his mother or Miss Betsy. Her hair was very black. Her skin was clear, almost white with a faint blush of pink. Her eyes were as blue as the sky on a clear winter day. She had straight white teeth and dimples when she smiled. She took off her outer wrap, and underneath was a dress of homespun. She moved gracefully as she walked to a cupboard from which she took a bag of raisins. She said something which Klaus understood and then handed them to him. She smiled and then indicated that he should go out with the boys and that Betsy could go with them.

"We'll go around to the other side, sit in the sun and have our treat," said Klaus. "Then I'll give the rest of the raisins to my sister to see that all the children get some. I don't think you should eat many at a time. I don't know what they could do to you, but you better wouldn't take any chances."

Abner popped a few in his mouth and enjoyed the little bits of sweetness. "Tell the lady we thank her," he said. "It was nice of her to give them to us."

"She was upset because all of youse were so thin," said Klaus. "She really is a very nice lady." He hugged the boys and said, "We must get back. It's a wonder to me that she allowed us both to be gone at the same time."

The boys stayed in the sun until Schotzy got red. "I forgot about sunburn, but I'll remember it tonight," he said.

Minnie and Mary came by. Minnie was burned almost as badly as Schotzy. "I do believe so half that the salve that Father Werner gave me will help take the fire out of sunburn," she said. "I'll put some on it the soonest I can. After that, we better would hole up a few days," she said. "Unless, that is, the cooks decide we're baked and ready for supper."

"You're funny," said Reuben who was darker complexioned. Neither he nor Mary were burned at all.

"Trudy gave us some raisins," said Minnie. "Ooh, they were good. Did you get some? Maybe we won't starve to death after all."

A man strolled by who was dressed differently from anyone else. He wore a big black hat and had buckles on his shoes. "Karl told me that man is dressed like William Penn used to dress," said Willy who stopped when he saw there was food to be had. "That's because he's a Quaker. All Quaker men dress like that."

The women had turned the bedding in the sun for several hours until most of it was dry. Everyone had gone up on deck except Herr Flickinger and Widow Schneider. All of the hatches had been opened and the place aired out making it drier. It smelled better and promised to be a healthier place.

One evening before preparing for the night's rest, the boys sat around and talked amongst themselves about their exploits back home.

"If I were home, I'd find a freshly laid egg and cook it in my secret hideout back in the woods," said Willy. "I had a nice frying pan and everything. I didn't stay hungry very long."

"I knew where each and every fruit tree was and when the owner would be around," said Schotzy. "I knew where the wild berries were, too. I'd pick people's strawberries and eat them, but not all."

"I, me, I find, I eat," said Reuben making motions with his hands. "Lady know I eat, no like. Catch, spank. No like spank. Cucumbers on ground, glundachs[90] eat, but not all. I, me find cucumbers, wipe dirt, chew part, eat, not all. Lady not know me eat, think glundachs eat." Reuben laughed, remembering the days when he was a homeless beggar with no one to look after him. He crooked his neck up and said, "Drink from cow. Eat egg, no cook."

Willy said, "What did he say? I didn't get it."

"I'll tell you what he said," replied Schotzy. "The lady who let him stay in her barn did not like it when he ate her cucumbers. She would spank him if she caught him. Then he saw that the glundach had let the cucumber on the vine and ate only part of it. After that he didn't pick cucumbers but would crawl along on the ground, wipe off the dirt and eat part of it. The lady thought the glundach ate it."

Willy nodded and said, "He's a pretty smart little boy."

Seth had been sitting quietly listening to the rest. "I growed up hungry," he said. "After my dat left, we never had enough to eat. He ran off quick and went to Pennsylvania. I

---

[90] glundachs: animals similar to groundhogs. Dachshunds were bred to catch them.

think I told you that my dat was a good man, at least that's what my mam said, but sometimes I wonder." He hesitated as if he should not have mentioned what he had just said and then continued, "One time some of the village boys tricked me into joining them in a shed back of an old barn. They said that they wanted to be my friends, and I believed them. I thought we would just sit around and talk like we're talking now but when I got there, they grabbed me, took me down and tormented me. Then one of them named Ernie asked me if I knew why they were getting even with me. I said I had no idea. I thought they were just mean. Then Ernie said that it was because my dat killed his uncle. He said that my dat got drunk sometimes, and when he did, he got mean. That's when he killed Ernie's uncle and ran off. My mam always said he was a good man, but sometimes I wonder. I never talked about it before, but sometimes I can't get it off my mind. My family was hungry a lot so if I found something to eat, I took it to them because they were hungry, too. I wonder how they're doing, my mam, my brother and my grandma. I miss them." He wiped his eyes and blew his nose on an old rag he had picked up somewhere. "I hope I find my dat when we get to Philadelphia. I think I will, don't you? Then I'll find out the truth about him." After Seth had finished talking, no one else had anything to say.

On a night when there was a full harvest moon that shone so brightly that it even cast a little light down in the lower deck, Herr Flickinger became very sick. He coughed and wheezed most of the night. Widow Schneider tended him until she began to cough and wheeze, too. It was then that Rachel got up and went to her. "I will watch him, and Trudy will help," she said. "You lie down and get some sleep, or you will be the next to go."

"I think I will," said Widow Schneider. "I'm so tired." She was soon snoring.

"She's getting no rest," whispered Abner to Schotzy whose bedroll was next to his.

"She must have a cord of wood sawed by now," answered Schotzy. "That poor old lady. Have you taken notice how old and skinny she looks? She used to be good sized and not bad looking for a lady her age. This trip has been really hard on her. I hope she makes it."

"Me, too," said Abner, wondering if he really meant it.

A couple of days went by and Widow Schneider seemed to be too tired to care who watched after Herr Flickinger as he got worse day by day. She did not seem to be as proud as she had been or as angry with Trudy and the rest of the world. It was as if she simply did not have the energy for it.

Herr Hartzell, who had taken a turn sitting with the old man, was giving his daily message to his people. "I'm afraid the old powwower has pneumonia and will not live much longer," he said. "We must treat him kindly and show him what Christian love is. Minnie, I know you won't want to do it but it would be a good thing for you to tell him that you forgive him for treating you badly. You are the only one on this ship who can make a difference with the end of his life, perhaps even bringing him to believe in the saving power of our Lord."

Schotzy whispered to her, "I think, too, that you should. You'll feel better when you do it and get it over with."

"I don't want to."

Schotzy looked her straight in the eye and said, "That doesn't matter how you feel. It needs done, so do it. Don't let something like this get to you. Now go!" He gave her a push. "Go."

"Just hold it. I have to think about it. Herr Hartzell, sir, is it true that an old person who has pneumonia always dies from it?"

"Ya, Minnie, that's true."

"How long do you think he'll last?"

"Not long. If you go, we'll pray for you all of the time you're with him. You don't have to be afraid at all."

Minnie took a deep breath, let it out slowly and said, "All right, I'll do it."

"We'll pray that God will send his ministering angels to watch over you and give you the right words to say."

"Thank you," she said and then made her way to where Herr Flickinger was lying. "Wie gehts?" she asked.

He shrugged and did not answer.

"I came to say," she stopped, thought a bit and then looked at him. She saw not the forbidding figure that had frightened her for so long, but a sick old man who was dying, an old man that no one really cared about. Suddenly she realized all he had done for her. She began again, "I came to tell you how much I appreciate all that you taught me. I mean about the plants and healing. I appreciate that you took me different places, and I got to see things that most children never get to see, like beautiful big churches and nice little churches, different towns and villages, beautiful countryside and rivers and lakes. You taught me how to meet people, talk to them and not be shy. Sometimes you were mean to me, and I forgive you for that."

Herr Flickinger looked at her without changing expression. It was hard work for him to breathe, and he took in his breath before asking, "What brought this on?"

"I now believe in Jesus."

"So?"

"I'm supposed to forgive people and love them and help them believe in Him," she replied. "I think you'd feel better if you believed in Him, too."

It took him a long time to get his words out, but Minnie was patient. He finally said, "I don't disbelieve in Him. I learned about Him when my papa used to beat the living daylights out of me for rutching around in church. That's when I started serving the one I serve." He stopped to cough and continued, "I've never been sorry." Another cough shook his body. "I'm glad I could teach you. You have a gift for it. Too bad you're now serving the other side." He gasped for air and said, "You could be a powerful witch still. It's not too late, you know. Everything I have is yours, my money, my books, everything you need for it." Another gasp, and then he added, "Run along and get me some beer, and I'll teach you more when you get back." He coughed and said, "And tell that old lady who's been hanging around me to go somewheres else. She's a pain you know where." Minnie could tell that Widow Schneider heard what Herr Flickinger said. She went to get the beer, and when she got back, he was dead.

Minnie made her way back to Herr Hartzell and her hands were shaking when she said to him, "Can you take this beer before I spill it? Herr Flickinger is dead. He said I could have everything that was his. What should I do about his things?"

"Sit down. I'll send Schotzy or Abner for Jake. Whenever you want, I'll help you. I think you'd best to get rid of the books."

"I've never looked at them books, but I know that one tells the powwower what to say when casting a spell or a hex. He looked at that one pretty much."

"Did he have any other things he wanted done?" asked Herr Hartzell.

Minnie thought about a half a second and then said, "He wouldn't want a service. He's always been a follower of the other one."

CHAPTER TWELVE

With Herr Flickinger gone, there seemed to be a better atmosphere in the air. Before, it always seemed as if something evil were hovering over everything. Now that feeling was gone. Karl brought the biscuits and the bucket of whatever it was, and commented, "What happened in here? It's not the same." He shook his head as if to get rid of something. After that comment he did not seem to want to leave. It was as if he knew he was among friends who had become very dear. He added kindly, "The captain is worried because so many of youse are dying. It took him long enough. He doesn't make money off dead people," he added sarcastically. "So from now on everyone will be allowed up on the deck for a few minutes each day as long as there are not a lot of you up at the same time and no one annoys the other passengers." *That's good,* thought Abner. *It will be good to get some fresh air and sunshine. Herr Flickinger being gone does make a difference.*

Minnie asked Schotzy to help her and Herr Hartzell go through Herr Flickinger's things. Widow Schneider obviously wanted to get in on it, but Minnie did not allow it. However, she did stay close to watch. Her place was there, and they could not ask her to leave. This meant that Abner could not get close, so he chose to ignore the whole thing. He, Reuben and the dogs went up to get air and walk around the deck.

Princess, who had been in the cage since Herr Flickinger's offer of a reward for killing her, was let out to roam once more.

There was a ship not far from them, and the captain must have signaled for it to come alongside. It flew a British flag just like the one flying from the mast of the *Augusta Margaret*. Abner came upon Klaus standing outside his employer's cabin just as the two captains of the ships were close enough to talk to each other. As they spoke English, Abner did not know what they said, but later Karl told Klaus that they were about two days away from the American coast. "We're pretty far north. It will take about five days to get to Philadelphia if the wind is favorable," he said. "They have extra water which they will give us and some apples."

Abner and Reuben watched the supplies being brought on board. The apples looked good, and he felt that he could hardly wait to sink his teeth into one. Reuben's eyes shone when he saw them. "Good apples," he said. "Climb tree, get apples, eat." He shook with anticipation. "Good apples," he said again.

They continued walking around the ship. When they came upon Klaus the next time, he knocked on the lady's cabin door, and Betsy answered. "Little cakes," he said. Betsy closed the door and came back with two big cookies. "For you," she said to the boys with a smile.

"Thank you, Miss Betsy," said Abner.

"Hanku, Miss Betty," said Reuben, his dark eyes shining with delight.

Betsy reached down and hugged Reuben, patted Abner on the back and returned to the cabin. She came out one more time with crackers for the dogs and a bag of dried apricots. "Share," she said. The boys made short work of the cookies, ate a couple of the apricots and used the crackers to teach the dogs to stay.

After a while, Minnie and Schotzy came up and joined them. He was excited. "You should have saw all the stuff Herr Flickinger had," he said. "That old man was a packrat. You wouldn't believe it until you saw it. I can't see how a cripple like him could have carried it all."

"Ya," said Minnie. "And it was a mess because it was all in through each other.[91] There was magic stuff mixed with money and clothes. Then there was good stuff like scissors, lots of scissors, and needles, packs of needles, butcher knives and other kinds of knives, embroidery thread, balls of woolen yarn of different colors and knitting needles, too. He must have figured on being a huckster[92] when he got to Pennsylvania."

"Some of the scissors and knives got wet and we'll have to work on them so they don't rust," said Schotzy. "We could sell everything like it is, but Minnie would get more for it if we polish it up and sell it to people who can't buy such things where they live."

"Whatfer magic stuff did he have?" asked Abner.

"Ach," said Minnie, with a shiver. "I'll let Schotzy tell you."

Schotzy reported with the enthusiasm that only a ten year old boy could muster. "There was stuff like dried toads, dried salamanders, small dried hearts of some kind of an animal and a dried bat."

"There were all sorts of medicines, all different colors," cut in Minnie. "Bright yellow, I know that's sulfur. Bright greenish, that's copper something. The reddish brown stuff is probly dried blood, and there's different colored stuff in packages and bottles."

"Your grandfather thought we best just toss that stuff overboard," said Schotzy. "He's going to look at the books and see if any are worth keeping. There was a good bit of

---

91   all in through each other: tangled together
92   huckster: peddler

money, too. Widow Schneider thought that some of it should go to her for taking care of Herr Flickinger like she did. Trudy told her that she got what she deserved for making a fool of herself. And the old lady didn't even get mad. That surprised me. She's lost a lot of pepper."

"You're right," said Abner. "This trip has been hard on all of us, but her especially. Remember the day we had dinner at her house? Minnie, you wouldn't believe how much food was on the table and how good it was! She piled it on Schotzy's plate, and he ate until he got sick. I hope she lives to cook more meals like that." Suddenly Abner knew that he did mean it when he said that he hoped Widow Schneider made it safely to Pennsylvania.

"Ya," said Schotzy. "I ate myself full that day."

"Ya, that's for sure," added Abner.

"My pappaw stole her good luck pfennig, and everything went downhill for her from then on," said Schotzy. "I don't really believe that the bad luck was caused by the loss of the pfennig, but it gives a person something to think about." Schotzy stopped, was quiet for a bit and then went on, "It's strange how many people believe in so many superstitions. That day may have been the start of bad luck for Widow Schneider, but it was the start of a good thing for me. That was when Herr Hartzell said he would take care of me. I was bound out to him a few days later. Being bound out was the best day of my life because I had someone who really cared for me." Schotzy's eyes lit up, and he added, "And that was the day you came into my life, Big Angel. I never told you this before, Minnie, but this is what happened. I ate way too much after just about starving all winter. Then I got so sick I thought I died, and a big angel came and carried me to heaven. It was Klaus who came along and carried me to Hartzell's! That's how I got my Big Angel.

"It wondered me where that came from," said Minnie. "Tell me, when did you get the gold?"

"That was just a cuppy days later. Ya, I had the gold, and the house was mine, too. I shoulda been set for life." Schotzy shrugged his shoulders. "Herr Hartzell told me he would release me, and I could stay in Rittendorf if I wanted to, but I had no family there. I figured I may as well go along to Pennsylvania and be part of the Hartzell family. The house will be there if I ever want to go back."

The children stood quietly enjoying the cool sea breezes when Reuben pointed to the sky, "Birds," he cried out excitedly. "Lots of birds!

Karl who had been walking by with a mop looked up and said excitedly, "They're shore birds. That means we're not far from land. What a good omen! We'll be there soon." When land was sighted, it proved to be Cape Henlopen near the entrance to Delaware Bay. The captain chose not to navigate into the river that night but waited for a pilot boat to guide them to port the next day. It would not be long before they would set foot on Pennsylvania soil.

What will happen to me now, thought Abner. *I'll be glad to get off this ship, but I'm afraid. Dear Lord, keep your hand on me. Let me be with someone who will be as good to me as my grandpa is to Schotzy. But there is no one else in the world as good as my grandpa. I just want to stay with my family.*

As they prepared to leave the ship, Karl cautioned them, "Do not drink the water from the river. It looks good and clean, but more than one person has become very sick from drinking it. Another thing you will want to remember is that today is the first day of November. The trees should still be pretty. You have never seen anything prettier than an American hardwood forest in autumn. I wish you the very best luck in the world. Keep warm. Auf Weidersehn, until we meet again."

"I like him," said Seth. "Sometimes it seems like you meet someone that you really would like to be friends with, and then they go one way and you go another."

Jake was there, too, giving good advice. "One thing I forgot to tell you about is the snakes. There are many kinds of snakes, and a lot of them are poisonous. There are many more here than there were back home. It's cold now, but any sunny day they will be out on the rocks trying to get warm. You must keep a sharp lookout for them especially this time of year when the nights are cold and the afternoons are warm."

Alice was immediately paralyzed with fear. "I hate snakes, and I'm not getting off this boat," she said, "and you can't make me."

Herr Schmitt took hold of his middle daughter and said, "Now quit acting like a baby. You must get off unless you plan to go back and marry Otto." Since he knew she did not like Otto, he was making fun of her.

"Papa, please, I don't know what to do."

"Get hold of yourself. You're not the only one who has fears. How do you think Abner feels about having to be bound out?"

Alice found Abner and asked, "Are you afraid to be bound out?"

"Ya, some," he admitted.

"You don't act afraid," she said with her teeth chattering. "I'm afraid of snakes, and I can't bear to get off this boat and go walking around where there are snakes hidden under every rock and bush."

"Grandpa told me to remember to say, **'He has not given me a spirit of fear, but of power and love and a sound mind.'**[93] He said to remember that Jesus is with you. He will

---

[93]   II Timothy 1:7

take away your fear. You still have to keep an eye out for the snakes, but you will see them, and you don't have to be afraid." He smiled at her and said, "Thank you."

Alice looked surprised. "What are you thanking me for? I didn't do anything."

"Oh, but you did. You helped me to remember not to be afraid. Thank you, again. And there is something else I want to say to you." Suddenly he was shy. He wrung his hands and stuttered, "I, I, I like you a lot. W, w, will you be my girlfriend?"

Alice did not hesitate. "I thought I was your girlfriend."

Abner looked at her and no longer felt shy. "You are my girlfriend," he said, "but I never asked you. I just wanted to be sure." He leaned over toward her and whispered, "We're not big enough to kiss, but I promise you that some day when nobody else is around, we will."

Alice beamed and whispered back, "I promise, too."

A few minutes later Herr Schmitt spoke to his wife in surprise. "What's with Alice? Just a bit ago she was kicking and screaming, and now she's as happy as a pig in a wallow. I have three daughters and a wife, and I sure don't understand females."

"You told her to talk to Abner," answered Frau Schmitt with a smile. "Are you ready for this? I think she's in love."

Before the passengers were allowed to leave the ship, the captain spoke to them and Karl translated, "Those of you who signed papers to be bound out and the ones who have sold themselves into bondage with me are allowed to roam freely in Philadelphia until you are sold," he said. "Do not even think about escaping. There are many bounty hunters out there, and there is really no place to run to. Anyone who tries to escape will have added on to his indenture twice the number of days he was gone plus a fine for the money expended for him to be captured. Are there any questions?"

Looking around and seeing no hands raised, he continued, "I repeat, do not try to escape your servitude. You don't know the territory and neither do I, but I have been told that the wilderness is very close. Out in the wilderness are panthers, wolves and bears which you would not want to tangle with. There are many poisonous snakes on the land and in the water. There are also big black snakes that wrap themselves around your legs and try to eat you. You are too big for them to swallow, but they don't know that, so they try to hold on to you until you are dead. You need to turn yourselves in on the second Monday from today. That's when your auction will be held. Enjoy your freedom because you will be slaves for the next two, four or seven years." He saluted them smartly and returned to his cabin.

"It's really going to happen," said Abner to Alice. "I never thought about being a slave and having somebody buy me like they buy a pig at the farmer's market. Some stranger is going to buy me!"

"Maybe it won't be so bad," encouraged Alice. "Just think of something nice that could happen."

"I don't know what that would be," said Abner. "Let's talk about something else. Here comes Klaus. He looks happy. He and Miss Betsy are getting married today or tomorrow. Imagine that, and they don't hardly speak each other's language."

"My mom says it's all right that they don't speak the same language," said Alice. "She says men and women never speak the same language. What do you think she means by that?"

"I don't know," answered Abner. "I don't understand what ladies say half of the time."

"When will Trudy and Jake get married?" asked Alice.

"Not until all of us indentured servants are sold and taken away," Abner replied bitterly. "That's ten days, and that means that I won't be able to go to their wedding." He had to bite his lip to keep himself under control.

Happily, Alice did not notice his state of mind. "What happens next?"

"I must get Hoke's belongings off the shelf and tie up my bedroll. Then we leave the ship. I'll be glad to get off this old tub and get something fit to eat. I've heard that they have good food here in Pennsylvania. See ya later, liebling."

Abner had not gone through Herr Hoke's belongings because somehow it did not seem right, but now he was eager to see what was there. As he thought about it, he decided that it would not be anything exciting like Old Flick's junk, but it should be interesting. Abner remembered going through the things that had belonged to Schotzy's Uncle Pete who died, and the things in Schotzy's house that had been locked up for many years. He did not expect anything like that amongst the Hoke's belongings, but one never could tell. The idea of looking through the stuff gave him something different to think about besides having to be auctioned off like a cow or a pig. Anything to get his mind off that was welcome.

At long last the *Augusta Margaret* landed in America. Abner got his things together and made his way off the ship. He remembered how his legs felt when he got off the ship in England but this time it was much worse. He started to join his parents who were waiting for their belongings to be unloaded, and his legs just about gave out.

"Whatsa matter, Abs?" Willy called out. "You shoulda stayed away from that strong drink. You're fersouffa."

"Let me see you walk," Abner called back. Everyone was in a jolly mood, laughing and joking. The French were going to a settlement of Huguenots east of Lancaster so there was a possibility they would see them again. Antonio was going into Philadelphia to see if he could find friends. He planned to rejoin the Brethren and go along with them.

"Where will we stay tonight?" Abner asked his mother after they had said farewell to their fellow passengers.

"I don't know," Rachel replied. "I do believe that the company that Jake works for has made arrangements for these next few days. We'll make our own arrangements to buy a horse and wagon. Jake will see about the land we are going to buy. There is a place called Yorktowne that has been laid out but not many people live there. It's about ten days journey to the west, and that's where we're heading. Here comes Jake now."

Cousin Jake was all business. "See those wagons over there behind the horses with braided tails? Pick one of them and load all of your things on the same wagon. We will be going to Germantown which is about five miles northwest of here. The people you'll be staying with are Mennonites, so you know they'll take good care of you."

"I'm glad to hear that," said Matthias.

"I won't be able to leave here and lead you to Yorktowne for about ten days. In the meantime you will get a chance to come back to Philadelphia to look the place over. It's a beautiful, clean city. There are broad streets that the women sweep every day. They even go right out after a horse passes to clean up after it. That helps to keep the flies down. That's one thing you will notice in the spring and summer. There are many more bugs and flies here than back home."

"That does not make me happy to hear," said Rachel, "I hate flies and bugs."

"I'm sorry I got off the track of what I was talking about," said Jake. "I want you to know that the route to Germantown takes you past the place where the redemptioners are auctioned off. There are other interesting places that the driver will point out to you."

Abner felt as if there were a knot in the pit of his stomach when Cousin Jake mentioned the auction. *I'll get over this some way or other,* he thought. *But I don't know how.*

"Rachel, I'm asking a favor of you," continued Jake. "Will you please ask Trudy and her mother to stay with you until we are married? I would appreciate it very much. Klaus and Betsy are going to get married and they'll be gone. I'd feel so much more satisfied that Trudy is safe if she's with you. And besides, that way you can help Trudy get ready for our wedding."

Rachel beamed, "I'll be more than happy to have her company and help her get ready for the wedding. I can't imagine anything I would like more."

Abner did not feel the same. *Trudy comes and so does her mother,* he thought. *Here it is my last few days with my family, and she has to be with us. I think I'll just go out and croak.*

"I'll treat all of you to breakfast before you head out to Germantown," said Jake. "I'm hungry, and I know you are, too. There's an inn not far from here where they used to serve a decent breakfast. You don't order. You just get what they have, but I was never disappointed. It's not far. We can walk."

The inn had a huge dining room, and the smell of the bacon met them as they made their way down the street. It was late morning so the room was almost empty when Jake walked in and inquired as to whether the establishment could handle the Brethren group.

"We take care of as many as show up," answered the buxom young woman who was in charge. "Just seat yourselves together so our girls don't have to run all over the place to find you. You tell me how many, and the food will be out shortly." Abner did not even question that she spoke the same language he did.

It was not long before another young woman, bigger and broader than the first, brought out pitchers of milk and put one on each table. Next she brought warm potato rolls, butter, applebutter and smiercase.[94] Herr Hartzell asked God's blessing on the food.

Abner felt as if he could not wait until the blessing was finished to begin eating. Grandpa had hardly finished saying "Amen," when he reached for a roll.

"Slow down," said Rachel. "The main part is coming. You are not used to eating a lot. You can have all you want, but don't punish your stomach."

Abner had never heard his mother say "punish your stomach" before. He thought it was funny, but with the way he felt about being bound out, he did not feel like laughing.

Seth, who sat at the next table next to Aunt Edda, did laugh. Since they had been baptized at the same time, Seth and Edda had formed a special bond. He was in a good mood thinking about seeing his father. "My dat should be around here someplace," he said. "I really want to spend my time with him before I go into bondage. If I can find him, that is. It shouldn't be hard to find him beins he was such a good man. Probly everybody knows him. If he is still here, that is."

Aunt Edda patted him on the knee and said, "He'll be here."

The serving girl who was carrying in big plates of food set one down in front of Seth and inquired, "What's your dat's name, young man?"

"Abe Kunkle. Do you know him? Lotsa people must know him. He's a good man."

"Ya," the girl replied. "He was a good man all right, but I never heard of him having a family across the water. This will come as a surprise to you, but he was murdered day before

---

94   smiercase: soft cheese, cottage cheese

yesterday. His funeral is this afternoon. Oops, I shouldn't have told you until you were done eating."

Seth turned pale and asked, "He's dead? How can it be?"

"He, his wife and his children, were out walking when a man his wife never saw before jumped out of the bushes and stabbed him to death."

"His wife and children?" gasped Seth. "He had a wife and children?"

"Ya, they'll miss him, but with all of her money, she won't have any trouble getting another man, even if she is dormlich."[95]

"Maybe there's another Abe Kunkle," suggested Herr Hartzell, seeing how upset Seth was.

"There was only one Abe Kunkle, and this young man here is one he couldn't deny,"[96] insisted the waitress. "Except Abe put on some weight, and this young man looks like he could stand some."

The older waitress came over and said. "Grace, there are plates full of food ready to be served. Now quit blabbermauling and get to work."

"Sorry," said Grace. "I was just telling them about Abe Kunkle. The funeral is this afternoon, you know. I'd like to go. It would give me a chance to get inside that house."

Jake stood up and said, "I'm sorry about your father, Seth. We'll see about your going to the funeral. I can't go with you, but perhaps this young woman could show you where he lived. Who would you like to go with you?"

"Herr Hartzell and Willy."

Jake addressed his group of Brethren, "I know that all of you support Seth but you really need to get to where you will be staying. So eat your breakfast. I'll arrange for a buggy

---

95   dormlich: homely
96   one he couldn't deny: He looks so much like him, it's obvious he's his son.

to take Seth to the funeral and then out to Germantown for the night."

Abner was shocked by the news but he was hungry. On his plate were two fried eggs, a big piece of ham and some white things that were browned and crisp. He wasted no time. When he came to the white things, he said, "This is good. What is it?"

"It's fried potatoes," replied Jake. "Americans eat them all the time, morning, noon and night."

"I can see why," said Abner, forking in another mouthful.

"Oh look," said Minnie. "Here comes Klaus with Miss Betsy and the mystery lady. Right behind them is Father Werner."

Klaus seated the mystery lady, and then went immediately to Widow Schneider taking his fiancée with him. "Mother," he said. "This is Miss Elisabeth Winslow, my bride to be." "We're going to get married as soon as we can. We'll catch a ship to Baltimore that is leaving later today. I'm inviting you to come to the wedding. I really would like you to be there. Will you come?"

Abner could see Widow Schneider's face contorting while she made up her mind. Her thoughts flashed across her face. *Dear Lord,* he thought. *Let her be nice.*

She smiled and answered graciously, "I'm glad that you asked me, son. Why in the world are you going to Baltimore? We just got here."

Klaus lowered his voice and said softly, "That is the easiest way to get where we're going. My lady does not feel safe here in Philadelphia. Finish eating your breakfast, and we'll eat ours. Then we'll go. The magistrate is not far from here."

Klaus then spoke to Jake. "My lady wants to hire a young man to go with us to act as a guard while I'm sleeping, someone I know who would be generally helpful. I suggested Willy. She will pay for his passage if it can be done."

Jake nodded between mouthfuls and said, "I don't see any reason why not. I'll see about it."

Trudy interrupted her brother, "Would we have time to take a room here for a bit so that we could clean up for the wedding?"

Betsy said, "I'd like that, too. Please see about a room or two. We won't take long."

Klaus arranged for the rooms, and then called Willy to his table. "My lady is looking for a young man to work for her. She will pay your passage and also pay you for working for her. She believes in treating people fairly. We will leave here today still, and I have no idea when we'll be back, if ever. Would you like to go along?"

"Sure. I'll tell my mom and pap I'm going," said Willy, without thinking about it. "But I told Seth I'd go with him to his dat's funeral this afternoon."

"I see you're done fressing. Let's go talk to Seth." Somehow it was all worked out. Seth said that after Willy, his second choice was Abner, and so it was arranged. Jake was to be Klaus's best man, and Trudy was to be Miss Betsy's maid of honor. They would take Widow Schneider. Matthias and Rachel would take Willy, Schotzy and Reuben. Minnie and Mary would take care of the dogs, go with the Schmitts, and stay with them. The rest of the group would go to Germantown.

While Seth, Abner and Herr Hartzell waited for Grace to get ready they spoke to Father Werner. "Goodbye, my friend," said Herr Hartzell to him. "It has really been a pleasure to know you. I wonder if we will ever meet again."

"We will," replied Father Werner. "If not in this world, surely in the next."

While Klaus waited for his womenfolk he sat down and had a cup of tea. Schotzy and Reuben went to him with sad faces. "I'll miss you, Big Angel. Must you go?" said Schotzy.

"I have to protect my lady and my Betsy," replied Klaus. "Besides that, I have to earn a living,"

"There are Indians where you are going," said Schotzy. "It might be dangerous. I'll pray that God sends a Big Angel to protect you. That way I'll have a Big Angel and you'll have a Big Angel."

"I have Big Angel, too," said Reuben. Both boys climbed on Klaus's lap and sat there until the women were ready to go.

Abner bid Klaus and the Willy goodbye and left when Grace was ready. She was dressed in a red plaid coat and a red knitted hat. She had not had time to go home and change clothes, so she wore her work dress under her coat. When she got into the buggy, she took up a major portion of the seat, and Abner had to squeeze in beside her. Seth sat beside Grandpa with their backs to the driver. *These Pennsylvanians grow bigger than the people back in the old country,* Abner thought. *It's no wonder, the way they eat! I'll get fat, too, if I eat like that all of the time. What I had for breakfast would hold me for days.*

Seth, Abner and Herr Hartzell were not dressed for the cold weather. It was about four miles to Seth's father's house, and Seth sat rubbing his arms to keep warm. The three new arrivals sat shivering and not saying a word. Grace started to point out different places of interest, but as the others did not seem interested, she stopped talking. Abner was glad to see his grandpa put his arm around Seth and talk to him gently. "We don't know what will happen, but whatever does, know that God is always there for you. He will give you strength to get through this. Trust Him. There will be a blessing in it for you one way or another. Do you believe that?"

"Ya, and I do, sir. It's hard to imagine, but I do believe it."

They were driving by a large brick house set on a little hill with beautiful grounds all around when Grace pointed and called out, "That's it!"

Seth, his eyes wide in surprise, said, "That's a mansion!" Abner and Herr Hartzell just stared. The driver pulled on the reins and backed the horse to the driveway. Then he drove up and parked under the portico where he stopped and let them out. He said something, pointed to the barn and nodded. Abner supposed that the man said he would wait. He hoped so.

"Now what do we do?" asked Seth. "I'm scared to death, and I'm mad, and I don't know what to do. I've never been in such a house, and I don't want to make a fool of myself."

"You'll be all right. Just take it as it comes," said Herr Hartzell.

The door was answered by a pale, thin young man in a formal coat. He looked at them as if they were vermin, told them to wipe their feet, and led them to the living room. They were the first ones there. The body was in a casket on a table, and the room was filled with chairs. "They must be expecting a lot of people," whispered Abner. His grandfather did not answer but motioned for him to be quiet. Seth went to the casket and looked at his father. Herr Hartzell walked along and held his elbow. Abner and Grace went immediately to comfortable chairs and sat down. *I don't want to look like I am gawksing around,* thought Abner, *but if I can't talk, I may as well look.*

The room was more beautiful than any he had ever been in. The walls were deep, rich cherry wood paneling. *It would be a pleasure to rub my hands over them,* he thought. The draperies were heavy golden silk. The rug was a deep red with designs in blue and gold. The chairs that belonged to the room were covered with striped material with the stripes being the same colors as in the rug, and the material the same as the draperies. The fireplace had a mantel with a mirror over it. On another wall was a painting of a man that Abner thought must be Seth's father, and a woman that no one would ever call beautiful. They were both wearing velvet outfits. *These people are rich! I wonder what Seth will say about that.*

The room began to fill up with people dressed in fine quality wool and velvet suits, satin gowns and coats with fur collars. When it became completely full, except four seats in the front row, the man in the formal suit came to them, looked at them haughtily and asked them to stand in the back. Abner started to protest, but his grandfather whispered, "Be still. We should be glad he lets us stay." A man with a clerical collar came in from a side room. He was followed by a woman and three children, all dressed in black. They sat in the front row.

Finally the service began. The preacher had a long sermon and then asked if anyone had anything to say about the deceased. The oldest boy, about Reuben's size, stood and said, "My papa was the goodest man you could ever meet." He started to cry and sat down. His mother put her arms around him and comforted him. Then five men, one after another, stood and said what a wonderful man of the church Abe Kunkle was, what a sober self controlled person he was, what a wonderful leader in their city, what a generous and caring person.

As they kept on talking, Abner could see Seth becoming more and more agitated. Finally he could stand it no longer. He almost ran to the front, shaking his fist and yelling, "It's a lie. A big, dirty lie! All of it! I'm Seth Kunkle, Abe Kunkle's son from the old country. What you're saying is a lie, I tell you. I just got off the boat. Seven years ago my father ran off and left my mother, my crippled brother, his mother and me. We never heard from him again. We nearly starved. Imagine that, we nearly starved and look at this house where he lived!" Seth flung his arm around in disgust, and then continued, "This Abe Kunkle that you think so highly of, he never sent us money not even a pfennig. My mother always told me he was a good man." Seth was shaking, but he shouted even louder, "It was a lie. He was drunk, and he killed a man. That's why he left us."

Seth broke down and began to cry. He could hardly stand, but he took hold of the table and steadied himself before continuing. "The brothers of the man he murdered wanted to kill him for revenge, but he ran away before they could get him. When they couldn't find him, they decided to torment me until I was grown and then kill me. I had to sneak away and sell myself into bondage to get away from them. I wanted to see my dat. I wanted to give him news of the family, to tell him his wife and mother still love him. I wanted him to know that they believe the murdered man tormented him and brought it on himself. Besides that, I wanted to see if he was all right. You bet he was all right. Look how he was living!" Seth pointed around the room. He was so angry he was out of control. His face was deathly pale, his chest was heaving, and he was clenching and unclenching his fists. "Do youse think he would have been happy to see me? Do youse still think he was a good man?" With that he collapsed, banging his head hard on the table and then on the floor.

CHAPTER THIRTEEN

Silence came over the room. The guests' mouths were open and their eyes wide in surprise. Herr Hartzell, Abner and Grace went to the front and knelt before Seth, rubbing his hands and talking softly to him. The woman dressed in black motioned for the butler to get a blanket, and for the minister to continue the service. She was shaking and looked as if she might faint, too. "Is this true?" she whispered to Abner and Herr Hartzell. Both of them nodded. "What shall I do?"

"Tell your man where we can put Seth, and then go along to the cemetery," said Herr Hartzell. "You have to do what you have to do. We'll be here when you get back."

"People expect to come back here and eat," she whispered.

"Do what you have to do," he repeated. "We'll be here when you get back."

"Do you have to be here when I get back? Can't you just take him and go?"

Herr Hartzell looked at her as if he could not believe what she said. "No, we're not leaving," he said. "Seth deserves an explanation."

Some of the mourners wanted to view the remains, but Seth was on the floor directly in front of the casket, so they followed the minister out the door.

The butler called in another man, and Seth was carried into a room off the kitchen. Before they put him on the small bed they lay him on the floor while they hunted for an old blanket to put over the clean bedspread. Abner could see by the look on her face that this made Grace angry, but she did not say anything.

"Do you have a rag that we could wash his face?" asked Herr Hartzell after Seth had been picked up and placed on the bed.

"No rags, sir," said the butler with his nose in the air. "We have only cloths."

"Get a basin with warm water, too," said Grace. "And don't put on airs with us. I know who you are."

"Yes, Grace, I know who you are, too," he replied. "I don't see where you come off telling me what to do." She did not answer but motioned for him to go.

When he brought the items requested, Grace took the cloth, wet it, wrung it out and then asked, "Don't you have any face soap?" He brought the soap. She smelled it. "Nice," she said. She washed Seth's face and neck, rinsed him off, and then washed his hands and arms while keeping him covered with another blanket that had been at the foot of the bed.

"I don't think my lady would want you to use that blanket," said the butler.

"Too bad," answered Grace, as she kept on with Seth's bath. She took off his boots, taking notice that he had no socks. Then she washed his feet which were filthy. After his feet were washed, she asked for clean water. All of this time, Seth was still unconscious.

"I wish he would come to," said Abner. "This has me worried."

"We aren't supposed to worry," said his grandpa. "I just wonder how the Lord is going to work this out."

"Frau Kunkle is a kind lady," said Grace. "I just think that she will accept this young man more readily if he's clean. I hate to tell you, but youse really stink."

Abner lifted his arm and smelled himself. *She's right,* he thought. *I do stink. I didn't think about it before. She'd stink too, if she hadn't had a bath for months.*

"If you'll help me lift him," said Grace, "I'll take off his shirt and finish the job. I had to take care of my brother for many years so I know how." She called to the butler, "Gottfried, do you have any clothes around here that would go around this young man? He just got off the boat, you know. He's just about as tall as his father was."

Showing complete disapproval, the butler brought out a shirt with a worn out collar and some old pants. "Go find better clothes," said Grace. "He needs warm pants, long underwear, socks, boots, a sweater and a coat. His father won't need them any more." She turned to Herr Hartzell. "I think he's coming around."

Seth moaned, opened his eyes and looked about wildly. "Where am I? Who are you? Where's Herr Hartzell?"

"Hush, hush, young man," said Grace gently. "He's right here. You banged your head, but you'll be all right. I promise."

"I remember now, you're the lady from the inn. I best get up. I must get out of here. Where are my clothes?"

"Just stay still. You can't go anywhere, I've got your pants," she laughed and then turned to the butler who had not moved when she told him to get more clothes. "You can bring the clothes later. Get him some soup or something light to eat. Maybe a scrambled egg with cheese, and some butterbread and milk. Ya, that would be good. The poor soul was about to eat when I shot my mouth off and told him his dat was dead." She turned to Herr Hartzell and Abner, "How long has it been since he had a good meal?"

"Not since we were in Holland and that was way last summer," said Abner.

Grace tried to stare the butler down, but he refused to be intimidated. Grace then said, "Do as I say. Herr Kunkle was his father, and he deserves to be treated well." The butler still did not move. Grace looked at him as if she could take him apart and put him back together different. She was taller than he and probably weighed twice as much. "Look," she said. "I told you that I know you, Gottfried Ludwig. You are no better than you should be. Your mother goes to my mother's church, and she is so proud of you and your job that she brags you up every chance she gets. She tells my mother and the other ladies what good things you bring home. Food, the best a person can get, all prepared and enough for the whole family. Towels, good towels. Comfort covers. A gold watch even! It's hard to believe they'd give you a gold watch. And blankets. Tools. Perfectly good clothes. Toys for the children, and sugarloaves. Ya, sugarloaves! No one else in the neighborhood has sugar in their tea. Only rich people can afford it, but your mother always has sugar in her tea." Grace reared up as tall as she could and looked down on him. "Now you do what I say or you will be sorry. Go!" The butler caved in like a pat of butter on a hot day.

"She should be a sargeant in the army," whispered Abner.

"That's the truth," nodded Grandpa with a smile.

Seth put his hands over his face, and Abner could see he was trying to control himself. He looked up teary eyed and said, "My dat is dead, and he was not a good man, even if my mother did say he was. But even so, how could he marry such a woman? She's beyond dormlich, she's greistlich."

Grace kindly said, "I'm sure there's an explanation. You just wait here until Frau Kunkle comes back."

Gottfried brought in a cup of clear chicken broth. Grace took a spoonful and held it to Seth's mouth. "It's good," he said. "Thank you, I can feed myself." He sat up and finished the soup just as the butler brought in the scrambled egg. "Thank you," he said as he put it away hungrily. "I'm kinda cold. Did you give me a bath while I was out?"

Gottfried returned with a full set of good woolen clothing. Everyone left the room and allowed Seth to dress. He finished just as the funeral party returned from the cemetery. Frau Kunkle, looking as if she had herself under control, immediately came to the little bedroom. "Seth, I've been expecting you," she said. "I'm glad my man bathed you and got you some fresh clothing." She smiled at Gottfried. "You're a gem to think of Seth's needs. I truly appreciate that. There will be a little something extra in your pay this month." Grace made a face, and it was all Abner could do to keep from choking.

The funeral meal was a grand buffet but the people who came for it did not stay long. Then it was time for the lady of the house to sit down and talk with Seth.

"Do you want us to leave so you can talk privately?" asked Herr Hartzell.

Without hesitation both Seth and Frau Kunkle said, "No, you stay."

It was the first chance that Abner had to get a good look at the second Frau Kunkle, and his first thought was, *She has a face that would stop a clock.* She was a rather dark heavy-set woman with a wide nose set in big face. She had dull gray hair pulled back in a bun and deep set, beady brown eyes. Her teeth were crooked with some missing. Her skin seemed thick, and there was a big yellow pimple on the left side of her nose. On her upper lip was a mustache of fine black hair, and there were many dark hairs growing under her chin. He was surprised when he noticed her hands. They were beautifully shaped with soft skin and long fingers.

"You said you were expecting me," said Seth. "Why did you say that?"

"Just last week, your father said to me, 'Agnes, it's seven years since I left the old country, and the time has come for me to pay my bills.' I didn't understand, and asked him what he meant. Then he told me that he had killed a man, and he expected the man's brothers would come and get him soon. I was upset, and then he said for me to be ready for it. Just before we went for our walk he said, 'Aggie, be good to Seth if he arrives after I'm gone, and treat him fairly.'"

Herr Hartzell interrupted. "Did you know Abe Kunkle was married and had a family back in the old country?"

"I didn't know when we got married, but gradually he let things slip. Then last week he told me things I didn't know before."

"Would you tell us about it?" asked Herr Hartzell. "Seth deserves a full explanation."

Frau Kunkle got a strange look on her face and stared at her hands. She thought a bit and then said softly, "I've never told anyone this before. I'm ashamed of it, but like you said, Seth deserves an explanation. I'll begin back before I met Abe, back to where I lived as a girl. French soldiers came and burned our whole village, all of the houses, churches, shops, and barns, even the outhouses. My mother was caught in the fire and died. The soldiers killed all of the animals, and then pulled up the fruit trees and grapevines. Just before they left, they fouled the wells. Where there had been a nice little village, there was nothing except chimneys and stone walls. I had no place to stay, so my father put me in a convent. I lived there while my father went to America. After many years, he returned for me. I met Abe on the ship as we came across the ocean. I had never been around men. When he winked at me, I was immediately in love."

Agnes Kunkle stopped, and Abner could see that she had broken out in a sweat. She reached down the front of her dress but could not find her handkerchief. She wiped her forehead with her sleeve and continued, "He was funny, and he'd make a little joke for me, or he'd smile in passing. He did not go out of his way to be with me, but I made it my business to know his every move. I know now that he was just being kind to a poor soul who was lonely. When he got sick on the ship, I made my father ask for him to be brought to our cabin. It was tight quarters, but I slept on the floor and took care of him day and night. If I hadn't, he would have died. Abe never touched me or said anything that would make me think he wanted me. I threw myself at him, but he did not respond." She took a deep breath, and wiped her forehead again.

Grace got up and started to go to her and then changed her mind. "Do you want a handkerchief?" she asked, taking a clean one from her pocketbook.

Frau Kunkle took it, wiped her face and continued, "One thing Abe told me was that he had had a business of buying, selling and fixing things. When we got home, I told my father that I thought he was the right man to help him in his store. I persuaded him to get him as an indentured servant. Abe lived at our house and was polite. He paid no attention to me no matter what I did. I wanted him, and I was determined. One evening I went to his room. My father knew where I had gone. Abe and I talked a little, and he got really nervous. My father walked heavy and we heard him coming. I quickly put my arms around Abe and tried to kiss him. He struggled to get away, and we fell over on the bed. Right then my father walked in with a gun and asked, 'Is there any reason you cannot marry my daughter?' If Abe would have said he was already married, my father would have shot him then and there, so he said, 'No.' That's how come we got married. So you see, he was a good man."

"My mother will be glad to hear that," said Seth.

No one said anything for a bit. Abner knew he should keep quiet and he did, but he looked around. There was Gottfried just inside the next room, listening.

"Did Herr Kunkle say anything else about Seth?" asked Herr Hartzell.

"All he ever said was, 'Aggie, treat Seth right.' But actually, according to the British law, Seth owns this house, everything in it, the stores, everything. He is the owner's eldest son and that's the law. I hope he will treat me and my children right. Even though it was my father's estate, when he died everything went to my husband and then to my husband's oldest male heir. That was not a problem until Seth arrived."

Seth stared at his father's wife in surprise.

"What good news!" said Abner excitedly. "Seth, you won't have to be sold at auction like a slave! You own a house! You have a business! Are you ever glicklich!"

"What are you talking about, Abner?" asked Seth. "I didn't do nothing to earn this lady's money. It wouldn't be right. I might take some if I knew my father earned it but otherwise not. Like I said, it wouldn't be right."

Just then the children's nanny came to the doorway, and Agnes left to see to the children's needs. As soon as she was gone, Grace got up, shut the door and began talking. "Seth, listen to me. Did you see that Gottfried listening? I can tell you that if you do not accept your inheritance, he will have it in no time."

"But," he interrupted.

"No buts. Like I said, listen. Herr Spangler, Agnes's father, had one little bitty store. Your father brought in different kinds of merchandise and built up the business. Then he got the idea of outfitting hucksters to go out into the wilderness and sell things to the white people and Indians. He let the hucksters take a whole pack of things with a promise that they come back and pay him after everything was sold. He even bought redemptioners, and they were all able to pay off their debts in two years and make a good living, too. Some of the hucksters bought carts, filled them up with needles, scissors and little things, plus plows, spinning wheels, dress goods, pots and pans, shovels, picks, grubbing hoes,[97] saws and axes, hinges and locks, nails and panes of glass, heavy things that a man couldn't carry on his back. They went to New Jersey, down into the Delaware counties, and Maryland, as far west as Lancaster and even across the big, wide Susquehanna River. Your father ordered good materials from across the water that no one else was bringing into this area. I'm telling you that your father was responsible for the success of the business, and you must accept your inheritance."

"If Herr Hartzell thinks I should, I will," said Seth. "She said, Miss Agnes, I mean, she said this house is mine." He looked around and saw that Herr Hartzell was smiling and nodding his head. "This house is mine! I must let my mother know. I've never even been in a house like this before and neither has she."

"Don't worry," laughed Grace. "You can get used to it."

Herr Hartzell spoke up. "Miss Grace," he said. "You are a godsend. I don't know the English laws, and I must move on in about ten days. Do you know anyone who has studied the law, an honest counselor whom you trust? Seth will need one."

Seth looked back and forth between Grace and Herr Hartzell. "Thank you for watching after me. I never had anyone watch after me before."

"I told your mother I would."

---

[97]   grubbing hoes: mattocks, heavy hoes used to dig out roots of trees and other heavy work

There was a knock on the door, and Agnes reentered followed by her children. She looked different, with a determined set to her jaw. "I'd like to introduce you to my children," she said. Her face softened, and it was plain to see that she loved them with all her heart. She placed her hand gracefully on the oldest boy's head and said proudly, "This is Samuel. He's six years old. He spoke at the funeral." She moved her hand to the middle child, a girl. "This is Christina, and the youngest is Charles. Children, the older boy standing there is Seth. He says he's your brother, but we don't know that for sure. If he is your brother, then your father was married before, but on our marriage license it says that he never was. Do you think he is your brother?"

"No," they answered. "Our papa wouldn't lie. He was a good man."

Grace stood and walked to where Agnes was standing, looked down at her and said, "You've been talking to Gottfried. He told you to say that, didn't he? Not ten minutes ago, you told us one story, and now you're telling us another. You know and I know that the spirit of a murder victim is not free to go until things that are concerned with his death are cleared up to his satisfaction." She stopped talking, lowered her voice and began speaking in a sort of spooky voice, "The spirit of Abe Kunkle is still in this house. I can feel it, and I can prove it." She pulled up her sleeve and showed Agnes that her arm was covered with goose bumps. "See that? Now do you believe he's here?" Agnes shivered and turned pale. Grace continued, "You said you loved your husband. Well, if you do, you would not want him to be forever wandering this earth trying to make things right. Abe's ghost will haunt you all the days of your life if you do not treat Seth right as he told you to."

Agnes started to sway. Herr Hartzell jumped up, took her arm and escorted her to the nearest chair. "Put your head between your knees," he said. "We don't want you to pass out on us. When you're all right, we'll talk."

Grace went to another room, came back with a small glass of brandy and gave it to Agnes. She downed it in one swig. The children sat on the floor and waited for their mother to feel better. After a short while Agnes looked up and said, "I'm sorry, Abe. I will treat Seth fairly as you said. I want you to rest in peace." Then she spoke to her children, "I am sorry to tell you that your mommy is a bad woman. I lied to you, and now I ask you to forgive me." She paused, wiped her nose and added, "Seth is your brother from the old country. Your papa told me about him. He will be living here as long as he wants all of us to live under the same roof." She got up, put her arms around Seth and said, "Welcome, son. Children, welcome your brother."

Grace stood and said, "I must get back to the inn. It's time for me to slop the hogs again."

Christina looked at her with big eyes and asked, "Do you really slop the hogs?"

"No, little darling," she answered. "I serve great big platters of food to people, and they eat like hogs."

Samuel laughed. "You're funny. I like you."

"No fair," said Seth. "I saw her first." And then everybody laughed. Seth turned to Grace and said, "Miss Grace, don't you like your job?"

"It's a job, but a person gets awful tired by the end of the day. If I could get another one, I'd be glad."

"Well, if this house is mine as Miss Agnes says it is, we will be needing someone to take Gottfried's place. Would you like to work here as my housekeeper?"

Suddenly Grace was all respect. "Yes, Mr. Seth, I would be pleased to work here as your housekeeper. But at the inn they are expecting me to work the supper shift tonight, and it's too late for them to get someone else. I'll come tomorrow, and we can work out the details. I must get back."

"Before you go, a cuppy more things," said Seth. "Abner, will you ask your Aunt Edda to come to see me soon? Tomorrow would be good. Ask Jake Altland to come, too. Also, I'd like you to have a nice warm blanket, make that two, to throw over yourselves to keep warm on your way to Germantown."

As he snuggled under the blanket next to his grandpa, Abner felt like he could not wait to tell everyone what had happened that day and to hear about Klaus's and Betsy's wedding. "I know everybody will want to see Seth's new house," he said. "Besides, Jake will have to talk to him about paying for his passage. What an exciting day, and it isn't even over yet. I wonder how he will let his mother know about his good fortune."

"If I know Seth, he'll figure it out," said Grandpa.

They dropped Grace off at the inn and kept on going to Germantown. It was just about dark, and they arrived at the same time as Abner's parents, Jake, Trudy, Widow Schneider, Schotzy and Reuben. Schotzy was full of news. "I was never at a wedding before. The mystery lady gave a big party just for us. We couldn't have a rattleband,[98] but even so, it was so much fun. You shoulda been there. Willy was excited about having a job and not having to be a bound out. He found out that in Maryland, they can't have white bondservants, they can only have black slaves. So when he gets there, he'll be free. I never saw anybody so happy in all my born days."

Most of the day had gone by, and Abner had not thought about being sold into bondage to strangers at the auction. Suddenly here it was worse than ever. He walked away thinking, *I have to get away so no one sees me blubbering.*

---

[98]   rattleband: Neighbors and friends gather outside newlywed's quarters and make noise by banging on pots and pans until the newlyweds invite them in and feed them.

Schotzy has lots of money and Reuben, too. They'll be living with my grandpa. Minnie has money and will be living with my parents and her sister. Seth has brothers, a sister, a business, money and a house. Willy is free and has a job. Dear God, forgive me for being jealous. If this is what you have laid out for me, help me to accept it, to be obedient to you and to my master. Help me to have a good attitude. Help me, Lord Jesus. Help me, help me. It's harder every day. Amen.

Jake saw him walk away, went to him, put his arm around him and said, "Your parents and your grandpa haven't seemed to have noticed that you're upset lately. Trudy noticed it first and asked me to talk to you. Will you tell me what it is that is bothering you?"

Abner tried to keep himself under control, but he could not. Tears came, and suddenly he felt as if a dam burst. At long last someone noticed that he was miserable. He was going to be able to tell someone his feelings about being sold like and animal, the next thing to being a slave.

"In just a few days I, I, I'm going to have to go be auctioned off like a cow or a pig," he said, trying valiantly not to lose control. "Strangers are going to feel my ribs and look in my mouth. Then one of them is going to buy me. I'm going to have to go live with strangers, eat their food, work at whatever jobs they have for me, and sleep wherever they put me. My family will go far off into the wilderness, and I have no idea where I will go. No doubt it will be far from them, and I won't see them for a long time. I try to be brave, but it is hard."

Jake looked at him in surprise. "Abner," he said. "Abner, hush. Hush and listen to me. I had no idea that was what was eating you. It's not going to happen. I thought you understood. I would have set you straight in a minute. When the Hokes left the ship, they told you, and they told me that everything of theirs was to be yours. Is that not right?" Abner nodded, and Jake continued, "Their tickets for passage across the ocean were paid so I put your name and your father's name down on the manifest instead of theirs. In fact, your ticket didn't cost as much as an adult's so you get some money back. I just settled up today. Here, I'll give you your money right now." He took out a money pouch, dug around, got out two pounds British Sterling silver and handed it to him.

It was too much. Abner stared at Jake and blinked in disbelief. The money was in his right hand, and it was shaking. He put his left hand under it to steady it. "This means I don't have to be sold like a pig. Oh, Cousin Jake, you can't know what I've gone through! When I think there are black people out there who are sold like animals and are never going to be free, it breaks my heart."

When Abner awoke the next morning, he could not remember where he was. The windows were six small panes over six small panes, and there were no curtains. He was lying on a featherbed with fat down pillows and a down comfort. It did not take a second to remember, but it was a strange feeling. He, his parents, Trudy and her mother were staying with an elderly couple named Hermann. They were Mennonites who believed, as did the Mennonites in Holland, that God had abundantly provided them with worldly goods so that they could take care of refugees from religious persecution as they passed through. Their house was large, but not fancy. When Abner went to bed the night before, he had been exhausted. The day had been very full coming right after the voyage to America, and his body was making up for it. It was late morning when he awoke. The sun was bright in a clear sky, and suddenly he was filled with happiness. He started to get dressed when he saw a pitcher of water, a basin, a towel, a washcloth and a dish of soft soap. He washed quickly, even shampooing his hair.

He ran downstairs as hungry as a bear and was greeted by the elderly lady who lived there. She gave him a piece of some kind of bread that reminded him of the mystery mush, but it was good when buttered and sweetened by what she called molasses.[99] It went well with a large glass of rich milk. "That will hold you for a little while," she said. "It won't be long 'til dinner. My man is taking your parents and grandfather around to see our farm. It has taken more than fifty years for us to get it in the shape it's in."

Abner was busily eating, but he stopped and exclaimed, "Did you say more than fifty years? When did you come here?"

"We came in October 1683 on the *Concord*, the second boatload of Mennonites to come to America," said Frau Hermann. "The Reverend Doctor Daniel Francis Pastorius was the leader. He came on the first boatload. It sailed up the Delaware River and landed in Pennsylvania in August six weeks before we did.

Abner was so interested in what she had to say, he forgot to ask what kind of bread he was eating. "If you were among the first to get here, where did you stay?"

"It wasn't quite as late in the year as it is now, but close. There wasn't time to build a house for us to live in before winter, so as soon as the men felt strong enough after the long ocean voyage, they dug cellars and put a cover over them. We lived in those holes in the ground for about a year. The men had to build a shed and a pen for the animals so the wolves and panthers wouldn't get them. We always laughed that the animals were taken better care of than the people. Our holes in the ground weren't comfortable, but the Lord provided enough food. There was a huge harvest of chestnuts that year. I've never seen a bigger crop since.

---

[99] molasses: What he PA Dutch call molasses is more like dark Karo than Bre'er Rabbit.

There were also black walnuts and grapes. Such tasty grapes! We picked watercress until the frost hit it in the middle of November. My man shot a deer. We shared the meat with others, and they shared with us. We put the deer hide on the ground floor to help keep us dry. Next, my man shot a bear. We shared the meat and put the bearskin across the opening to keep the cold out. We had brought some chickens with us, and we let them run wild, bringing them into our cozy home at night. We ate some of the eggs and hatched the rest. We brought a cow, and we had milk, cheese and butter. There were rabbits and squirrels to eat, as well as the chestnuts, walnuts and hickory nuts."

"Cousin Jake said something about there being dangerous wild animals and poisonous snakes. Were you never scared out here in the wilderness?"

Frau Hermann smiled and said, "We figured that God chose us to come here and make a path for others to follow. We knew that if He chose us, He would equip us with whatever we needed to more than just survive. We believed that He would help us to live more abundantly than we had lived back home. That didn't mean that we didn't have to work hard, because we did, but He gave us the strength. We knew that if we were obedient, God would provide us with all of our needs, and more than we could imagine or ask for."

"You talk like my grandpa," said Abner. "We tried to bring our three cows along, but they didn't make it."

"Your grandpa told us you lived in the Palatinate[100] which is a lot farther than where we came from. We came from a place very close to the Holland border, so it took you much longer than it did us. I doubt if our cows would have lived

---

[100]   Palatinate: A very fertile area in Bavaria and the upper Rhine Valley that belonged to feudal lords. The people living there were serfs. pronounced puh LAT in ate

through such a difficult journey either. But you did have their milk for many months, not? Praise Him for that."

"Ya, I will. Thank you for reminding me. There are many things to pray for, especially for us to be safe from things that can hurt us. I want to know about the dangerous animals and poisonous snakes. What about them? Are there many? Do you ever feel afraid?"

"God gave us brains," she answered, "and we better would use them. He gave us eyes to see, ears to hear, feet to run, and voices to raise if need be. Snakes like sunny places. We keep an eye out for them. We also keep a hoe handy to whack them a good one. I've killed all kinds. Don't like doing it, but we do what must be done, same way with dangerous wild animals. If I see one, I run or holler, or both! I always let my man kill them. I don't use a gun."

"I want to learn to shoot a gun as soon as I can," Abner said. "I got some money, and I'm going to buy me a gun with it."

"I've been told that Pennsylvania gunsmiths are the best in the world. You learn to shoot straight but never use the gun to fight. That's how we live." She looked at the clock and added, "I've enjoyed talking with you, Sonny, but I must get moving on dinner. Some of the neighbors are bringing food in, but I must do my part. Just go out that door and look around. No doubt you will find someone you know."

"Thank you for the food, and thank you for telling me how it was when you first got here," said Abner. "I really enjoyed both."

Abner went outside and joined his parents and Trudy. He wondered where her mother was but did not ask. Herr Hermann was also telling them about the early days. "The first year was hard," he said, "but the next year was bountiful. I made a brave little dwelling house over the cellar that we had lived in the first winter, and it was snug and warm. I had a shop with all kinds of goods that I brought along. Sometimes I rode out with merchandise and sometimes brought something back from the Indians. I had no rent or tax to pay. I had a cow which gave plenty of milk, a horse to ride around on. My pigs increased rapidly. At first I had only two, but the next summer I had seventeen. I had many chickens and geese. My garden did well, and I ordered trees from England to begin the orchard that you see here."[101]

"I hope we do as well," said Matthias. "We will be going to the wilderness beyond the Susquehanna River. The William Penn Land Company just opened it up for settlement."

"You will do well if you trust in the Lord as we have," said Herr Hermann. "I can't see how people can get along without Him."

"Neither can I," said Matthias. "As long as we are talking about the time you settled here, could you give us any advice that would help us get started and be successful?"

"What you want to look for is the best soil available. A limestone base is ideal. The best tip I can give you is to look for the tallest black walnut trees. They grow best on soil that's on a limestone stone base. Save the cow manure and always spread it on your fields. The soil is a gift from God, and it is up to you and me to protect it for all the generations to come."

"I've heard that your people really did not want to leave Switzerland," said Matthias.

"That's true. The Swiss leaders would order the Mennonites to leave. When they didn't, the soldiers would take them to the border and force them to leave with nothing but the clothes on their backs. This usually happened in wintertime. A large number of the Mennonites went to the Palatinate,

---

[101]   Herr Hermann's quotation here is from a letter written by Cornelius Bom to Rotterdam in 1684 and quoted in The German and Swiss Settlements of Colonial Pennsylvania, by Oscar Kuhns, pgs. 41, 42

where the soil was so rich that they could make a good living. Others went to Holland and England. They would build up their resources, and then back they would go to Switzerland. My people were pretty determined; some might even call us stubborn," Herr Hermann added with a chuckle.

"This forced leaving and returning went on until the French, who wanted all of the Rhine Valley but had no claim to it, decided to ruin it so that no one else could benefit from it. They came through and burned villages, killed people and cattle. They left the land in ruins. My ancestors could not make a living there any more so they went back to Switzerland. This was after the Thirty Years' War. The next time the Swiss government said the Mennonites had to go, the governments of Holland and England objected. They said said that the Mennonites could not arrive penniless and expect the English and the Dutch to accept them like they always had. Finally Switzerland allowed the Mennonites to sell their property and take their belongings. The government even agreed to pay their passage on the Rhine River boats just to get rid of them. That made the difference. The Mennonites sold out and stayed in Holland and England until they began to migrate to Pennsylvania."

"Why did the Swiss persecute them?" asked Abner. "Was it on account of their baptism like us?"

"Yes and no. It was more complicated than that. The Swiss have a standing army of 80,000 men, and most of their soldiers have been forced to join. Other countries use these men to fight in their wars. The money that those countries pay to the Swiss government helps to keep the government going and the Swiss taxes down. The Mennonites refused to be part of it. This is how they did it: they would not baptize their babies because the church keeps records that are available to the government. The government keeps track of the boys in order that they can be drafted into the army when they reach eighteen. The Mennonites, like I said, are stubborn. They wouldn't baptize their babies so the government couldn't keep track of them so easily. When the government caught up with them, they wouldn't go into the army. If they were forced in they wouldn't fight."

It was obvious that Herr Hermann was getting a bit tired; so the Hartzells and Trudy thanked him, excused themselves and went looking for the rest of their group. "They must be around here someplace," said Abner. The first person they saw was Alice. The children were playing Hide and Seek and Alice was it. She was hiding her eyes while the others hid, so he ran to her and said, "I'll help you find them." When they got inside the barn, Abner said, "Wait. I've got something to tell you. I'm not going to be bound out after all."

Alice threw her arms about him and gave him a kiss. "I am so happy," she said. "I've never been so happy. Did you hear that everybody?" she shouted, "Abner is not going to be bound out!"

"Why are you saying that, Alice?" asked Matthias. "He should have known that his passage and mine were paid for when the Hokes left the ship."

"Well, we didn't know that," she answered. "After this when something important happens, I hope somebody tells us about it." Matthias was taken aback and amused by Alice's response. "I think we have a daughter-in-law all picked out," he said to Rachel later.

CHAPTER FOURTEEN

Herr Hartzell had passed the news about Seth's good fortune, and everyone was pleased for him. Aunt Edda and Cousin Jake had gone in to see him as he had requested; and Abner felt as if he could not wait to see what that was all about. In a short while the dinner bell rang. Everyone washed up at the well and went in to eat. Widow Schneider sat at the end of the table next to Trudy, but far from Abner. He missed Willy and Seth who always knew what was happening and gladly shared the information with everyone.

The food was much the same as back in the old country, but different. There was a large piece of roast beef surrounded by mashed potatoes, buttered carrots, buttered squash, creamed cauliflower, sweet and sour coleslaw, pickled red beets, red beet eggs, hot spinach salad, dried corn, lima beans, chow-chow,[102] pork and sauerkraut, celery, sweet pickles, corn bread, white bread, butter, apple butter and honey. There were many desserts on the sideboard such as walnut cake, apple cake, ginger cakes, sugar cakes, apple pie, dried cherry pie, mince pie, pumpkin pie and shoo-fly pie. The Brethren group and their hosts sat at one table and everything was passed around. Abner decided to taste everything but his

---

[102]   chow-chow: pickled mixed vegetables

plate was full before half of the food had reached him. And the pies! In the old country there had been meat pies but never fruit or sweet pies. It was a great surprise to discover how good they were.

He sighed and said, "I better wouldn't punish my stomach. If I keep eating like this, my belly will be out there where I can keep my eye on it." He laughed and knew that this was one of the best days of his life. The burden that he had carried for months was gone.

After dinner Herr Hermann said that there were plans to butcher a hog in a couple of days, and he and his sons would welcome all of the help they could get. "I'd be glad to help," said Matthias. "How about you, Abs, would you like to help, too?"

"Well sure," he said. "I never helped much at home, but I'm bigger now. How about you, Schotzy? Did you ever measure a pig's tail?"[103]

"Ya, Abner, I did," he said, making a face. "You ain't gonna catch me with that trick."

"Since they're going to butcher day after tomorrow, could we go see Seth tomorrow?" asked Abner. "It wonders me how he is making out. I'd like to go to his store and see whatfer stuff they have there." *What I really want is to get something for Alice, something for my mother and something for Trudy's wedding present,* he thought.

The next morning Herr Hermann allowed the Hartzells to borrow a horse and buggy to visit Seth and to see about buying a horse and wagon for themselves. Herr Hermann suggested that they buy the cows, pigs, sheep, chickens, and geese in Lancaster when they were closer to their destination.

---

[103]   Measure a pig's tail: a dirty trick played on first time helpers

It was a cold windy day when Matthias, Rachel, Abner, Schotzy, Herr Bollinger, the shoemaker and Herr Rohrbaugh, the tanner went to see Seth. When the two craftsmen heard about his good fortune, they decided to ask him to buy them and let them work for him. They had been friendly with Seth since he had joined them, and closer still after they had been baptized at the same time. They thought it might turn out to be a good arrangement. Rachel wanted to go along just to get away from all of the people she had been with for so many months. Reuben did not want to go, and Herr Hartzell said he would stay back and let Abner show the way. Although he was not absolutely sure he could find Seth's place, he did not let on that there might be a problem. His grandpa, just to make sure, gave Matthias directions.

"Do you mean to tell me that this is Seth's house?" exclaimed Schotzy when they drove up to the large brick house. "It's perfect! Imagine having a house like that. Minnie's gotta see this. I want one just like it."

Rachel nodded and said, "It would be nice."

Schotzy jumped out of the buggy, ran up to the door and banged on it.

"Whoa!" shouted Abner. "You don't do that. You use the knocker."

"Ach well, I didn't see it," he said just as Frau Agnes Kunkle answered the door. Even though Abner had seen her the day before, he was not prepared for the way she looked this day. Her hair was uncombed, and she had on a washed off[104] old dress that could not have been pretty even when it was new. In the sunlight little black pimples showed up on her temple between her eyes and her hairline. She was barefoot, and he noticed that she had a bunion.

Abner rushed to the door and said, "We're sorry to have bothered you, but is Seth here?"

---

[104]   washed off: well worn and faded

"I don't know where Seth got to," she said crossly. "He fired Gottfried without asking me, and I don't know when the new girl will come. Looks like I must answer the door myself."

Rachel was at the door by now. Abner had not described her to his mother, and it did not occur to her that she was speaking to the lady of the house. She thought Agnes Kunkle was a scrubbing maid. "Please take us to Frau Markle," she said.

"I recognize Abner," Agnes said as she stared at Rachel. "I don't know you. Just stand back and wait until Frau Markle comes." She slammed the door in their faces.

"Ach du lieber," said Rachel. "What do you call that?"

"That was Frau Agnes Kunkle, Seth's father's second wife," said Abner.

For once, none of the others could find words to say. "Why didn't you tell us?" demanded Rachel after she got over her initial shock. "You just said that Seth inherited a house."

"Well, he did." Abner could not see why the others were upset with him.

After a fairly long wait, Aunt Edda came to the door. She hugged her sister and asked all of them to come in.

"Why did Seth want to see you?" asked Rachel as soon as she got inside, wasting no time to get to the point.

"Come in and sit down," said Aunt Edda, leading them to the beautiful room that Abner had been in before. When all of them were comfortably settled, she began the explanation. "Seth and I became quite friendly after we were both baptized at the same time. I remember him asking me if I ever got sick on the ship, and I told him I never did. I remember telling him that I would really enjoy it if I had a cabin to myself."

"I didn't know that," said Rachel. "Go on."

"His family was the first thing he thought of when he found that he had something coming from his dat. He thought about how to get money to them, and he came up with this idea. He wants me to go back to his village and take it to his mother. He wants me to bring her here if she can come, and tell her what happened to him and his father."

"But you can't go across that ocean to England, and get on another ship, catch a river boat, and go up the river to his village all by yourself," objected Rachel.

"I'm not going all by myself," said Aunt Edda. "He's asking Karl, remember the sailor on the ship that brought us the food? That's the one. He's going to ask Karl to go along with me and be responsible for getting some of the money to his mother. Seth will pay all of my travel expenses. After I get back here, I'll be free, and he'll pay me something besides." Abner looked at his aunt and thought she had never looked better. She was so excited her eyes sparkled with happiness at the prospect of being free and earning some money as well.

"How soon will you leave?" asked Rachel.

"A week, maybe ten days, I think, but I'm not sure. Seth hasn't talked to Karl yet, but he sent for him. Seth isn't sure that Karl will accept his proposition. I can't imagine that he wouldn't. And Rachel, I have another idea, and I'm excited about it. I might ask Seth if I could buy things over there for his store. There should be a good profit, and I would like doing it. I could look in stores here, and then see what is over there that they don't have here. I saw a lot of nice things when we stopped at the different towns along the river. I know I'd like to have them, so I know other women would like to have them, too. I'm full of ideas! It is something what you can do when you have a little money!"

"Edda, you amaze me," said Rachel admiringly. "I never knew you had it in you."

Edda laughed. "I amaze myself," she said. "You know, this is America, where people don't look at things the same as they do in the old country. That's what Jake said anyways. We don't have to do things the way everybody always did."

"That's a little scary, isn't it?" asked Rachel. "If we do things the old way, we know that way works."

"Not necessarily," replied Edda. "Just think about all of those hungry children in the old country, and then think about Seth's father coming to this country without a pfennig and ending up a rich man in just a few years. I like that idea. It couldn't happen where we came from, but it can happen here. I think I'll see what I can do to get a fistful of money. I wouldn't mind living in a house like this and being able to call it mine."

"My, you do have big ideas."

Edda shrugged her shoulders and asked, "Why not?"

Schotzy looked around the room like Abner had when he was first there. "Just think that here in this Pennsylvania, ordinary people can get houses like this!" he said in awe. "I can't get over it."

"I wish we could look all over the house," said Abner. "I know Seth wouldn't care, but I guess we daresn't." He peeked at his mother and saw her shake her head.

They sat quietly for awhile, and then there was a rap on the door. Abner looked through the glass and saw that it was Grace. He raced to answer and pulled Grace into the room. "It is good to see you, Miss Grace," he said. "I heard that Seth fired Gottfried, and somebody is mad about it."

"Mr. Abner," she said, pinching his cheek. "You know and I know that I can't comment on that." She looked around. "Where is Mr. Seth?"

"We don't know where he got to. We just dropped in. We thought he'd be here." Then remembering his manners, he said, "I want to introduce you to everybody. I know you saw them at the inn yesterday, but you don't know their names. This is Herr Rohrbaugh, he's a tanner; next is Herr Bollinger, a shoemaker. Then comes my mother, Rachel Hartzell, and my father, Matthias Hartzell. That there's Schotzy, my best friend. Then comes my Aunt Edda Markle. Seth asked Aunt Edda to go back to the old country and take money to his mother. His grandma is old, and his brother is not right so she had to stay behind."

"It's nice meeting you," said Grace. "And Frau Markle, when will you be going back across the ocean?"

"As soon as the ship we came on is ready to go back."

Grace looked at Edda's flimsy clothes and worn out shoes. "I've heard that it is bitter cold on the North Atlantic in winter. You must get new boots, new shoes, wool stockings, a new coat, some dresses and, just about everything. When Mr. Seth gets back from wherever he went, we must talk to him. I think he'll probably want to send clothes to his family as well as money. Herr Bollinger, do you have any leather?"

"Ya."

"I know that Mr. Seth hasn't ordered new shoes and boots for Frau Markle, but I know he will. Why don't you measure her foot now, because as soon as he gets here, that will be one of the first things he will ask you to do. Now, Frau Markle, we will have to find someone who has a coat your size to sell or find someone to make a good warm one. This is exciting. I love doing things like this."

Abner spoke up, "I forgot to tell you that Miss Grace is going to be working for Seth."

"Anything else you forgot to tell us?" asked Rachel, shaking her head.

"Leave me see, did I forget anything?" Abner then remembered Agnes Kunkle telling how she tricked Seth's father into marrying her. *I better wouldn't say anything about that*, he thought.

A horse and buggy pulled under the portico. Seth jumped out, followed by Cousin Jake, Karl and another man.

Abner opened the door, and he could tell that the stranger was a Quaker by the way he was dressed. The men came in with a blast of cold air. "Brrr, it feels like winter," said Seth. He introduced Herr Barclay as the lawyer recommended by Grace and then added, "Look at me, I won't mind winter one little bit here in this grand house and with these new clothes of my dat's. He had lots of clothes, and I want to give them to youse. Why not? I can't wear them all at once. I never had more than one pair of pants at a time in my life. I was lucky if I had a shirt and a coat. Let's go up to the wardrobe and get them out. I really want youse to have them. Youse were good to me, and now I can repay you."

"Mr. Seth," said Grace. "Mr. Barclay may have other things he has to do today than to watch you give away your father's clothes."

"Truly, Miss Grace, I don't mind," said Mr. Barclay. "I think I would enjoy seeing him be generous with his father's belongings. There are so few generous people in this world that it is refreshing when you meet one. Lead the way, Mr. Seth."

Rachel, Edda and Grace remained downstairs while the men followed Seth. "Look at this staircase," he said. "It's all carved from one piece of wood. Can you imagine how big the tree was that it was carved from? And look at these rooms! I just can't get over it. Never in my wildest prayers could I have even imagined to pray for so much. I just can't get over it! And take notice of this bed. It was my dat's, and I'm supposed to sleep in it! I kept waking up last night and thinking that someone was going to come and throw me out. I just can't get over it. What started out as something awful has turned out to be a great blessing to me. It's almost too big to take in."

The men stood quietly and then Seth said, "Ach, ya, I almost forgot what we came up here for!" He opened a wardrobe and showed them the shelves full of clothing. "Frau Agnes told me that there is a chest or two of her father's clothes, boots and shoes in the back bedroom that youse may as well take along if they will fit anybody you know."

Seth started to pass around clothing. The men and boys looked at the pieces and passed them on. Before long, Matthias called downstairs, "Rachel, this is woman's work. Come up here and give us a hand. We aren't used to such."

Rachel, Edda and Grace were laughing as they came up the steps. "It wondered us how long it would be until you hollered for us." In short order the clothing was given out, the women folded them, and the men tramped downstairs with their arms full.

After all of them were back downstairs, Seth asked Grace to see if she could prepare dinner for them, and then the men began to talk. Herr Rohrbaugh and Herr Bollinger asked about working for Seth. "That's a great idea," he said. "But I don't know. I'll have to talk to Mr. Barclay about it."

"Money will be no problem," said Mr. Barclay. "Also the law says that a man and his wife cannot be separated when they are sold into bondage, so the wives must be bought, too. How many children are there in the two families? You could afford to buy them, too, if you wish. Are any of them under five? Children under five cannot be sold."

"We were baptized together," said Seth. "That makes us brothers. I would never separate a family if I could keep them together." The look of pure joy on the two men's faces was a sight to behold.

Then Herr Bollinger looked around and said, "God has been so good to us. I remember the night that we first met these people. Rohrbaugh, here, a man named Lutz, and I decided to rob them after they passed through our village. We had no money, you see, and we figured it would be the easiest thing in the world to take theirs. We tried, but we couldn't do it. Herr Hartzell prayed, and I swear the angels sang. Then he told us about ourselves. After that he said we should join up with them and go to Pennsylvania." It was plain to see that Herr Bollinger was very touched by the remembrance. Then he spoke to Abner. "Young man," he said. "You gave us each three pfennig, and I have a feeling that it was all you had. I could never thank you enough for that gesture of generosity. Even though it was only three pfennig apiece, it actually saved our lives. We were starving and that meant the difference." He looked up toward heaven and said, "Thank you God, for sending us to these good people. We will always try to do good for others as these have done good to us."

Herr Rohrbaugh shook hands with Abner, Seth and Jake. "Thank you from me and my family, too."

"What about Herr Lutz?" asked Herr Bollinger. "He should be here with us. What did Father Werner have to say about him?"

"He said that Lutz came back to the rectory and told him that his wife had drowned," said Jake. "Then he and his little girl left. He hadn't seen them since."

Grace returned to the living room and said to Seth, "I'm terribly sorry, but alls I can come up with is just a little bit. I thought there maybe would be leftovers from the funeral meal."

"That's all right, Grace," replied Seth. "We aren't used to eating much."

Rachel and Edda got up to help in the kitchen, but Grace motioned for them to sit. "I can handle it," she said. When she called them, they were surprised to see so much on the table. There were fried eggs, fried potatoes, slices of ham, buttered carrots, cole slaw and fresh apple slices. "I am so sorry this is all there is to eat," Grace said. "Another time we'll have a decent meal."

"After what we had on the ship, this is a feast," said Seth. "Thank you, and by the way, have you seen Frau Agnes?"

"I do believe she's holed up in her room," answered Grace. "The nanny took the children somewhere."

Seth seated Edda between Karl and himself so Edda could listen as Seth filled Karl in on his plan. "I'll be glad to do that," said Karl. "I signed on for a round trip, and that is a contract that I must fulfill. I'll be able to watch after Frau Markle on the ship, and then I'll be free when we get back to England. I'll be glad to go up the Rhine to find your mother. The only problem I can think of is that the North Atlantic is terribly cold and stormy this time of the year. Does Frau Markle have proper clothes and boots for the trip?"

"We'll see to it," said Seth, his eyes sparkling. "This is exciting. I wish I could go back, but I better wouldn't. You can't ever tell what would happen here if I left."

Mr. Barclay nodded and said, "That's wisdom, Seth."

Abner saw his Aunt Edda look around as if getting up her nerve. Finally she said, "Seth, when we were in the old country I saw many things in the shops along the river towns that I think women in this country would like. Would you let me have some money to buy nice things and then sell them in your store when I get back. I think we could make a good bit doing that. What do you think?"

Seth looked at Mr. Barclay. "What do you think?"

"You are trusting her with money for your mother," said Mr. Barclay. "Therefore I think you must trust her with money to buy goods to sell in your stores. I think it's a good idea to give it a try. After all, you have to get merchandise somewhere."

Edda beamed, and Abner said, "I know you'll do a great job."

Rachel hugged her and said, "Abner is right. You know, this trip has been long and hard, but the good part about it is that I've learned to love you, my sister."

"And I you," said Edda.

It was time to leave and let Seth talk to his lawyer. "Herr Altland," he said. "Will you and Fraulein Trudy stay here with me while I talk with Mr. Barclay? You can help me understand and decide on things." He called for Grace. When she joined them, he continued. "One thing that bothers me is whether to tell my mother about Miss Agnes. I get the feeling that unless my grandmother and my brother have passed, and my mother could come back with Frau Markle, there is no reason to tell her that my dat remarried. It would break her heart. Another thing, I know I've made over this house, but I don't feel like I belong here. I would like to work in the stores and learn the business, but I don't want to live here. This is Frau Agnes's home, and I can't take it from her."

"Seth, you have a good heart," said Cousin Jake. "I'm sure there are places you can stay."

Grace looked around to make sure Agnes Kunkle was nowhere within earshot. "I have a feeling she has some plan. I hear things. She has a lawyer, and you never know what one of them will come up with." She glanced at Mr. Barclay and said, "Sorry."

Mr. Barclay raised his left eyebrow and asked, "Do you think I don't know?"

Abner, his father, mother, Aunt Edda, and Schotzy left the lovely mansion and went to Kunkle's Store. Edda in particular looked things over closely as if trying to memorize everything that was there. Rachel wanted woolen material, but it was very expensive as was the linsey-woolsey.[105] "I guess we'll have to wear layers of whatever we have until we raise sheep and flax to make our own," she said. "We'll make do somehow."

---

[105]   linsey-woolsey: A woven cloth that is part linen and part wool

"I don't know what to buy," said Abner. "I forgot to check out the things that belonged to the Hokes. I'll have to look at them as soon as I get back to the Hermann's, and then I'll know. We will be coming back here, won't we?"

"No doubt, so us men can leave now," said Matthias. "The women are not done fingering everything, so we can go do what we want and come back for them." Just as Matthias, Abner and Schotzy were about to leave, Jake and Trudy arrived.

"That Grace is something!" said Trudy. "She speaks both English and Dutch, she knows a lot about the law, and she knows of a place that Seth can stay. He didn't really need us. She'll watch over him like a big sister."

The men went to look for a horse and wagon for the Hartzells and a horse and buggy for Cousin Jake and Trudy. The boys watched as Matthias and Jake examined the horses. As they went over them carefully, they pointed out what to look for when buying one. They settled on two chestnut mares that seemed to be gentle, yet strong.

Next to the horse dealer was a buggy, cart and wagon maker. It would take five days to complete the ones he had started, but he would lend a buggy or two to buyers until the new ones were finished.

"We're getting closer to being ready to head for the wilderness," said Abner. "What more do we need to do?"

"Klaus would tell us to get a gun," said Matthias. "I wonder if a person can buy one or if they must be ordered."

"We'll just have to find out," said Jake.

"I want a gun," said Abner, "but I'm surprised we're getting them. I thought we didn't believe in guns."

"We don't believe in going to war and shooting people with guns," replied his father. "But we can shoot wild birds or deer to eat, or kill something that might harm us or attack our animals." It was was not too far to walk to the gunshop, and Abner enjoyed looking into the shops as they passed. There was a clockmaker and repair shop, a cutlery shop and a silversmith before they got to the gunsmith's.

"I got one gun here that a man ordered and couldn't pay for. I told him I needed the money," said the gunsmith. "I can let you have that one and take a deposit on as many as you want. You got lucky because there's a waiting list for my guns. This morning I decided I'd sell this one to the first person who showed me the money. It will be three or four months until I can have the others ready for you."

Matthias turned to Jake, "Do you mind if I pay for this one?"

Jake nodded in agreement. "You'll need shot and powder, lead and a mold," he said. "I'll show you how to use it."

"We may as well order guns for the rest," Matthias continued. "You want one too, don't you Schotzy?"

"I never thought about having a gun," Schotzy answered.

"You need one in case you want to shoot a deer or a turkey," said Abner. "They say them turkeys make good eating. I'm excited about getting me a gun."

"I don't know if I want a gun or not," said Schotzy. "Like I said, I never thought about it."

"We could learn to shoot together," said Abner.

"Not now," said Schotzy, "maybe when I'm bigger."

Jake gave his deposit. Matthias then paid for his and put a deposit down for Abner's. He picked up his gun, and all of them walked back to Kunkle's Store.

"I want to ask you a question, Papa," said Abner. "Have you ever shot a gun before?"

Matthias shook his head, "No, never did."

As they approached Kunkle's Store, Jake spoke up, "One thing you need is a couple or three grubbing hoes," he said. "When you get your property, it will more than likely be covered with trees. Englishers gird the tree and plant around the roots, but we Dutch dig out the roots because with the roots still in the ground, you are more than likely going to break your plow. You use grubbing hoes to dig out the roots."

Abner made a face. "That sounds like a lot of hard work."

Cousin Jake nodded. "It is, but then if you take care of your ground, it will last your lifetime and many more lifetimes. My father told me that members of our family farmed the same ground back in the Palatinate for thirty generations. That's eight or nine hundred years. The soil is still good because they took care of it."

Their shopping done, the men hooked up their new horses, tied Herr Hermann's horses to the backs of the buggies, picked up the women and went back to Germantown. The first thing Abner did upon his return was to look at Herr Hoke's bedroll and belongings. When he unrolled the bedding he discovered that it consisted of a heavy wool blanket, a light wool blanket, two linen sheets and a small pillow. Inside he found a moneybag with a string so it could be worn around the neck. In it were two pfennig. He immediately put his other money in the bag and put it around his neck. Next, there were good quality old tools made mostly of wood. He could tell that they had been used hard and were well cared for because the handles had the finish that comes only from years of toil and sweat. There were two planes, one small and one somewhat larger, a level, two wooden clamps, a drill, a hammer, a screwdriver, a wooden mallet, a hatchet, a shovel, a hoe, a T- square, an ax, a pair of stockings and a pair of gloves. *These tools are nice,* he thought. *It was nice of Herr Hoke to think of me and I'll always think of him when I use them. It wonders me where the Hokes are and how they are doing.*

Supper was ready. Afterwards everyone went to bed early in anticipation of the butchering which would start at dawn. Abner was not yet fully rested and did not feel as if he had stayed in bed long when it was time to get up. Even so, he could tell that others had been up for a good while. After he had eaten and put on an old sweater that had been laid on his bed, he and Schotzy went out to see what would happen. Out in the back was a trough with a fire under it that was used only for slaughtering pigs. When the water started to boil, the pig was brought out and knocked in the head with a sledge hammer. Next, its throat was cut, and it was allowed to bleed. Then it was hoisted into the boiling water and turned over with long forked poles. Next, the men reached in with scrapers and began scraping off the pig's bristles, being careful not to scald themselves.

"Ach, this stinks as bad as the ducks," said Abner.

"Well, at least we aren't in there getting it all over ourselves," said Schotzy.

When the men were certain that all of the bristles were off and the pig was clean, it was pulled out of the water and strung up by its hind feet. Now the work began in earnest. The pig's belly was carefully split. Its intestines, heart, liver and kidneys were caught in a pan and given to the women. Next, the men took long knives and began to cut the fat off the pig's back and sides. This fat was cut in blocks, put in a large kettle and set on the fire. It was not long until the fat began to sizzle and pop. The lard was fried out and the cracklings[106] remained. Abner knew that some people considered cracklings to be a treat. Not him. When he was little, he had eaten too many at once and got sick from them. He had no desire to ever taste them again. The cracklings that were not eaten as well as old grease and lard, would be used later to make soap.

While Abner and Schotzy where standing around waiting for something to do, Schotzy said, "This is interesting. I've

---

[106] cracklings: fatback after the lard is fried out

never seen it done before. It's too bad they didn't let the little ones see what's going on, but I guess they'd get underfoot."

"Where is Reuben anyways?" asked Abner.

"Martina is watching him and Mary. He likes them both, so he doesn't mind."

"They make sure he talks right when he's with them," said Abner.

Once in a while one of the men would say, "Here, boy, take this over to the women," and either Abner or Schotzy would do what was asked. Whenever he carried something into the summerhouse[107] Abner marveled at how wonderful it smelled, except for the one time when the women and girls were cleaning the intestines. They would be used for sausages. The women washed them and then went over them several times sniffing them to be sure the casings, as they were now called, were very clean.

The boys were kept busy fetching and carrying all morning until they were really hungry. "What do you think we'll have for dinner?" asked Schotzy after his stomach growled so loud Abner could hear it.

"I don't know, but one thing I do know, it will be good."

The men and boys were served first. Abner took a large potato roll and buttered it. He had had one the first night and he knew it would be delicious. There was all of the great food that was always served at these affairs. The first thing that was passed to him was fresh liver fried with onions. Next came pork with sauerkraut and roasted chickens with filling.[108] After the meat came dishes of cauliflower with cheese sauce, carrots and peas, cabbage filled peppers, lima

---

[107] summerhouse: a building adjacent to the house where food was cooked in the summer in order to keep the regular house cool. This little house was also used for preparing the meat after butchering.

[108] filling : dressing

beans, corn pudding, snitz and knepp,[109] bread and butter pickles, pickled watermelon rind, celery, string beans with bacon, buttered noodles, candied sweet potatoes as well as mashed potatoes with lots of butter. The boys could not get over how good the mashed potatoes were. "I could eat these smashed potatoes and nothing else, I do believe," said Abner. "And to think that I never tasted them before a cuppy days ago!"

"Wait," said Schotzy. "See those men putting pork and sauerkraut on them. Let's try that."

"Ummmm," answered Abner after his first bite. "I think I have found a new favorite."

"And look over there on that sideboard," said Schotzy. "Pies. I think I'll try the raisin. There's apple, too. There's one called shoo-fly pie[110] and one made with dried cherries."

"What's the brownish one?" asked Abner.

"That's pumpkin," said the lady who was serving the pie. "It's a custard made with pumpkin and spices. What kind may I bring you?"

"It is so hard to decide but I think I'll try the apple. I really like pie," said Abner.

"I'm sticking with raisin," said Schotzy. "I'll try another kind next time."

"There are four kinds of cake, too," said the lady.

"Thank you, but don't talk about it," said Abner holding his stomach. "I ate myself full."

---

[109]   snitz and knepp: dried apple slices cooked with ham and dumplings

[110]   shoo-fly pie: brown sugar, butter, molasses, hot water and baking soda topped with crumbs and baked in a traditional crust. There are wet bottom and dry bottom recipes. They are so sweet they draw the flies which have to be shooed away.

It was a long day. The pig had to be cut up, and then the women fried the chops. After they were cooled, they laid them in crocks and poured fresh lard over them to seal them. The meat would not spoil for as long as it was kept cold. Some meat was ground, seasoned with salt and pepper, and put in the casings for sausage. All scraps were thrown into a large kettle. Some of the scraps, as well as the meat from the head, would be boiled, cut up fine and thickened with corn meal for scrapple. Some of the scraps and some of the liver and kidneys would be cooked down into what was called puddings. This was served hot on pancakes for breakfast. The hams and the undersides of the belly, which became bacon, were put in a salty-sweet solution to soak for three weeks. After the soaking, they would be put in smokehouse for one day with a smoldering fire made with hickory wood. The hams and bacon would keep and be good to eat for a long time. The lard was stored in crocks to be used for cooking, baking and frying.

"You'd think we were back home, ain't?" said Abner. "It's no different except for the potatoes and the pies."

The next morning there was scrapple for breakfast with molasses poured over it. "Don't tell Mom," Abner whispered to his papa, "But this is better than the scrapple we had at home." Matthias nodded and kept on eating.

CHAPTER FIFTEEN

The day was cold for November with a deep frost. Abner heard his father, grandfather and Cousin Jake discussing the weather. "You know," said Jake. "I'm wondering if we should stay in Philadelphia for the winter. Winters here in Pennsylvania can be pretty ugly, and then again they can be fairly mild. I heard that last year was terribly cold. You just never can tell. They tell me there were very few black wooly bears this year and most of them you see are blond. Also squirrels' coats aren't as thick as they are some years. Those are signs of a mild winter."

"What are you getting at?" asked Matthias.

"What if we leave here and get across the Susquehanna and there is no place to stay? We could be out in the snow with no shelter for months. When the ground freezes a person can't even dig a cellar and live in it. We would all have to sleep on the ground and live in a lean-to with little protection from the wind or the wild animal. Panthers, bears and wolves are out there. On the other hand, it could turn be mild. In that case, we could get where we're going and have decent shelters built before winter sets in. The winter might even be open, that is, no snow. We must decide what we want to do."

"We'll pray about it and ask for God's guidance," said Herr Hartzell. "I must not be the only one who seeks God's guidance on this, though. You two need to hear from Him, too."

"Personally, I would be in favor of going on," said Jake. "We'll pray and then we'll see. I want to talk to Trudy and find out if she will be ready to get married on Monday. I've a little business yet."

"We're going to see Seth again, aren't we?" asked Abner. "I want to know how he's doing."

"We could go this morning," said his father. "I'll ask if your mother wants to go and maybe the girls. Michael Becker walked out here last night to make up with Martina. He must have got over his mad. We can see if he wants to ride back in with us."

"That's too many for one buggy, but maybe some of them could ride along with Cousin Jake," said Abner. "I know everyone wants to say good-bye to Seth."

"I'd like to take Reuben in and see if I can buy something for him to wear this winter," said Schotzy. "I could wear something warmer, too. Widow Schneider cut down some men's pants for me last time when I needed them. Maybe she would do that again with a pair of Seth's dat's."

There was a good bit of talking back and forth until everyone who wanted to go to the city had a ride. When they were all ready, Frau Hermann's hired girl brought out bearskins and hot bricks to keep them. At last they were off, laughing and chatting and looking forward to a great day in the city.

Jake had to stop at the William Penn Land Company first to see about business. He said he would join them at Kunkle's Store as soon as he was finished. The rest went straight to the store. Seth was excited to see them and motioned for all of them to come to the back where he could talk to them.

Here he goes again, grumbled Abner to himself. *He will talk and talk, and we have other things to do.*

"I have work to do so I can't talk long, but I wanted you to know this," said Seth. "I told Miss Agnes that I didn't want her house, and I didn't want any money that came to her from her father. I also told her I would always see that she was well taken care of. Mr. Barclay is writing up a paper about it. I also said that when they were grown my brothers and I could work things out as far as ownership and running the stores.

"After we had all that worked out, Miss Agnes surprised me. First she cried. Then she said that if I had kept the house and the business, she would have gone to the judge and told him in court that she and my dat weren't married because he already had a wife. Since my dat and her were not legally married, my dat should not have inherited her father's estate. In that case, I would have nothing coming to me. She did not want to do that to her children, because children of unmarried parents are at a terrible disadvantage in this world. Even so, she said she would have done it to make sure she had property and money to care for them. I am so glad that God put it in my heart not to be selfish. If I had been, I would have ended up with nothing. Grace had told her that my dat would haunt her, but she said she had to do what she had to do. He stopped, shook his head in wonder. "I was tempted to say I wanted the house, but I knew it wouldn't be right. Just think, I'd have lost every thing. As it is, I am the main heir and will take over the business whenever I'm ready."

He turned to a frowning Englishman who was standing next to him. "This here is Mr. Asher Morton who is general manager of this store. He will teach me about buying and selling and keeping the books. Grace found a nice place for me to stay near here. The landlady will cook my meals, clean my room and do my laundry. I'm all set." Seth smiled a big smile and added, "Please look around. I'm not in a position to offer you a discount right now, but I'm glad for your business." He motioned to Edda and dismissed the rest.

Herr Hartzell, however, was not finished. He patted Seth on the back and said, "I want you to know I am proud of you. You did the right thing and God has rewarded you for it. Edda, please tell Seth's mother that I am pleased with her son. He is a good man. And Edda, here is a letter I have written to Frau Grim. I want her to know that we arrived safely, and we miss her. Also, when you return from Seth's mother's will you stop by and see if she has written a letter back?" *Hmmmm,* thought Abner. *Grandpa sounds excited about sending his letter. Hmmm.*

"I want to buy presents for my mother and Alice and Trudy," said Abner to Schotzy while they were looking around the store. "Come over here and see what this is. I asked Mr. Morton and he said that it is a rollingpin. He couldn't believe I didn't know what it was used for. He said that using it makes it easier for ladies to make pie. We all like pie, so if I get one for my mother, one for Alice, and one for Trudy, it will make it easy for them to make us pies. Those are good presents, don't you think?"

"Ya, them are real good presents," said Schotzy. "I'll get Minnie one, too."

Abner could not wait. He had to know whether the ladies liked their presents. As soon as he paid for them he gave them to Rachel and Trudy. *They must like them because they laughed,* he thought. *It wonders me what Alice will say.*

Abner heard the door open and saw Cousin Jake come in and go straight to Trudy. *He looks upset,* he thought. Trudy could tell immediately that something was wrong. "What is it, Schwiesshart?" she asked.

"Seth and Edda will have to be auctioned off, as well as the Bollingers, the Rohrbaughs and the rest," he said. "I was told by my bosses that that's the way they wanted it handled.

They did not like that Willy and Klaus left. They said I would have to pay the same amount for them as whatever Seth brings. It made me so mad I had a hard time holding my temper, but I knew I better would if I didn't want fired on the spot. I must tell Seth. Perhaps Mr. Barclay will do the bidding and take care of it for him. I'm sorry that's the way it has to be. I tried. When I got to the office, there was a weasely, sissified looking young man who came out. He smirked when he looked at me as if he knew me or something about me. It was strange."

"It was probably someone you knew before you went back to the old country," said Trudy. "He was surprised to see you back."

"I don't think so," said Jake, shaking his head. "I wanted to get married and spend a few days with you before we headed west. Now this! I really can't leave here until after the auction because part of my pay is based on how much money is brought in. Those men said I do not need to be there but I don't trust them. These Englishers think all of us Dutchmen[111] are dumb. I could tell them I know this much: the only pirates aren't out on the rivers or oceans."

"What will you do if the ship leaves before the auction?"

"We'll worry about that if the time comes."

"Ach well, we'll get married one of these first days," said Trudy with a smile. She started to laugh, but when she saw that Abner had been close enough to hear what she and Jake had said, she became serious and added, "I want to show you this very special present that Abner gave us for a wedding gift. He said that it would make it easier for me to make pies for you."

Jake looked at it and said, "That's a smart boy, my little cousin." Abner pretended he had not heard what had been

---

[111]   Dutchmen: people from the Deutchland, i.e. German States, not Holland

said about him. "I must tell Seth and Edda about the latest development," added Jake. "I can't tell you how much I hate this. I just have this feeling that someone is behind it, someone who knows that Seth cannot be sold into bondage and still run the store. It smells bad."

Grace greeted Jake when she saw him and Trudy. "I came to see about helping Frau Markle get some clothes quick so she'll be ready to go on the ship. We don't have much time. I located a dressmaker who will work long hours until they are finished. Unfortunately, the only material available is tow.[112] If we can't get anything else, what she'll have to do is wear three or four dresses made of tow at the same time. But I still don't think it would be warm enough. I've been scouting around to see if anyone her size has died lately. Maybe the heirs would be willing to sell the clothes. That's the best bet for getting any warm clothing quickly."

Abner had been ready to go for awhile. *Will those women ever get finished?* he thought. He had looked at everything in the store more than once. *When I get rich, I'll have me a gold watch. I'll buy one for my papa, too.* The time dragged on and then suddenly the Schmitt family and Michael were at his elbow. He looked down at the rollingpin, knew Alice would like it, thrust it at her and said, "Here."

Alice opened it, looked at it and asked, "What is it?"

Michael laughed and said, "It's a rollingpin. He wants you to make pie for him. He gives you a present so you can make him pie." By then the entire Schmitt family, except Alice, were howling with laughter. "You got a fine boyfriend, Alice," Michael added, still laughing, "He doesn't even know what kind of a present to get a girl."

Abner ran out of the store and down the street until he could run no more. He sat on someone's front step until he

---

[112]   tow: coarse linen cloth; pronounced toe

got his breath and then slowly made his way back to the store, getting there just as his father and Schotzy were setting out to hunt for him.

"Are you feeling better now?" asked Schotzy when they were riding back to Germantown.

"That Michael Becker made fun of me because I gave Alice the rollingpin. What did he get Martina?"

"Nothing. He doesn't even have one pfennig."

"Were you talking to him?"

"Ya, he was walking around the store looking at things and we got talking. He's an orphan like me, only he doesn't have anyone to look after him like I do. The only relative he has in the world is that uncle who cheated him out of his inheritance. They were the only ones in his family to survive a plague that came through their village. Michael is educated and used to having money, and then all of a sudden, nothing. He felt that he had no choice but to sell himself into bondage. Before he left home, his uncle cornered him and took every valuable thing he tried to bring along, even his father's gold ring."

"I'm sorry to hear that," said Abner and realized that he meant it.

"He's jealous of you, you know."

Abner looked at Schotzy in disbelief. "Me? Why would anyone be jealous of me?" he asked in surprise. "I've got nothing to be jealous of."

"You do so," replied Schotzy. "You have two parents and a grandpa who love you. People like you. You're smart, and you're lucky. Look how Herr Hoke left his things to you and how you don't have to be sold at the auction."

"I'll have to think on that. I never thought of myself having anything anyone would ever be jealous of. It always seems to me that I have more troubles than enough."

"You are luckier or more blessed, however you say it, than most. Think about it."

Time passed quickly, and soon it was the day of the auction. Abner did not understand why, but he felt he needed to be there. Jake was going to take Edda and pick up Seth. Abner asked his father if they could go. He said they could but they would have to drive another buggy. Schotzy asked to go, too. "I don't think it would be a good thing for Reuben to see," he said. "And he's content to stay here and play."

"It will be all boys and men," Matthias said with a grin. "Won't that be great? We won't have to wait for the women to make up their minds, and we'll check on the buggy and wagon while we're there."

"Can we ask Grandpa, too?" asked Abner. "He'd probly like to get away from the women." That was how come four men were in a buggy headed for Philadelphia on a cold November day in 1735.

On the way to the auction, they saw a white man striding along followed by a black man with a heavy load on his back. The white man was yelling at the black man to walk faster and not be so lazy. It was plain to see that the black man's load was very heavy, and it was impossible for him to keep up. When the black man stumbled and fell, the white man beat him with his walking stick. "Isn't there anything we can do to stop that man from doing that?" asked Abner.

"No, there isn't," replied Matthias. "Jake says that slaves have no more rights than animals. Masters can even kill them. There is no law against it."

"That's terrible," Abner replied hotly. "It's just not right."

Auctions in the summer were held outside but because it was cold, this day it was held in a barn. Abner knew just exactly how they felt, the poor souls to be auctioned off. He even got a pain in his stomach seeing them up on a sort of stage being examined by potential buyers. Seth, Michael,

Edda and most of the people from Abner's village of Rittendorf were there, as well as the glass blower and the Bollinger and Rohrbaugh families. Each person to be auctioned was asked his or her age and other personal questions. When Seth's turn came there were a number of bids and his price went above ten pounds sterling, which was a very high price for a boy of his age. Abner turned to stare at the person who was bidding. It was Gottfried Ludwig, Agnes Kunkle's former butler. When the price went above fifteen pounds, Mr. Barclay stood and shouted, "I demand an explanation, and I challenge that young man to show his money." The auctioneer asked Gottfried to see his money. He had twenty pounds on him. The bidding for Seth began again, and Mr. Barclay paid twenty-one pounds for him.

Edda, dressed in a threadbare, washed off dress, her hair scarcely combed, limped onto the stage. She slumped as she stood in front of the crowd, looking as if she had a bad back. The frown on her face looked like the old Edda, not the one Abner had seen lately. In reply to questions, she said that she was thirty-five years old, a widow with no children. *I wouldn't buy her,* thought Abner. *She looks like a hag. I hope no one wants her.* The bidding went to three and a half pounds and Mr. Barclay bought her for four. He had just paid for her when Grace came running in, moving fast for a person of her size.

"We must hurry Edda," she said. "The ship is leaving this afternoon. You're all fixed up for clothes. I found a family who had wool blankets and nice warm clothes they were willing to part with. There are enough for you, Seth's mother and his grandmother. Herr Bollinger brought your shoes and boots to the store, and I have them. Seth gave all his dat's clothes away, and I had to hunt some more for his brother." She shook her head and said, "That boy!"

Grace had her own buggy and volunteered to take Edda to her place and get her ready for the trip. Matthias said that he would go to Germantown and get Rachel so she could come and say goodbye.

"That's all right," said Edda. "We said 'Auf Weidersehn' this morning, just in case. One more thing, Matthias. I want to thank you for being a good husband to Rachel. When she married you, I thought she was ferdudst, totally off in the head, for choosing a person who was into all that religious stuff. But now I know she was right. See you next year." She hugged Abner and whispered, "Tell your papa he is not the only good actor in the freundschaft."[113]

Abner went back to watch the auction and saw that Gottfried was bidding on Herr Bollinger and family. Mr. Barclay bought them after the bidding went unusually high for a cobbler. *There's something strange about this,* Abner thought. *Ya, really strange. I don't know if I trust that Mr. Morton. If Seth hadn't showed up, Mr. Morton could have done what he wanted with the stores, and Miss Agnes wouldn't have known the difference. Even now, Mr. Morton could cheat Seth, and he wouldn't know. I must think about this. Should I say anything to my papa or Cousin Jake about it? They don't know that Seth fired Gottfried and made an enemy. I'll tell them when I get back, but first, I need to go to the outhouse.*

Abner went out the door and around back where he saw Mr. Morton giving Gottfried money. He ducked down and hoped they had not seen him. He went back into the auction barn and looked for Seth. Gottfried came back in and began bidding on the Rohrbaughs. Abner found Seth and whispered, "I just saw Mr. Morton giving Gottfried money."

"I'll tell Mr. Barclay," said Seth. "I felt he might be underhanded, but Miss Agnes said he was to be trusted."

"She trusted Gottfried, too."

"If Mr. Morton doesn't help me, who will?"

---

[113]   freundschaft: extended family

"Herr Bollinger and his wife ran a cobbler's shop together. They'll help. Don't forget Grace. She knows just about everything. Mr. Barclay will help, too."

"That's a great idea. You're a good friend, and I shall miss you."

"Seth, remember the day we met? I traded a belt for the birdcage to put Princess in. You said the villagers would kill her. That was the day we ate the whole horse and cow. You joined us that night. It's fun to remember those days but I must go." he took care of his need and then went back to watch more of the auction.

Michael Becker was one of the last. Abner did not feel like talking to him, but he knew he must. He and Alice had not been alone together since he had given her the rollingpin, and he did not yet have all of his feelings sorted out. Still, he knew that he had to talk to Michael, to forgive him and to tell him so. *Father,* he prayed, *You know I don't want to do this, and I know You want me to, so please give me the right words to say. Thank you, Amen.*

Abner walked to where Michael was sitting. "Wie Gehts," he said.

Michael shrugged his shoulders and said, "The same way you'd feel if you were in my shoes."

"I'm sorry," said Abner. "Herr Hoke gave me something, and I want to pass it on to you." He pulled out the little bag from around his neck and took out fifteen pfennig. "When he gave it to me, he said that a boy needs some money."

Michael pushed the money away. "I don't need it."

"Of course, you do." Abner put the money on the bench beside Michael and walked away.

"Why should you give this to me?" Michael called to him.

Abner turned around, walked back and answered, "Before we left our home, my papa was forced to work for the king.

I promised God that if my family could be together, I would always help people who needed help. You happen to be part of that promise. If you ever want to pay me back, give it to someone else who needs it." Abner shook hands with him. "God go with you," he said.

"And with you, also," Michael replied.

Jake came looking for them. "There was something rotten in there," he said, "but there was nothing Mr. Barclay or I could do about it."

"I know," said Seth. "Mr. Morton just lost his job, but he doesn't know it yet. I'm asking Grace to help me. Herr Bollinger will help me, too, I'm sure. We'll do fine. Thank you. I wish you the best for your marriage."

"I hope you can come," said Jake. "We would be disappointed if you didn't."

"I'll try," said Seth.

Matthias had had enough of the auction and wanted to go. "Abner, where have you been?" he called out when he spotted him

"Saying goodbye to Michael," was all he said.

"The wind's changed and it's warmer now," said Matthias. "We'll probly go west soon, and I want to leave so I can check on the wagon and buggy. After that we'll go back to Germantown unless there is something someone else wants."

"I've been thinking," said Herr Hartzell. "I should have a buggy, too. Maybe I can get a second-hand one."

"In that case, you'll need a horse," said Matthias. "It's too bad you weren't with us when we came to town the first time."

"I'll get one," said Grandpa.

"Like I said before, the wagon and buggy will be done on Tuesday," the proprietor at the buggy shop told Matthias. "But sitting here is a buggy that someone ordered and then could not pay for. It's extra nice. If you want it, you can have it right now."

"I'll have to think on it," said Herr Hartzell.

"I'll pay for it," said Schotzy.

"Ephraim, get in the buggy!" said Herr Hartzell sharply. Turning to the proprietor, he said. "What are you asking for it?" The proprietor told him. "Is the price firm?" The proprietor shrugged and raised his eyebrows. "Well, if it is here still on Tuesday, and I don't find another, we can talk."

When all of them were back in the buggy, Herr Hartzell said, "Ephraim, when someone is buying something, never interrupt, and I mean never." Schotzy, who had never heard him speak in that tone, seemed to be frightened. Herr Hartzell continued, "I want you to remember not to take anything at the first price. There is always room to negotiate. Do you understand?" Schotzy nodded. "As long as we are talking about money, I want to tell you this, don't ever let others know how much money you have and don't ever act like you have plenty. It simply is not wise to advertise it. It does not matter how much money you have, it can be soon gone. 'A fool and his money are soon parted,' is one proverb. I know you are not a fool, so I shall believe this one about you, 'A word to the wise is sufficient.' Sufficient means enough, so I shouldn't have to say anything more about it. This goes for you, too, Abner. All right Matthias, let's go see the horses."

Herr Hartzell looked over several mares. He asked Abner and Schotzy what to look for as if testing them on what Matthias and Jake had told them a few days back. "Which one would you buy?" he asked each boy.

"I'd get the gray one," said Abner.

"I like that one, too," said Schotzy.

"I agree," said Herr Hartzell. "If I get the buggy at a good price, I'll see about getting it on Tuesday. We can go now."

Matthias turned to his father, "Papa, when do you think we will head west?"

"It's warmer, and that's a good sign," he said. "Tomorrow is Sunday. Monday Jake and Trudy will get married. Tuesday we'll get the buggies and wagon. We can say goodbye to Seth and pack up. If this weather holds, we can leave early Wednesday morning."

As they had done in Holland, they attended church with the Mennonites the next morning, and Herr Hartzell held a service for the Brethren in the afternoon. He finished the service and asked if anyone wished to put his or her trust in Jesus Christ, be baptized and become a member of their church. Herr Schmitt, Frau Schmitt and Martina stood up and went forward. Abner could see the surprise on his grandpa's face.

"Before I baptize you, I want to know why you are joining us," said Herr Hartzell. "You were always very strong in the church you were brought up in."

"We have been with you people since we left home," Herr Schmitt answered. "We have watched you, and we and know that you really live your faith." The baptism took place in the cold creek that afternoon. Abner stood beside Alice as they watched her parents and sister being baptized. *I wish I could put my arm around her,* he thought, *but I guess I better wouldn't.*

The next morning was the wedding. "It wonders me if my mother will come," said Trudy to Rachel. "We stay in the same room and sit beside each other at mealtime, but she isn't speaking to me still. It breaks my heart."

"Just assume that she's coming," said Rachel. "Pray, and when the time comes, you'll know what to say. Then see what happens."

Antonio arrived shortly after breakfast. He was driving an old buggy pulled by an old swaybacked horse. "It was the best I could afford," he said. "I really don't know anything about horses. I'm afraid I may have been taken across." Abner looked at the horse and thought, *Whatever he paid for that old nag, I'm sure he was robbed.* Antonio continued, "I saw Seth on Saturday, and he told me about the wedding. I was sure I'd be welcome. Another thing, you know I'm planning to go along with you to Yorktowne. I think I could open a school there."

Just before the ceremony, which was to be held at the Hermann's house, Seth arrived bringing the Bollingers and the Rohrbaughs with him. Frau Bollinger, carrying a small package in her hand, said, "I want to see the bride right away. I have something here she needs." She disappeared up the stairs and came back down smiling.

When it was time for the ceremony, Widow Schneider came down the stairs with a smile on her face. Trudy followed and she was smiling, too. She looked lovely in the. ivory colored dress of silk lace. Schotzy had found it in an old trunk at his house in the village where they had lived before becoming refugees. Abner remembered the morning he had found it. It was just before the trouble started that had forced them to leave home. *That was last spring and now it's almost winter,* he thought. *It seems like a long, long time ago.* He looked at the guests and realized that many of the villagers who had started the trip with them were not there. *We spent all that time together and we may never see each other again.* He looked around, saw Alice and winked. She winked back. *I'm glad the Schmitts are still with us.*

There was another feast following the wedding. Afterward Jake and Trudy drove away to be together until the group would leave on Wednesday morning. After they were gone, Abner heard Frau Bollinger say to his mother, "The salt I brought broke the Gypsy's evil spell."

"What do you mean?" asked Rachel.

"I took salt up to Gerty Schneider and Trudy. I told them that no doubt the Gypsy cast a spell on them that they did not speak to each other. To break the spell, each of them had to throw the salt over her left shoulder with her right hand. You saw how happy they both were at the wedding. It worked! I just didn't have any salt to give to them before."

"I'm glad the quarrel is over," said Rachel, "no matter what healed it."

Abner pondered what had been said and then thought, *I don't believe the Gypsy cast a spell on Widow Schneider, and I don't believe that the salt took it away. The Gypsy and Widow Schneider didn't talk to each other, and I have my doubts that the Gypsy even took notice of her. I believe that contrary old lady was ready to make up. She missed being able to ask Trudy to do things for her. The salt gave an excuse to make up without having to apologize.*

After the bride and groom left, the group said goodbye to Seth, the Bollingers and the Rohrbaughs. "I'll be coming to Philadelphia now and again," said Cousin Jake. "In the meantime, may God keep you close."

As they were driving away in a buggy that had belonged to Seth's father, Abner shook his head in wonder. "When I think of what has happened to Seth," he said to Schotzy, "I just can't get over it."

The next day was a busy one. Grandpa, Matthias and Jake went to the city to buy the horse and buggy for Grandpa, and to pick up the new buggy, wagon and supplies. Abner was expected to help pack and do some work around the place for the Hermanns. As he and his mother were packing, Rachel saw Herr Hoke's wool blankets. "I have no warm clothes," she said. "I hope you don't mind if I use one of these blankets to make a dress."

"If you need it, use it. Use them both," he said. "We have enough other covers." She chose the lighter weight one, immediately got out her scissors, needle and thread. She measured herself with a string, marked the measurements on the blanket with charcoal and then began to cut. After that was done she began sewing the pieces together. Before long she had a new dress to wear.

Abner looked at his mother with admiration. "I didn't know you could cut and sew like that," he said. "It really looks nice on you."

"Thank you," she said. "It's plenty big. I can get fatter or get uf gie bindle again and there will be plenty of room. For now, I'll wear my old dress underneath, and this one on top. That will help to keep me warm." She looked at the pieces left over. With the help of Frau Hermann and Widow Schneider, she made mittens and hats for Abner, Reuben and Schotzy. "I've just sat around for the last two weeks," she complained. "I could have been sewing."

"You rested because you needed to," said Frau Hermann. "All of you refugees need to rest after you get here."[114]

Wednesday dawned bright and clear, a perfect fall day with a clear blue sky. Cousin Jake and Trudy pulled up in plenty of time to help with everyone's last minute packing. *They look happy*, thought Abner. *I'm glad they're finally married.*

Herr Schmitt had bought a used wagon that was in good condition. It and Matthias' wagon were piled high. Some of the children rode on the wagons, and others rode in the buggies. A huge breakfast had been provided and the leftovers were packed into baskets for dinner. "Here we go again, not knowing where we'll stay tonight," said Abner who was riding on a wagon with Schotzy, Reuben, Minnie and Mary.

---

[114]　The Mennonites of Germantown often kept religious refugees in their homes as guests for two weeks after they arrived in Pennsylvania.

"This is almost like we were when we left Rittendorf," said Minnie. "We pulled your ears for your birthday, and your papa yelled at you because we fell off the cart."

"You know what?" said Abner. "He doesn't yell at me so much as he used to."

Before long they came to the Schuylkill River. "Is this the Suquehanna?" asked Mary.

"Not yet," said Matthias. "After we cross this one, we'll have to travel for seven or eight more days before we get to the Susquehanna. Jake says that the Susquehanna is a lot wider than the Schuylkill."

"There's no bridge," said Mary. "How do we get across?"

"See the ferry hooked to the thick rope? The thick rope is a loop, and is strung between those two poles on either side of the river. The man across the river will pull the rope and take us to the other side when it's our turn. The ferry will not hold all of the buggies and wagons, so it will take awhile until all of us get a turn to cross. If you don't understand what I'm saying, just watch and you'll see."

"Thank you Uncle Matthias, said Mary. "We went down a lot of water, but this is the first time we've been pulled across water."

"I do have good news, too," said Matthias. "Your Cousin Jake said there is a new road between here and Lancaster. It was begun two or three years ago when he was here before. It should be about finished. It will make traveling easier. We shouldn't bounce around so much."

"Cousin Jake said the new road has pretty many places to stop and pay toll," said Abner.

Matthias scratched his head, looked a little off in the head, and said, "It wonders me where I heard that before."

Abner laughed, "Papa, you're funny."

When it was their turn on the ferry, they paid the toll and drove the wagon on board. As they crossed the river the ferry rocked back and forth.

"I scared," said Reuben. "Water makes fast. Me hold on tight."

"Ya, little brother," said Schotzy. "It will be a relief to get back on land."

Traveling on the new road was much better than some of the roads they had been on. It was fairly smooth, and the low spots had been filled in with flat stones from the fields. The days passed and each evening they stopped at a farm and asked if they could stay the night in the barn. "Why don't we stay at an inn?" asked Minnie one evening when it was about time to stop.

Jake, who was driving the wagon answered, "Only men and rich women stay at the inns. A woman needs a room by herself but the innkeeper can put six or eight men in a room because when the beds get full the late comers sleep on the floor. You can see that he gets a lot more money by renting only to men. In most places someone will rent out a room in their home to women. I'd rather sleep in a barn because nearly everyone who stays at an inn goes away with more than what he came with."

"What do you mean?" asked Mary.

"I mean little visitors, the kind that jump around from one head to another."

"Oh, you mean head lice," said Mary. "Herr Flickinger had some. I used to pick them off and kill them for him. Widow Schneider had some once in awhile, too."

"It's good the inspectors didn't know that," said Jake. "People who have head lice are forced to have all of their hair cut off before they can leave the ship. If Trudy's mother would have had that happen, she would have made awful." Jake put his hand to his mouth. "Ach du Lieber, I shouldn't have said that." Everyone who heard him nodded in agreement.

The countryside was different from what they were used to in Europe. Nevertheless, it was interesting. The trees were past their peak of autumn color but they were still beautiful. There were many herds of whitetail deer grazing in the meadows, many cottontail bunnies hopping around, and gray squirrels gathering nuts and burying them. "We should gather some nuts too," said Abner. The next time they stopped for a break Matthias pulled under a hickory tree where there were many nuts. Abner got out Herr Hoke's hammer and Matthias cracked them on a rock until everybody had some. Then they gathered some up to take along.

One day there were children standing by the road with baskets of apples. Herr Hartzell bought some and shared them with everyone. As Reuben bit into his, out came another tooth. "I keep. I find rathole," he said, remembering the superstition that says putting baby teeth down a rathole brings good luck.

Later that day they saw brown stalks stacked together out in the field. It was obvious that they had been cut and stood together. "What are those things, and why are they standing that way?" asked Abner of Cousin Jake who was driving the wagon that afternoon..

"Those are corn shocks," he answered. "The ears grow on them. In the fall they cut them off and stand them up together like that. That way they dry better. No doubt we will see them shucking the ears before we go much further."

Farmers along the way often asked them to stay for supper and gave them milk for the children. "This is what God has put us here for," they would say. One noonday they happened upon a corn shucking party and were invited to the meal that had been prepared. Afterward all of the men and boys went out and shucked corn for a while. Abner discovered that shucking, or pulling the husks off the ears, was not an easy job. *Shucking is something else I now know how to do now,* he thought. *A body never knows when he'll need to know how to do something like that.*

CHAPTER SIXTEEN

As the children rode along on the back of the wagon, Mary often talked about Herr Flickinger and what he had taught her, even though Minnie told her not to. "He told me that he taught you to powwow," Mary said one day to her sister. "That's why he couldn't teach me, because he already had taught you. Did you know that a powwower has darest to teach only one other person? So if you know how, why don't you powwow?"

"I don't want to."

"He said that when Widow Schneider was screaming on the boat, you should have run your finger between her toes, and then put your finger under her nose. That stops it every time."

"I wasn't about to touch her stinky feet," said Minnie with disgust.

"And he said if you have a sore throat, drag your fingers between your own toes, smell your fingers and breathe deep," added Mary.

"That would probly kill me," said Minnie. "Talk about something else, or don't talk at all." She looked away from her sister and began to whistle.

Mary became panicky. "Minnie, don't whistle. You don't have darest to whistle." Minnie continued to whistle. Mary begged her sister. "Minnie, please, please, please, don't whistle."

"You talk about Old Flick, and I'll whistle if I want to."

"But you daresn't whistle! Herr Flickinger said, 'Whistling girls and crowing hens, always come to some bad end.'"

"That's silly," said Minnie.

"No, no, it's not. Girls who whistle end up having babies like you. Herr Flickinger said so."

Minnie stopped whistling and stared at her sister. "What do you mean, like me?"

"I mean babies who don't know who their papas are."

Before Mary took knew what happened Minnie jumped on her sister. She sat on her, pulled her hair and banged her head on the wagon bed. "If you ever, ever say such a thing to me again, you will be sorry you were ever born," Minnie said angrily. "You were bound out to the Slaybaughs and I should have left you with them." She kept on banging Mary's head.

"I'm sorry. I'm sorry. I'm sorry," Mary cried. "Let me go. Don't be mad at me. I just wanted you to know what Herr Flickinger said."

"And I told you before, I don't want to know what Herr Flickinger said."

Abner and Schotzy pulled Minnie off Mary. Matthias stopped the wagon. Herr Hartzell who was following them jumped out of his buggy and ran up to the girls. "What brought this on?" he asked. Neither of the girls answered. "You must tell me," he said. Both girls hung their heads and remained quiet. Turning to Abner and Schotzy he asked, "Do you two know what happened here?"

Abner looked at Schotzy and saw that he was not going to answer either. *How can I say it that it won't hurt Minnie's feelings?* he thought. *There's no way. I may as well just out with it.*

"Mary was talking about Herr Flickinger," said Abner. "Minnie told her to stop. Mary kept on talking about him, and Minnie started to whistle. Mary said Minnie daresn't whistle because if she did, she would have a baby like herself, one that would not know who its papa was."

"Minnie, my dear Minnie girl," said Grandpa in the gentlest, kindest voice Abner had ever heard. He put his arms out to her and held her close. "It doesn't matter under what circumstances you were born, I want you to know, you are a beautiful person." Minnie began to sob, and Herr Hartzell continued, "You have grown in the Lord so much on this trip. I can see it in the way you talk and the way you act." He stroked her hair as he added, "I apologize for not helping you keep Mary away from Herr Flickinger. I am at fault for this. Will you forgive me?" Minnie muttered something, and Herr Hartzell added, "I am so sorry that these words were spoken and that they hurt you so badly." Tears came to his eyes.

At the sight of his tears, Minnie looked at him in surprise and stopped crying. "Herr Hartzell, it wasn't your fault," she said. "It was Mary's. She knew that back home people teased me about it all of the time. Hardly a day went by that someone didn't cast it up to me. They would sing out, 'She doesn't know who her papa is,' just to make me mad, just to torment me."

Herr Hartzell stroked his beard, thought a bit and said, "But if I understand it right, Mary did not say this to be mean. She was trying to protect you from something she perceived could hurt you sometime in the future." He turned to Mary and asked, "Is that right?" Mary nodded, and he turned back to Minnie. "Please don't hold this against your sister. She loves you. All of us love you, but most important of all, God the Father loves you. **Psalm 27:10** says**, 'When my father and my mother forsake me, then the Lord will take me up.'** So you see, even though your earthly father never acknowledged you or took care of you, our Heavenly Father will always be there when you need Him."

Minnie lay her head against Herr Hartzell's chest and relaxed. Abner could see the stress leave her body as she smiled contentedly.

Herr Hartzell continued, "Jesus says in **Hebrews 13: 5 and 6, 'I will never leave thee nor forsake thee.'** Then Paul says**, 'The Lord is my helper, and I will not fear what man shall do unto me.'** When you asked Jesus to come into your heart, He sent His Holy Spirit to live in you. That means your body is a holy temple of our Lord. You belong to God. In no way are you inferior to anyone else in this world." He took his arms from around her and she sat up. He turned to Mary, hugged her and asked, "Are you ready to tell your sister you are sorry you hurt her feelings and ask her forgiveness?"

Abner could see where the tears had run down her dirty face. "I said I was sorry. Minnie, please don't stay mad. I'll try not to talk about Herr Flickinger any more."

Herr Hartzell turned to Minnie and said, "Now it's your turn."

"I should have known you wouldn't hurt me on purpose 'cause you're not a mean person," said Minnie. "I hope I didn't hurt you. Please forgive me. You are my sister and I loved you from the day you were born." The girls hugged each other; Herr Hartzell got back in his buggy; and the caravan resumed its journey.

They had stopped to pay another toll when everyone could hear the sound of horses galloping towards them from behind. "Do you remember," asked Abner, "when we were first on our journey and we heard horses in the night? We were so scared that we hid in the woods. Now we don't have to be scared. We're in Pennsylvania. We're safe here from soldiers who would take my papa back to work for the king.

We don't have to be afraid that someone will put us in jail or torture us for worshiping God as we believe we should."

"I remember," said Schotzy. "It's a good feeling not to be running scared."

The riders had to stop at the toll gate, but when asked for money, they did not seem to understand what they were being asked. "Them are different looking," said Alice. "Them are not Englishers. What are they?"

"I do believe them are Indians," said Abner, as Pearl and Werner began to growl. They were nearly full grown by now and commanded respect. Rufus yapped and Reuben took him in his arms to quiet him.

"They don't have Indian clothes on," said Alice. "They're dressed like ordinary people."

"And look at that!" said Abner in astonishment. "They are wearing red barred[115] coats just like Grace's."

Beyond the tollgate was a table and out farther an outhouse. The mothers decided that it was a good time and place to eat dinner and take a break.

"You got eat?" asked one of the Indians who suddenly appeared at their table.

"No," said Frau Schmitt, waving her hand. "Go away."

"Hold it," ordered Herr Hartzell. "Don't you remember Jake's story about the Hochstetler family who were murdered for refusing to give the Indians what they asked for? We must not act as if we're afraid of them or don't trust them. They don't like that. Now smile and offer him something."

Frau Schmitt's hand was shaking as she offered the Indian a piece of bread. He did not take it but reached over and took the loaf she had cut it from. She watched the Indian bite off large pieces, chew them up and swallow them.

---

[115]   barred: plaid

Alice grabbed Abner's arm. "You said we wouldn't be scared after we got here, but I think I'm scared," she said.

"Don't let on." When the Indians had eaten nearly all of the food, they each took several apples, got on their horses and left.

"Now what are we going to do?" asked Rachel.

"We'll share what we have left, and then just keep on moving like we did before," said Jake.

That evening when it was time to stop there was no house, barn, or town to be seen. It was getting dark as Jake pulled his buggy off the road onto a level spot. The rest followed. "We'll stay here," he said. "We can pull the lower branches off pine trees and make a windbreak and barrier. Then we'll build a big fire in front to keep us warm and to keep the animals away. Trudy, where is that big kettle we bought?"

"What do you want it for?"

"To make supper."

"What are we having?"

"Get it, and I'll show you."

The men constructed the shelter and the boys gathered wood for the fire. Then Antonio showed the boys how to lay pine boughs on the ground to make mattresses that were much better to lie on than the bare ground. "I never slept on pine branches before," said Abner. "Don't they smell good!"

The boys fetched water from a nearby creek and Trudy put it on the fire to boil. Then Jake poured corn meal into the boiling water while stirring hard. He added a little salt, and after a bit of cooking, he ladled some out to everyone. Antonio offered honey to sweeten it, and everyone agreed it was not half bad.[116]

Abner took one bite and shouted, "That's it! He's solved it. The great mystery is no more." Everyone looked at him

---

[116]   not half bad: an idiom meaning, pretty good

as if he had left his brain some place along the way. "Don't you get it?" he asked. "Cornmeal is the stuff that the mystery mush was made of, at least part. I thought that when we got off the ship once, we would never have to eat mystery mush again. It wondered me from the first day what was in it. Didn't anybody else think about what was in it?" No one answered. *I don't care,* he thought as he giggled to himself. *I think it's funny. I could point out that there is no pepper in it with little legs and wings, but I won't.*

After supper, everyone sat around talking when someone asked Martina if she ever found out why Michael Becker hated Catholics so much.

"Ya, he told me," she said. "Thirty-six of his relatives near Heidleburg died fighting for the Protestant cause in the Thirty Years War. Every family in the area lost many members. Many lost their homes, cattle, crops and everything of value. Most of the people in that principality believed the teachings of the Reformed Church and the university was taught by professors who believed the same. The prince belonged to the Reformed Church and life was returning to normal. Then the Jesuits, who are Catholic priests, offered a free education to the prince's son. When the prince died the people discovered that when his son went to the university he had become a Catholic.

"The son knew that he could not make all of the people who belonged to the Reformed Church change back to being Catholic so he said that all of the churches were to be open to everybody. That meant that Catholic priests could use the Reformed Churches. Heidleburg University was forced to hire Jesuit priests to be professors. Michael's uncle attended the university, and became a Catholic. Michael's father died, and then his uncle cheated Michael out of his inheritance. Now he feels that everything that the Protestants fought for is going back to the Catholics.[117] It's as if that long war was fought for nothing. That's why he hates Catholics."

Abner thought about what Martina said for a long time. *I can see why he feels that way. It does seem as if that war was fought and all of those people suffered and died for no good reason. It wonders me if all wars are fought for no good reason. It seems to me that we who refuse to go to war are right. If everyone refused to fight, then God could take care of things in His own way.*

That night the men took turns standing watch and keeping the fire going. In the middle of the night when Abner got up to go to the woods to relieve himself, he looked up at the stars. They were bigger, brighter and closer than he had ever seen them. "Thank you God, for getting me up so I could see them, and thank You for creating them. They're beautiful." He was not aware that Pearl and Werner had followed him until they growled deep in their throats - always a sign of danger. Abner looked around and saw the fire reflected in several pairs of eyes.

BOOM!

"Ach du lieber!" Abner tore back to the safety of the enclosure.

"Didn't you see those wolves creeping up on you?" asked Jake excitedly. "I think I got one." The gunshot awakened everyone and there was no more sleep to be had that night. When it was daylight, Abner looked at the wolf. *Our dogs wouldn't have let them get me*, he thought. *But still, just looking at this one gives me the shivers.*

Jake skinned the wolf, stretched it and rubbed salt on the pelt. "I learned to do this from the Indians," he said. "I would like it to be made into a hat and mittens for Trudy. I've heard that her mother is very talented when it comes to such."

---

[117]   The area around Heidleberg became predominately Catholic at that time and remains so to this day.

After sunup when the boys went to the creek for water, they saw that the creek was full of fish. Jake got a net from his belongings, and in just a few minutes there were more than enough sunfish and bluegills for a bountiful breakfast.

Widow Schneider, after she had eaten breakfast and had a smoke, was in a good mood. "I'll be glad to make a hat and mittens for your bride," she said.

At the next little town there was a bakery that sold bread and soft pretzels. Each person got a big soft pretzel. Some spread soft cheese on them, and others spread mustard. "I never had anything like this before," said Abner. "It tastes good but it's chewy." He looked down at Reuben and saw him holding another tooth. "You keep this up and you'll have no teeth left," he teased.

Later in the day, they came upon a young man who was walking along the road. He waved them down and said, "My cows got out. Did any of youse see my cows?"

Matthias called back to the rest in the caravan, but no one had seen any.

Mary jumped off the wagon, ran up to the man and said, "I can tell you how to find them."

"And how would that be, young lady?" he asked.

"First you find a kie-hooler.[118] That's what the Englishers call a granddaddy-long-legger spider."

The young man nodded and said, "I know that."

Mary continued very seriously, "You must holler at it, **'Where are the cows?'** The kie-hooler will lift one of his long legs, and that's the direction to look for the cows."

"Thank you very much, young lady," the young man said politely. "I'm sure that would work in the summer, but now it is almost winter. I wouldn't be able find a granddaddy

---

[118] Kie-hooler: one who finds the cows. In some areas, the term is used for granddaddy-long- legs spiders.

long legger at this time of the year. Do you have any more suggestions?"

"No I don't," Mary added, still serious. "If I did, I'd tell you. You know, don't you, that it's bad luck to kill a spider."

"Ach, ya, and I do know that. My mother makes me carry them outside if we find one in the house."

"My mama made me do that, too, but she's dead now."

"I'm sorry to hear that, and thank you very much." He bowed, took her hand and kissed it. "You're a fine young lady." Abner, Schotzy and Minnie could scarcely keep from laughing. Mary looked at them, put her hands on her hips and said, "When I grow up and I have a farm, and my cows get out, I'm gonna try it. I'll find them, too. You just wait and see."

The next little village was named Kinzer. It was the place that the French people who had been with them on the ship were planning settle. "Are you excited about seeing Louie?" Schotzy asked Reuben.

"I glad see him." He looked at Martina who was mouthing words and said, "I will be glad to see him."

Louie was watching for them when they arrived. He waved until they stopped, and then he and Reuben hugged like long lost brothers. Then he ran to get his family. When they came out, Antonio translated for the group. The French, even though they were never friendly on the ship, were suddenly very glad to see them. They showed them the house that had been built for them. It was a nice house with decorative cutout woodwook called fretwork around the edge of the overhanging roof and balcony. Louie's grandmother insisted that they stay for a meal which was very tasty. When it was time to go, she invited them to stop every time they were passing through. As they were leaving Louie whispered something in Reuben's ear.

"What did he say?" asked Schotzy.

"He say he knows secret," whispered Reuben. "His grandpa has a barrel of gold."[119]

The weather had turned cold just before they reached Lancaster, and there were snow flurries in the air. Seeing the snowflakes excited the children but they could not get down and chase them because the drivers wanted to get settled for the night. Unfortunately, the town was full of other refugees and they found no place to stay.

"We don't have a choice," said Jake. "We'll have to buy food, a cow, some sheep, geese and chickens, and then keep on going." He turned to Herr Hartzell. "What do you think?"

"You're right. Our intention has always been to get across the Susquehanna as soon as possible. Since there is no place to stay here for the night, much less the winter, I think we should go to market, purchase the livestock and keep on going."

Just before nightfall a man west of town let them stay in his barn and showed them an Indian path that led to the river. The next morning as they traveled, they saw freshly harvested fields on both sides of the path. Farther on they saw men and boys cutting large leaves of something and hanging them in sheds to dry.

"It wonders me what they are harvesting," said Abner.

"I do believe that it's tobacco," said Cousin Jake. "That's their best crop. You saw how the people were buying it back in the old country. Which reminds me, I think I'd best see about buying some for Mother Schneider."

Jake stopped the wagon and talked to the farmer who was hanging the tobacco in the shed. As he did so, Abner noticed that the boards that formed the sides of the shed

---

[119]   There is a tradition in the Forry family that one of the ancesters arrived in America with a barrel of gold. His descendants have looked for it but if they found it, they did not let anone else know.

swiveled. "We wonder if we can buy some tobacco," said Jake. "And we wonder why those boards are hooked up like that."

"There's a simple enough explanation," said the farmer. "The tobacco must dry out and stay dry. It gets cut while it's still green, and it dries in the shed when the air makes through. If a storm comes up, we rush out and close up the sides. I have some tobacco still from last year that will be good to smoke."

Jake bought some and then asked, "Is this the right way to the river? We want to cross and go to a place called Yorktowne."

"You are on the right track," the farmer replied. "Just go past the big barn with white horses in the field. Then bear to the left. It will take you right to it. I do believe that Gideon Mummaw, the man that has the white horses, will let you stay the night in his barn. His wife she gets lonely way out there. She'll be glad for company, and they'll take care of you. They're good people." Jake thanked him, and they were on their way.

"We should've got down and run around when we were stopped," said Minnie. "I'm cold. I wish we'd get there onc't." Alice snuggled up to her and put her arms around her. They were huddled together trying to keep warm when they heard horses behind them. "They sound like they're coming fast," Minnie added. "I don't hope it's Indians wanting alls we got."

When the riders overtook them, one of them shouted, "We've come to talk to Jake Altland. Is he here?"

Jake waved and pointed to himself. "I'm Jake Altland."

"We've come to tell you that you cannot cross the Susquehanna now," he shouted.

Jake pulled the reins, and the horses came to a stop. He jumped off his buggy and asked, "Why? I have all of the papers. I was told that everything was in order."

"I brought official papers that will tell you all about it. Indians from the north fought and subdued the Susquehannock Indians who live across the river. When it was time to make a treaty so that white people could move into the area, the governor of Pennsylvania sent a delegation to the north and made the treaty with the conquering Indians. Thomas Penn, William Penn's son, just got here from England. As soon as he heard about that treaty, he said that it was a good idea, but there must also be a treaty made with the Susquehannocks. He says we must deal with them fairly. Plans are being made to talk to them early next year. That's the reason you may not cross the river now. You must wait until a treaty is signed with them. Thomas Penn wants no trouble. Do you wish to return to Philadelphia? It would be easier to find places to stay there than way out here."

"We've already talked about it," said Jake. "We do not believe in turning back." He turned to Herr Hartzell. "Isn't that right, sir?"

"That's right," Herr Harzell answered. "We've come this far, and we'll keep going until we get to a suitable place to stay for the winter. We'll be ready to cross the river when Thomas Penn gives permission."

"We never know what will happen next," said Abner to the other children. "I'm glad we aren't going to turn back."

"Ya," said Alice. "We'll go to the place with white horses. White horses are a good sign. I believe that will be a good place to stay."

"I like white horses," said Reuben.

When the group reached the Mummaw farm, Herr Hartzell explained the situation. "We need a place to stay for the winter and maybe longer," he said.

"Of course you can stay in the barn," said Frau Mummaw. "You will be our guests for meals until we get things set up so you can cook your own. Come in, come in. We may be a little crowded, but who cares? We haven't had company for a long time. Forgive me if I talk a lot, but I have words stored up inside me from a long time back. Put your coats on our bed, and I'll see what I can shake together for supper. So you thought you were going across the river! Don't worry, it will open up soon for settlement, and then there will be hundreds of people going by here. It is so interesting to find out where people are from. Gid, go cut off meat for these people from the deer you shot day before yesterday. Some fresh meat will be good for them. No, no, no, wait, wait, wait. Did you turn those ducks loose that you had penned up but were going to turn loose because they eat so much? If not, we could have them for supper."

"Hold it, Daisy," said Herr Mummaw. "The ducks are still there. Your jaw is flapping so fast no one else gets a word in."

"I was just trying to make them feel welcome," Frau Mummaw replied, not in the least bothered by his remark. She turned to the girls. "Do any of youse know how to pick and clean ducks?"

"We don't, but the boys do," answered all of the girls at once.

"Really? That's unusual."

"We're an unusual bunch," said Minnie, sounding very sincere. "Especially Abner. He loves to pick ducks."

"That's true," said Widow Schneider with a smile. "He is without doubt the best duck picker of them all. We're all proud of him."

Alice looked from Minnie to Widow Schneider to Abner as if trying to figure out the conversation while Abner stood there feeling silly. *They got me good,* he thought. *I've got to think about this. I can be ugly or I can be nice.* Then he remembered that before Klaus' wedding he had prayed for Widow Schneider to be nice. *If she could be nice then, I can be nice now,* he thought. He nodded his head in Widow

Schneider's direction, smiled and said, "Thank you. I am surprised that you took notice. I did try to do a good job." He turned to Frau Mummaw and asked, "How many ducks are there? Lead me to them. Schotzy, would you care to help? Or maybe Minnie would like me to teach her how to pick ducks beins I taught her to read and she loves to learn."

"No, thanks," said Minnie.

"I help," said Reuben.

"I'll help too," said Matthias.

"This will work out fine," said Frau Mummaw. "Gid, show them where the ducks and chopping block are and do not stand around and waste time. Anybody with eyes in their head can see that these people are hungry. After that you can show the men the logs you've gathered. You said just yesterday that you hoped someone would soon come along who needed to stay the winter so you could get them to help build the log cabins. So now go and take care of the ducks and then tell them what you need to be done. It looks to me like it can work out to everybody's advantage; and it just might be that the Lord's hand is in it. Wait, wait, wait! Boys, be sure you save the feathers. I'm sure you know that much if you are expert duck pickers. Here's a pillow case to put them in. Wait, wait, wait! Here's a crock to put the ducks in."

The women and girls stayed in the house while the men and boys followed Herr Mummaw to the barn where the ducks were. He picked up and ax and began cutting off heads until he had cut off a dozen. "That should do it," he said. All of the men and boys began to pick rapidly. Herr Mummaw gutted them and in no time all of the ducks were done. He took the birds into the house and returned immediately. "Do not tell my wife that I picked and gutted ducks," he said with a grin. "If you do, I'll deny it." He then changed the subject. "Do any of youse know anything about construction and building fireplaces?"

"You've got experts here," said Abner.

Schotzy jabbed Abner in the ribs with his elbow and whispered, "Remember about keeping your mouth shut when the men are talking."

Herr Mummaw took them around in back of the barn where there was a big pile of logs and a high pile of field stone. "Have any of youse ever built a log cabin?"

"We never have, but they don't look difficult," said Jake.

"How about a house?" Herr Hartzell, Jake and Matthias nodded. "What kind of a house?"

"I've worked as a stone mason so I can easily do as many fireplaces as you need, and my son will help me," said Matthias. He pointed to his father and Jake. "The three of us have worked on government buildings and built half timber houses."

"Wunderbar! If youse would be satisfied to stay here and build these logs into cabins, youse can live in them until spring," said Herr Mummaw. "To tell you the truth, they go together quick and easy. The only problem is that I don't have any glass panes for windows so they will be dark inside. After they're built, you can see about getting other construction jobs in the area until you're allowed to cross the river. There's a ferry right here that's been run by John Wright for five years or more."

"You say it's right here," interrupted Abner. "I don't see it. Where is it?"

"Just go to the edge of the yard by that crooked cedar tree," replied Herr Mummaw. "Turn to the left and run down a little way. You will see the sunset on the river just about now. It is a beautiful sight."

"The girls would like to see it, too. Let's get them," said Schotzy.

"I'll race you," said Abner. Accompanied by Reuben, the dogs and the other little boys, they ran to the house.

"Can the girls come out? Herr Mummaw says that the Susquehanna River is right down below the edge of his yard," said Abner. "The sun is setting and he says it's beautiful to see."

"All of youse go ahead," said Frau Mummaw. "The ducks are in the oven. I'll make some cornbread. It won't be long until supper's done, but you'll have time to see the sunset."

"Thank you," said Rachel. "I do want to see it. I'll get my coat." The other women followed her. When the men saw them headed for the river, they went along, too.

The sunset on the water was indeed a beautiful sight, and as soon as he saw it, Herr Hartzell began to pray. "Our Father, most gracious God, we can never thank You enough for bringing us this far. Our hearts are full of gratitude and joy. It was a temptation to worry about where we were going to stay this winter. We now know that because great is your faithfulness we were in the palm of Your hand all of the time. Forgive us for forgetting for even a little that You have never let us down since we left home all those months ago, Amen."

Everyone stood quietly taking in the beauty of the evening until Herr Hartzell quoted, **"It is of the Lord's mercies that we are not consumed, because his compassions fail not. They are new every morning: great is thy faithfulness. The Lord is my portion, saith my soul; therefore will I hope in him."**[120]

"It seems as if we need to have a service of thankfulness right now," he said. The rest nodded and he spoke, "God has been faithful. He is ever faithful, just as He promised. His faithfulness extends even unto death. I often think of my dear wife. She would not have had the strength to endure this trip. In His goodness the Lord let me keep her until very last day before we were forced to leave." He wiped his eyes

---

[120]   Lamentations 3: 22-24

and continued, "Look back and count the times He saved one or all of us from harm or death. He saved us from from neighbors in the village. He saved us from the pirates. He saved us from the soldiers. He saved back us in Seth's village when those people wanted to drown us. He saved Rachel when she fell into the water. Out on the ocean He brought us through the worst storm the captain had ever seen. Each day He provided us with places to stay and food to eat. Now we are almost ready to begin the next part. We know there will be danger, but we will depend on God and His mercies. We know they never fail. Indeed, great is His faithfulness. He has met all of our needs and given us the desires of our hearts."

He ended with another prayer, "Help us Father, to remember to teach our children of Your great deeds. Keep them ever fresh in our memories so that we can pass them on to coming generations. We know You are with us, and we know You have plans for each one of us. With Your help, we will do what You have sent us forth to do. We thank You and praise You because You are worthy to be praised, in Jesus' mighty name, Amen."

Abner opened his eyes and looked at the hills on the other side of the river. He remembered the day that both his grandpa and his father reminded him of the Bible verse, **Delight thyself also in the Lord; and He shall give thee the desires of thine heart.**[121] It had been a day when his heart was heavy at the prospect of being sold into bondage. God had granted him the desire of his heart and he did not have to become an indentured servant. He was free to go with his family wherever they settled, free to worship as he wished, free to be whatever he wanted to be. There were challenges ahead, but he knew that as long as he trusted in the Lord he would be able to meet them.

---

[121]   Psalm 37:4

EPILOGUE

In 1736 Thomas Penn signed a treaty with the Susquehannock Indians. It was then that the real Jacob Altland crossed the Susquehanna River and took ownership of property in what is now Dover Township, York County, Pennsylvania. He gave a portion of his land for Altland's Meeting House, a small church that is still standing. Lutheran, Brethren and Reformed congregations have all worshiped there. My husband and our children are among his many descendents. LMC

SELECTED GLOSSARY

A

all: an idiom meaning all gone

B

big feeling: arrogant, proud, feeling important
brutzich: whining or crying, rhymes with foot sick

D

daresn't: dare not, must not
darest: allowed, as in "Do you have darest to play now?" one syllable.
das es recht: That's right.
dear: expensive
dodger: hard, blah-tasting cookie or biscuit
doppich or doppy: clumsy, awkward
dormlich: homely
dumkopf: dummy, stupid person

F

ferdudst: crazy or at least rather mixed up, dud rhymes with stood
ferhuddled: confused, bewildered
fershimmeled: stressed out, shook up

fersouffa: drunk
filling: bread or potato dressing, stuffing
fractur: decorated birth or marriage certificate
fress: eat like a pig, gobble down
freundschaft: extended family

G

ge-pooped: tired, pooped out, or dirtied with feces
glichlich: lucky, pronounced glicklick
go both ways: vomiting and diarrhea at the same time
glundach: animal similar to a groundhog; Dachshunds were bred to catch them.
greistlich: ugly
grex and moan: complain
gut: good, rhymes with fruit
gutgucklich: good looking, gut rhymes with fruit, guck rhymes with look, lick

H

half timbered house: built with large timbers and stone
hex: curse or cast an evil spell on someone
hummy: calf

K

kie-hooler: granddaddy-long-legs spider, kie is pronounced key
kinder: children
kuttz: vomit; sounds like cuts

L

leave and let: these two words get mixed around
liebling: little love, darling
linsey-woolsey: a woven material that is part linen, part wool

long already: for some time

M

maidel: girl or unmarried woman
mansly: little fellow
maus: mouse

N

nebby: nosy; from nebbisch
nix-nooks: a naughty child, more than likely a boy, plural: nix-nookses

O

once: at once, an idiom meaning sometime or right now; also onc't

P

Palatinate: extremely fertile area along the Rhine River in southern Germany; many Pennsylvania Dutch came from there, pronounced puh LAT in ate
powwowowed for: having a powwower saying certain prayers or incantations
powwower: a healer or one who casts spells

R

rattleband: noisy gathering outside newlywed's quarters
raus mit du: get out; raus rhymes with mouse
rathaus: government building, sounds like rot house
rutch: wiggle; rhymes with butch

S

schmutz: slang for kiss, anything that can be smeared
schnuppisch: snoopy

schushlich: sort of shaky so that one shuffles one's feet; rhymes with push ly

schwiesshart: sweetheart; pronounced shweess heart

Simle gut: I'm fine.

smiercase: soft cheese

sneaky: persnickety, difficult to please, esp. where food is concerned

snitz and knepp: dried apples, dumplings and ham

so half I believe, or **so half I do believe**: I sort of think so, maybe

souffer: drunkard

strublich: uncombed or windblown hair

summerhouse: a small building near the kitchen where food was cooked in the summer and during butchering

swear: Brethren would not swear an oath. It is unbiblical to do so.

T

toodli: toddler: tood rhymes with stood

tow: coarse linen cloth: pronounced toe

U

umglich: not right, misshaped

W

wasn't so good: not well

wie gehts?: a greeting, how are you?

wonderful: can meant terribly: She was wonderful sick

wunnerschnitzich: overly curious, nosy

wutzies: little pigs; wutz: pig or hog, rhymes with puts

SELECTED BIBLIOGRAPHY

Anderson, Howard. A Lost Heritage, Living Pennsylvania Dutch, self published, York, Pennsylvania, 1988

Aurand, A. Monroe, Jr. Home Remedies and Superstitutions of the Pennsylvania Germans, Aurand Press, Lancaster, Pennsylvania, ca. 1920

Blank, Benuel S. The Amazing Story of the Ausbund, The Oldest Hymnal on Earth Known to Still Be in Continuous Use, Carlisle Printing, Sugar Creek, Ohio, 2000

Carter, W. C. and Glossbrenner, A.J.. History of York County (Pennsylvania) from Its Erection to the Present Day, York, Pennsylvania, 1834

Eby, Kermit. For Brethren Only, The Brethren Press, Elgin, Illinois, 1958

Eccenbarger William. Walkin' the Line, M.Evans and Co. New York, NY, 2000

Fisher, Virginia S. The Story of the Brethren, Brethren Publishing House, Elgin, Illinois, 1957

Hollerbach, Eugen. Father Rhine Tells His Sagas, Rahmel-Verlag GMBH, Germany

Klees, Fredric. The Pennsylvania Dutch, Macmillan Co., New York, NY, 1950

Kuhns, Oscar. <u>The German and Swiss Settlements of Colonial Pennsylvania,</u> Eaton and Mains, New York: Jennings and Graham, Cincinnati, Ohio, 1900

Moraley, William. <u>The Infortunate or The Voyage and Adventures of William Moraley, Indentured Servant,</u> New Castle, Great Britain, 1743. Introduction and Notes: Susan E. Klepp and Billy G. Smith, The Pennsylvania State University Press, University Park, Pennsylvania, 1992

Reynolds, Patrick M. <u>Profiles of Pennsylvania, Volumes 6, 8, 9, 12-15,</u> Red Rose Studio, Willow Street, Pennsylvania, 1982 – 1991

ABOUT THE AUTHOR

Known for her sense of humor, Louise M. Coffman, a Californian, accompanied her husband to his Pennsylvania Dutch country after WWII. The language and culture, so different from what she was accustomed to, made a lasting impression. Fifty years later she drew on those memories, her interest in history, her faith, her teaching, her mothering, and that sense humor to create *Abner's Story, Abner's Escape,* and *Abner's Journey to America.* She finished the third book just before her eightieth birthday. To help to preserve the rapidly disappearing Pennsylvania Dutch culture, she teaches and speaks publicly. She and her husband travel, are active in church, parents of three, grandparents of six and great grandparents of six. They live in York, Pennsylvania.

Printed in the United States
27320LVS00003B/52-270

9 781420 808629